COLL

BIOS

To,

Margaret,

Happy reading

and all the best

Love

C. Ward

x

Chiado Publishing

chiadopublishing.com

All characters and events in this publication, other than those clearly in the public domain, are ficticious and any resemblance to real persons, living or dead, is purely coincidential.

chiadopublishing.com

U.K | U.S.A | Ireland
Kemp House
152 City Road
London
EC1CV 2NX

Spain
Centro de Negocios Edificio España
Plaza de España, Nº 5 - 6
37004 Salamanca
España

France | Belgium | Luxembourg
Porte de Paris
50 Avenue du President Wilson
Bâtiment 112
La Plaine St Denis 93214
France

Germany
Kurfürstendamm 21
10719 Berlin
Deutschland

Portugal | Brazil | Angola | Cape Verde
Avenida da Liberdade
Nº 166, 1º Andar
1250-166 Lisboa
Portugal

Web: www.chiadopublishing.com | www.chiadoglobal.com

Title: A Promise For My Mother
Author: Caroline Ward

Graphic Design Ps_design – Departamento Gráfico

Printed and Bound by: *Chiado Print*

ISBN: 978-989-51-0443-7
Legal Deposit n.º 360278/13

Caroline Ward

A Promise For My Mother

Chiado Publishing

This book is dedicated to my mother,
Sandra McWilliam.

Contents

Foreword

'After all I've done for you! I'm your grandma – don't you speak to me like that!'

The number of times I have heard my grandma say that! All through my life I have had the only woman in who I could confide belittle, control and blackmail me. The only woman? Well, I never really had much time with my mother as she passed away when I was very young and my grandma has brought me up. Grandma is a small woman but very authoritative and, strangely, her wiry greying hair seems to shine.

My name is Caroline and I was born on 24th March 1965 to Ronnie and Sandy. My father left when I was quite young, after my mother divorced him for beating her and it is sad that a lasting memory I had of him was throwing me across the yard and breaking my arm. Still not quite sure if that was on purpose or a game gone wrong. I rack my brains at why I cannot remember much about my life as a little girl but, I suppose if I think a lot harder I might be able to piece together more. Oh, let's have a go!

As I sit here looking at my wonderful Christmas lights in my lovely home with my wonderful husband and fantastic little dog Tammey I wonder how I made it this far intact! Loving, caring grandma. Is... isn't that what grandmas are supposed to be? Maybe other people's are but I wonder why this was not the case with my grandma. Perhaps I had better get my memory in gear and relate my life. Then you might get an idea. Hopefully my story will be inspiring but, like many stories that are not very nice it does have a happy ending!

Early Memories

'There's a drink here and a biscuit, Caroline!'

I smiled at the voice of my mother announcing goodies and I just abandoned my dolls and ran into the house. We had come to my grandma and grandpa's cottage and I had been playing in the back yard as it was a nice day. I was five years old but, having no father for a year or so, I had grown up quite fast.

'Wash your hand my darling,' said my mum.

She ruffled my hair a bit and smiled and I ran back into the kitchen to wash my hands as instructed.

As I remember the cottage was a traditional one with a fireplace and beams and I used to squint at times when the sun hit the brasses at certain times of the day. It also had a small bar, which I wasn't allowed to go to of course! Grandma and grandpa kept it nice and I sat on the floor cross-legged munching my biscuits and slurping my lemonade, which had my grandpa laughing!

Then grandpa got up. 'Well, I'm off to the pub. See you in a bit. Make sure that Caroline tidies her dolls up. It's getting late now.'

As grandpa went out of the door I blew my cheeks out but dragged my feet as I followed mum's pointing finger to the back yard. I looked at the makeshift tents and dolls spread all over the yard and thought I should not have got so many out at once!

A little later after all my dolls were safely in the warm I was sat with my mother on the couch, my grandma sat on her favourite chair looking at the clock and wondering where my grandpa had got to, as usual!

Mum smiled. 'You know he will call at the chippy mum,' she said to my grandma.

I smiled. 'Oh, good. Will grandpa bring me a fish mummy?'

Mum nodded. 'Does he ever forget your fish?'

I looked up at mum and my eyes watered a little. Mummy, why did daddy have to go away?'

Mummy sighed. 'Things just didn't work out between us darling...'

'He was a bad 'un!' cut in my grandma.

My mum shot her a frowning glance and my grandma shrugged her shoulders.

The conversation was cut off as the door opened and my grandpa came in, smiling and accompanied by the wonderful smell of chippy fish!

'Grandpa!' I shouted and I ran over to him. 'Have you brought me a fish?'

Grandpa laughed and ruffled my hair. 'Would I ever forget?' He turned to grandma. 'Here you are Pearl. Go and dish out and get the tea on!'

After fish and chips my mum announced it was time to go. I didn't want to go as I loved it at grandma and grandpa's but we had to go home.

Grandpa ruffled my hair. 'Go on precious! Make sure your mum gets home okay.'

I smiled and gave him a hug. 'Bye grandpa. Thanks for the fish.' I went and hugged grandma. 'Bye grandma.'

My grandma said goodbye and hugged me but why did it not seem as lovely as grandpa's hug.'

When we got home my mum made me go straight into my room to get ready for bed. Afterwards we were sat having a drink and I was cuddled into my mum.

Mum stroked my hair as best as she could as I remember her hands not being so good. I loved her doing this and I started to drift off to sleep.

'Hey,' said mum twiddling my ear. 'Don't fall asleep here. Let's get you off to bed!'

I went to bed smiling and tasting grandpa's fish.

Christmas for a five year old is supposed to be magical, or so people have told me in my adult years. Actually, the Christmas tree at grandma and grandpa's is magical and I am sitting looking at the wonderful lights and mix of decorations, trying not to look at the presents underneath!

I look up at grandma and smile as she brings cake and a drink. 'Are some of these decorations old grandma?'

Grandma nods. 'Some. Some grandpa got the other day, from a man at the pub.' She shakes her head.

'Can we make some? Please?' I ask.

'Have we got anything to make decorations with mum?' asks mum of grandma.

'Decorations?' comes grandpa's voice as he closes the front door. 'Is someone making decorations?'

'Caroline wants to make decorations dad,' says mum. 'Have we got anything to make them with?'

Grandpa laughs. 'I tell you what Caroline. We'll go and look for things to make decorations with while grandma and mummy make the dinner.'

I jump up and follow grandpa upstairs to look for anything that we can use.

It's Christmas morning! We have come back to grandma's and the wrapping paper is all over the place! I eat some chocolate from my stocking and dance around the room with my doll.

'She's beautiful mummy! Thank you!

'Put her back at her desk,' says grandma. 'We'll be having dinner soon.'

'Come on,' says grandpa. 'Let's set the table!'

Christmas dinner is yummy! Everyone is tucking in and nobody is talking. Grandma, grandpa and mum are drinking sherry but I have to settle for pop!

Grandma finishes her mouthful and clears her throat. 'You know, Sandy, you can stay here tonight. It will save you going out into the cold.'

Mum shakes her head. 'No, it's okay mum. It would be crowded and we can go home. We're well wrapped up.'

'But are you sure you will be okay on your own Sandy?' asks grandma. 'I mean you know that...'

'Pearl, leave it alone!' cuts in grandpa. 'If our Sandy says she will be okay then she will!'

Grandma scowls at grandpa but grandpa just smiles at me and fills my glass with more pop.

Later, I am helping mummy clear some pots and I hear grandma and grandpa talking, but I don't know what they are saying.

'Mummy,' I say. 'Why is grandma angry?'

'I don't think she is angry darling.'

'But she sounds cross with grandpa mummy! Has grandpa done something wrong?'

Mummy puts her hand on mine and shakes her head. 'No, grandpa hasn't done anything wrong.'

I frown a little as mummy seems to stumble a little bit. 'Are you okay mummy?'

'Yes,' answers mummy. 'Now what are you going to call your doll?'

I smile. 'Katy of course!'

Mummy laughs. 'Of course!'

We go back into the house and grandma and grandpa suddenly stop talking loud and look at us both, smiling.

I hold out my doll. 'This is Katy!'

Grandpa laughs. 'So, she's called Katy then? Very nice Caroline. You take care of Katy and make sure she is happy!'

'Oh, I will grandpa, I will have Katy forever!'

I cannot look at the man that my mum is with and call him dad. I see my mum very upset and crying and a man that loves her can't let her be like that, can he? I sit in my room and cry – I want my mummy to be happy.

I am at grandma and grandpa's and I am crying.

'What is the matter Caroline?' my grandpa asks.

I answer through sobs. 'Why is mummy crying and not happy grandpa?'

Grandpa sighs. 'Your mummy is not very well sweetheart,' my grandpa answers. He hugs me. 'Let's go and get some lemonade and biscuits.'

My grandma frowns. 'Huh! Trust Sandy to find another bad 'un! What is she playing at?'

Grandpa throws grandma a curt look. 'Shush Pearl! As if it isn't bad enough for our Caroline!'

I start to sob again and grandpa hugs me tighter. 'Can't you see Pearl what is happening?'

Grandma shrugs 'Yes! Why else do you think I am complaining! She is putting our little Caroline through hell!'

Grandpa smiles at me. 'Come on precious. Let's go for a walk.'

I have got my new coat on and grandpa is taking me for a walk to the other end of the street. We bump into Mr Jones, a footballer with the local team, walking his dog.

'Afternoon,' says grandpa.

Mr Jones smiles at me. 'Hello gorgeous!'

I smile and then stroke the dog. 'Hello Mr Jones. Are you playing on Saturday?'

Mr Jones nods. 'Yes. Walking Lofty keeps me in exercise between training!'

Grandpa nods. 'Let's have a good result then!'

Mr Jones smiles. 'Always Mr Brown. Good day.'

We carry on for a while and when we get back to the cottage mum is dozing and grandma is making hot chocolate. The fire is going and I think it is really too hot. I take my coat off.

'Had a nice walk Harry?' asks grandma.

I smile. 'We've been talking to Mr Jones. I have been stroking his dog.'

Grandma smiles and grandpa raises his eyebrows, as if grandma doesn't smile very often.

'I hope you asked him to put in a good performance Harry!' says grandma.

Grandpa nods. 'Always Pearl. Always.' Grandpa ruffles my hair. 'I'm going to the pub. Be back for tea Pearl.'

Grandma shakes her head.

***

I am now eight and worried, so worried as my mum is not very well at all. My grandma has left grandpa and has come to live with us. Anybody would think that it would be a good thing for your grandma to live with you. Not so, not with the rotten miserable face and horrible way she treats me. I know grandma might be worried about mum but that's not my fault. At least that horrible man has gone out of our life! But why does mum bang her head on the floor? Surely that must hurt?

I go to hug mum. 'Are you okay?'

Mum smiles and strokes my hair. 'I'm fine darling! Go with grandma and she will take you to school.'

Grandma gets hold of my hand and marches me to the door. 'Come on Caroline. Get your coat.'

I kiss good bye to mummy and we go out of the door.

'Grandma. Is mummy going to be okay?' I ask as we are on the way to school.

Grandma sighs. 'I don't know Caroline. She is quite poorly and that idiot man didn't help! I'm glad he's gone.'

I smile at grandma. 'I am as well grandma. He was horrible to mummy.'

We get to school and grandma gives me a hug.

'See you later grandma.' I go into school and look back to see grandma walking off.

The light through the window looks like it is shining around mum and it makes her look like an angel. I jump onto mummy's knee with my drink of milk and she screws her face up a little as it must hurt her. But then she smiles and cuddles me. I cuddle into her and the world seems okay, just for a little while!

The next day at home mummy is making clothes for Katy as I come home from school with grandma. The ones she has on are looking a little bit mucky! Mummy's great at sewing and it seems to make her happy. I have grown, of course, but Katy hasn't so her clothes will always be the same size.

'Grandma. Why are you not with grandpa any more? I miss going to meet him from work.'

'Oh, just one of those things darling.'

'People sometimes just can't live with each other,' mum says.

'What, like you and that man mummy?'

'Yes. Like me and John.'

I frown. 'But he was horrible mummy and grandpa was nice.' I turn to grandma. 'Grandpa was nice grandma. So, why are you not with him any more?'

'It just didn't work out Caroline. Now. No more!'

I look at the door – I don't know why. Why is grandma being so horrible?

***

I am now old enough at nearly ten to know that something is really wrong with mum. Grandma keeps saying that it is just something and nothing but I know better. It isn't fair that I keep getting upset at school and I keep asking and asking grandma but she doesn't really say anything. Anyway, if there is nothing really wrong why am I going to grandpa's most days and not staying at home?

I sip my drink and look at grandpa. He doesn't look really sad but he doesn't look really happy either. I suppose he is just looking okay for my sake.

I tug on his sleeve and smile. 'Grandpa. Where's grandma?'

Grandpa smiles. 'She's looking after mummy darling.'

'Is mummy okay grandpa?'

Grandpa stares me in the eyes. 'She is very poorly darling.' He smiles. 'But I'm sure she'll be okay.'

I start to weep a little and grandpa hugs on to me tighter. All I want is my mum to be well but she isn't – and

I know that grandpa is trying to make out she will be okay but I have seen her banging her head again and I have seen her shaking and, oh! Why did she have to get ill?

Later on grandma comes to grandpa's and, after they have had quite a long talk with raised voices at times, grandma smiles at me a little and sits me down.

Grandma looks at me, looks at my watery eyes and shakes her head a little. 'You are going to live here with grandpa for a little while until mum gets better. I have to be with her a lot and I need you – mum needs you – to be brave and stay with grandpa. Is that okay Caroline?'

I start to cry again and look at grandpa. 'Grandpa?'

Grandpa nods. 'Yes, it's okay. I can take you to school and pick you up and go to work around it. We'll be all right.'

'When can I see mummy grandma?'

'I will pick you up from school tomorrow and we will go to visiting at the hospital. Grandpa is on a later shift so that works out okay.'

I smile a little at that and grandpa ruffles my hair. Come on! Let's go to the shop and get some sweets.'

'Is there anything else that you need?' The ward sister smiles at mum and when mum shakes her head she goes about her job.

I hold mum's hand and she smiles. 'So, how is school darling?'

'Okay mummy. Just the same really.' I frown a little. 'Are you going to be okay mummy?'

Mum sighs. 'I feel pretty rotten Caroline but the nurses here are very good. I'll be fine!'

'I am going to see your dad tomorrow Sandy,' says grandma. 'He doesn't know about this yet.'

I look up. 'My other grandpa? Can I come grandma?'

'No, you'll be at school. You can see him another time.'

The bell goes for the end of visiting and I hold my mum's hand tight. 'Do I have to go?'

Mum nods her head. 'I'm afraid so darling. Grandma will take you home to grandpa's.'

'Can I come tomorrow?'

Mum smiles at grandma. 'You can bring her tomorrow night mum. Harry will be going to the pub anyway!'

I give mum a kiss and then grandma gives mum a hug. As we go out of the ward I look back and see mum trying to smile. I know she is wanting to cry really. I go watery eyed again as we walk to the bus stop. Grandma says nothing.

The next night I am sat at the side of mum's bed and grandma is talking to the nurses. Mum and I are eating grapes – actually we are both sick of grapes – but it keeps mum smiling. Grandma comes back and sits down.

Mum turns her head to grandma. 'How was my dad? Is he coming to see me?'

Grandma nods. 'He said he is coming to see you tomorrow. He's been tied up today. Huh! Not surprised!'

Mum frowns. 'Now, mum. Don't be like that.' Mum coughs.

I hold mum's hand. 'Are you okay mummy?'

Mum nods. 'I will be all right. It will be nice to see dad.'

'Huh!' says grandma again.

The bell goes for the end of visiting. 'Can I come tomorrow with Grandpa Ronnie?'

'I don't see anything wrong with that. Do You?' asks mum of grandma.

Grandma shrugs. 'I suppose not. I'll sort it out. Come on Caroline. We need to get to grandpa's. He will go out for fish.'

I kiss mummy and she is really smiling today. We wave as we leave the ward.

Grandma says nothing again as we walk to the bus stop. In fact, she nearly drags me along! What is wrong with grandma?

The next evening I am walking up to the hospital ward with Grandpa Ronnie, in fact, I am skipping a bit! We go into the ward and my smile goes away as mum is not looking very well. Grandpa Ronnie asks the nurse and she says that mum has been coughing a lot and they have given her something to make her doze a bit. Grandpa Ronnie and I sit at the side of the bed. After a while mum wakes up and smiles at Grandpa Ronnie and then gets hold of my hand.

'Now then,' says grandpa, 'how's my Sandy feeling now?'

'Hi dad,' says mum. 'I am okay. Better for having a little sleep.' She turns her head to me. 'Go and ask the nurse for some fresh water Caroline please.'

I go and do as mum asks but I know that she wants to talk to Grandpa Ronnie on her own. When I get back they are laughing a bit. I smile and give mum the water.

'Thank you darling,' says mum.

'What were you and grandpa talking about when I was away mummy?'

Grandpa Ronnie laughs. 'Hah! You can't keep anything from Caroline, eh?'

Mum shakes her head. 'No dad! She's not daft isn't our Caroline!'

We all laugh and share *more* grapes! Then the bell goes for the end of visiting and I lean in and kiss mum.

'Bye mummy. See you tomorrow.'

Mum gives me a hug. 'Bye darling.'

Grandpa Ronnie leans in and gives mum a big hug and kiss. 'Bye poppet. You take your time and make sure you get better for a long time! See you in a couple of days. Got some new people in the guest house and have to settle them in.' He frowns. 'Oh, and your grandma isn't very well and is having trouble looking after her dog so I am taking it in for a bit.

'I give a big beaming smile. 'Oh, grandpa Ronnie. Can I come and see Tootsie?'

'We'll see Caroline, we'll see.'

The walk to the bus is much nicer with Grandpa Ronnie, although slower as he is limping a bit. This seems such a shame as he is a stocky man, large in a nice way and full of fun.

How was your visit with Grandpa Ronnie?' asks grandma.

'It was nice grandma,' I answer with a smile. 'Mum was doped when we got there but she woke up smiling.'

'Doped?' asks grandma. Grandma has taken me to grandpa's so they could talk a little.

Grandpa is in the kitchen cooking mackerel fillets under the grill and the smell is wonderful.

'She had been coughing a lot grandma and the nurses had given her something to make her sleep.'

Grandma frowns but soon has something to shake her head at. 'Blimey Harry! Could you not cut the bread thicker?'

'I have to finish the loaf off Pearl. Had the other half this morning with my bacon!'

Grandma shakes her head again. 'I don't know where you put it!'

Grandpa pats his tummy. 'Got the right job Pearl, got the right job! Delivering post keeps you fit!' He frowns a little and looks at me as he makes a mackerel butty. 'Will your mum be okay?'

'I don't know grandpa. She says she will be.'

Grandpa nods and takes a bite of his butty.

Grandma and I sit and grandma just sits and watches grandpa in between reading the newspaper. Grandpa finishes and then smiles. 'Right, who's for a sing-song?'

Grandma looks up from her paper and shakes her head. I smile and nod.

'Tie A yellow Ribbon?' asks grandpa.

Just a little Caroline before we go home,' says grandma.

***

Grandpa has picked me up from school again and taken me to his cottage. He has cooked a stew and is singing away to himself in the kitchen but the singing didn't seem very happy. It is the second week that I hadn't gone home and come to grandpa's after school. I hadn't seen grandma very much but grandpa said that she was at the hospital a lot with mum. Grandpa brings in the stew and we begin to eat it.

Grandpa can see my eyes getting watery. 'What's wrong Caroline?'

'When can I see mummy again grandpa?'

Grandpa lowers his head slightly. 'Soon Caroline. Soon.'

Later we have a sing-song and then grandpa ruffles my hair. 'Time to go to bed young lady. School tomorrow.'

I start to cry and grandpa hugs me. He then takes me upstairs and tucks me in bed.

'Can I have a story grandpa?'

Grandpa nods and then reads me a little bit of the Famous Five book and then I must have drifted off to sleep as the next thing grandpa was waking me up for breakfast.

That afternoon grandpa picks me up from school but he seems hurried and not very happy. He pulls me along to the bus and I think that this is not like grandpa! On the bus grandpa says nothing but holds my hand tight and then when we get to the cottage he gets me a drink of pop and a comic and then goes into the kitchen to make some tea. Then I hear grandpa sobbing a little and I go into him.

I tug on grandpa's jacket and he takes his head out of his hands and looks at me.

'What's wrong grandpa? Is it mummy?'

Grandpa sighs and then nods. 'Mummy has got very poorly Caroline. She isn't waking up very much and we are just a bit worried. That's all.'

I smile. 'Maybe the nurses have given her some of that doping stuff again grandpa!'

Grandpa smiles. 'That's it! You might be right!'

Grandpa and me watch telly for a bit and then he reads me a story while I have a hot chocolate.

'Everything will be okay,' says grandpa as he kisses me goodnight.

I smile and then snuggle down.

The next day is Friday and grandpa has taken me to the chippy after school. We are eating our tea when there's a knock at the door. It's grandma and I smile and hug her as she comes in.

'How's mum?' I ask grandma.

Grandma smiles. 'Well, she has been having a bit of a dance! Some of the nurses joined in as well so not so bad today!'

'Did you not dance grandma?' I ask with a grin.

'Me? Oh, no. Not me! You wouldn't catch me dancing!'

'Do you want some fish and chips Pearl?' asks grandpa. 'There's some left.'

Grandma smiles. 'Go on then. Any bread?'

'Nope!' says grandpa. All the bread has gone.'

'Typical!' says grandma.

The next morning I am woken up by the telephone ringing quite early. I hear grandpa talking and then he is sobbing a bit again. I get my dressing gown on and go down and grandpa is in the kitchen making a drink. He turns to me and his eyes are watery.

'Is mummy ill again grandpa?'

Grandpa doesn't answer at once but just takes our drinks into the living room. I sit opposite him and I see he is very upset.

'Is mummy ill?' I ask grandpa again.

Grandpa shakes his head. 'No sweetheart. Mummy is okay now. She has gone to Heaven and Jesus is making her better.'

I start to cry and then I cry out for mummy. 'Mummy, mummy! I want mummy grandpa!'

Grandpa hugs me and I am crying very loud. I cry for a long time and then grandpa gets up and picks up the phone.

He talks to the voice on the other end of the phone. 'Caroline won't be coming to school today. Her mum has passed away.'

He puts the phone down and then comes back to hug me. We both cry together.

Growing Up

'Caroline? Caroline!'

I hear grandma calling and I go to her.

'Yes grandma?'

'Get your coat. We are going to see your mum.'

I stare at grandma. 'Going to see mum? How?'

Grandpa frowns. He has his uniform on for delivering the day's post, making his tall but thin frame look quite distinguished. 'Is that wise Pearl? She is only a little girl!'

'She can say her goodbyes!' retorts grandma. 'It's her mum Harry!'

'Yes, but it's not very nice Pearl! It might frighten the poor girl.'

'Nonsense!' says grandma. 'It's life! She might as well get used to things seeing as it is now up to me to bring her up.'

Grandpa raises his eyebrows. 'Up to you?'

Grandma nods. 'Yes. Up to me. Sandy made me promise to bring up Caroline as she didn't want the poor girl to go to her dad. Very wise decision!'

I look at grandma. 'Grandma. I don't want to see mummy! I'm scared!'

'Pah!' says grandma. 'Get your coat Caroline. You can say goodbye to mum and then we will go home.'

I cry as I'm putting on my coat.

'What will you do now Pearl?' asks grandpa.

'I will wait until after the funeral on Tuesday and then I will have a think.'

I turn to grandpa. 'Are you coming too grandpa?'

Grandpa shakes his head. 'Not today. I am on Tuesday. Now, go with your grandma and do as she says. I'll see you later.'

I hug grandpa and then grandma and I go.

I am looking at mum and crying. She looks so peaceful and not in pain and I look up and say a little prayer to Jesus to look after her. I am shaking and I don't like it but grandma says nothing for a long time. Then she looks at me and turns me round, marches me towards the door. We get outside and I start to cry really loud and shake. Grandma shakes her head but the kind lady from the funeral directors gets hold of my hand.

'I know you are upset Caroline.' says the kind lady, 'but mummy is with Jesus now. She will be watching and she won't want you crying now, will she?'

I shake my head.

The kind lady turns to grandma. 'Don't be so hard on her! She is only ten and how do you think she feels!'

Grandma sighs and then ruffles my hair. 'We'll be okay Caroline. It's hard for me as well, you know.'

I hug grandma and then she turns to the kind lady. 'Thank you. We will see you Tuesday.'

'Can we take you anywhere?' asks the kind lady.

Grandma nods. 'You can take us home please. Yes.'

I don't remember much about the funeral but I do remember the people that were there making a big fuss of me. I didn't want a fuss making of me! I just wanted to go home to grandpa!

I am now sat in the chair at grandpa's with a drink. I can hear grandma and grandpa talking loudly and I put my head down.

'But, Pearl. How are you going to bring Caroline up? Do you have the time? What about work?'

Grandma straightens slightly. 'I am looking into taking a job as a warden. The position has a house with it so I will be on hand for Caroline as well. I cannot let Sandy's wishes down and this is the best I can do for now.'

Grandpa puts his fingers together and nods slightly. 'Well, I suppose it isn't a bad idea.' He smiles slightly. 'I know it is a lot for you to do Pearl but this is really a good idea.'

Grandma smiles back. 'Thank you Harry. It will be okay.'

'When do you start Pearl?'

'As soon as I have seen out the notice on the flat and got myself together, say, in about a month's time. Is Caroline okay with you until then Harry?'

'Of course Pearl. She can stay as long as she likes.'

They both look at me and see that I am crying. Grandma comes over and smiles, not a regular thing. 'We will get by okay Caroline. Everything will be okay.'

'I just hope you're right,' mutters grandpa.

Grandma throws him a frowning look.

The next month seems to go quick but it was a rotten time really. I still cry a lot and grandma doesn't seem to care very much. Grandpa is lovely as always and I keep thinking I am going to miss the fish and peas and the sing songs. I start to cry again.

'Oh, it'll be okay sweetheart. I will come and visit you as much as I can. I will even find a chippy near to you so as I can bring you a fish!'

I hug grandpa and smile. 'Thanks grandpa.'

‘Come on, come on Caroline. Let’s get your things inside. Hurry up!’

I get as much as I can in one go and drag them into the house. ‘Can I not get any help grandma?’

‘Someone will be over in a bit,’ answers grandma sternly. ‘In the meantime, hurry up and get your things inside.’

I start to take my things upstairs to my room and after I have laid my dolls out in a tea party I go down to grandma again. Grandma is sighing and standing with her hands on her hips.

She shakes her head. ‘How are we ever going to get straight?’

‘Get grandpa to help!’ I say smiling.

‘I might have to do that Caroline,’ says grandma and she actually laughs a little.

‘Can I have a drink please grandma?’

Grandma nods. ‘Let’s get the kettle on and get you a drink of lemonade.’

‘Good grief! Those blasted buses!’

I am at ‘big’ school now and it isn’t nice but grandpa has come to visit us and I am smiling as I can smell the fish! I had been in my room playing nurse to my dolls as they had all gone sick, giving them some ‘medicine’ and putting them to bed in their boxes! Grandma had shouted upstairs to tell me that grandpa was here and when I got downstairs I grinned and hugged him tight!

‘Grandpa has brought fish and chips,’ says grandma. ‘Go and wash your hands and then we can eat.’

After my fish and chips I go back upstairs and see how my poorly dollies are doing. I can hear grandma and grandpa talking downstairs but I don’t take much notice.

'How are you bearing up Pearl?' I catch grandpa asking as I am going upstairs.

'We are okay Harry. Don't you worry about that!' Grandma sighs a little. 'I have to tell you Harry that I have been out a couple of times with Ronnie.'

Grandpa frowns. 'Why?'

'Well,' says grandma, 'He is feeling a bit low as well with Sandy dying so we have had a bit to talk about. Just comfort, that's all.'

'Don't you go confusing Caroline! She has had enough to contend with.'

Grandma scowls. 'Don't get to telling me what to do Harry.'

Grandpa shakes his head. 'I am just looking out for Caroline, Pearl.'

'I know,' grandma answers, 'but I know what I am doing Harry.'

Grandpa shrugs his shoulders.

After a while grandma shouts that grandpa is going and I go downstairs and hug him then wave him off at the door. Later, grandma makes hot chocolate and then tucks me up in bed.

'When will grandpa come to see us again? I ask grandma.

'I don't know Caroline. Maybe next week.' She tucks me in a bit tighter. 'Grandpa Ronnie is coming to see you tomorrow after school and he says he has a surprise for you!'

I smile. 'A surprise? Grandpa Ronnie?'

Grandma gets up. 'Yes. Now go to sleep young lady. You have school in the morning.'

My face goes sad. 'I don't want to go to school grandma. Everybody is horrible to me!'

Grandma frowns. 'Horrible? Why?'

I sob a bit. 'I don't know grandma but I don't want to go.'

'I will see if I can talk to your teachers this week,' says grandma. 'Now, good night.'

'Good night grandma.'

I hug Katy, who is better now, and go to sleep sobbing.'

The next day when grandma picks me up from school we go back inside and I am told to wait in the corridor while grandma goes in to speak to my teacher. I can hear grandma's raised voice and then she comes out and signals me to follow her.

'Come on Caroline.'

I look back at my teacher who is waving. 'See you tomorrow Caroline.'

'Bye Miss,' I say waving back.

When we are on the bus grandma says, 'I have had a word with your teacher and she says that you have been picked on a bit. She will keep her eye on you.'

'Thanks grandma.' I smile. 'Grandpa Ronnie is coming after, isn't he?'

Grandma nods. 'Yes, after tea.'

After tea I am giving Tina my Tiny Tears doll her medicine again and then I hear a knock at the door and grandma lets Grandpa Ronnie in. I can hear Grandpa Ronnie laughing and I can also hear a dog yapping! I run downstairs and a poodle runs up to me and jumps up, barking.

Grandpa Ronnie holds his hands out and I run and hug him.

'I have brought something for you,' says grandpa Ronnie. 'I want you to have Tootsie.'

I jump up and then look at grandma. 'Can I grandma? Can I have her? Please?'

Grandma nods. 'If your grandpa Ronnie says she is yours then of course you can have her.'

I bend down to hug Tootsie and she licks my face. 'Come on Tootsie,' I say. 'let's go and check your temperature!'

As we run off upstairs Grandpa Ronnie frowns. 'Tootsie isn't ill!'

Grandma waves her hand. 'Oh, she has a makeshift hospital up there! It was only yesterday that we thought Wanita the Spanish doll would have to have her leg off!'

Grandpa Ronnie laughs. 'I see Caroline is doing okay then!'

'Hmm,' says grandma. 'She's having a bit of a bad time at school Ronnie. She's being picked on. I've had a word with the teacher and she is keeping her eye out.' Grandma frowns. 'I am a bit worried Ronnie.'

'Well Pearl,' says grandpa Ronnie, 'maybe Tootsie will make her happy!'

'That she might Ronnie,' answers grandma.

Later on I come downstairs, followed closely by Tootsie, and go into the living room where grandma and Grandpa Ronnie are talking and laughing a bit. It's nice to see grandma laughing a bit!

Grandpa looks at me. 'Ah, Caroline. Is Tootsie fit and well then?'

'Yes grandpa,' I say smiling.

'Don't encourage her Ronnie!' says grandma. 'I might find a thermometer in my mouth tomorrow!'

Grandpa Ronnie laughs.

'Are you staying for supper Ronnie?' asks grandma.

'Oh, please do Grandpa Ronnie!' I say, with Tootsie on my knee now.

Grandpa Ronnie shakes his head. 'Unfortunately a guest house won't run itself!' Grandpa Ronnie groans. 'Besides, my leg is starting to ache so I want to get home.'

I lower my head and Tootsie licks my face, which makes me giggle a bit!

Grandpa Ronnie gets up and ruffles my hair. 'I will come and see you in a couple of days poppet. Take care of Tootsie!'

'I will grandpa.'

'Go and get ready for bed and then we can have some supper Caroline,' says grandma as she sees Grandpa Ronnie out of the door.

'Bye grandpa! See you in a couple of days.' I turn to go upstairs. 'Come on Tootsie. Race you to the top!'

I bite into my toast and then smile at grandma, 'Is Grandpa Ronnie okay grandma? What's wrong with his leg?'

Grandma sighs. 'He has hurt his leg, that's all. Now, don't you worry about it! Grandpa Ronnie knows how to take care of himself.'

I stroke Tootsie on the head. 'Can she sleep with me grandma? Please!'

'Okay,' says grandma nodding, 'but no mess in the house. You take her out if she needs to go!'

'Okay grandma. I promise!'

'Now, go to bed. I promised Mrs Dutton I would look in before I finished. She's been having trouble with her tummy and her daughter is on holiday.'

I nod and then run upstairs. Tootsie beats me, of course!

Grandma shakes her head. 'What is the matter now Caroline?'

I am crying, the tears running down my face. 'They are horrible to me grandma! I can't help it if mum has gone!'

I have had another year almost at this horrible school and I am feeling terrible because of the teasing and bullying.

Grandma raises her eyebrow. 'Oh? Is that what they've been teasing you about?'

'Yes,' I say nodding. 'They pinch me and ask if mummy is going to make me better! Grandma, why did mum have to go?' I start to bawl and the tears run down my face again.

Grandma marches me back into school. She sits me in the corridor and then storms into the headmaster's room. I can hear raised voices and the headmaster isn't happy about grandma barging in unannounced. When she comes out grandma straightens herself and then indicates for us to go.

'Come on Caroline. The headmaster is well and truly told! You won't have any more trouble.'

'Thanks grandma.' I say between sobs.

But the next day grandma is in the headmaster's office again after school! I am crying again and a couple of the nasty girls come past – they had been on detention – and snigger and poke me and I swing my hands out but they just poke me again and tell me to 'go and ask mummy to sort it out!'.

I hang my head and cry and they run off laughing.

Grandma comes out and sees me crying. 'What has happened Caroline?'

'Some of the girls have come past and poked and teased me again!; I say in between sobs. 'Why can't they stop taking about mum? You are supposed to stop them grandma. You are my mummy!'

Grandma shakes her head and we march out of the school. When we get home I hug Tootsie and then go up to my room.

'I will get you a drink Caroline,' shouts grandma and then shakes her head when I don't answer.

Later I hear Grandpa Ronnie's voice and realise grandma must have asked him to come. I hear them talking quite a lot and then I hear Grandpa Ronnie shouting me.

'Caroline? Come down. Grandma and me want to talk to you.'

I trudge downstairs, followed by Tootsie, and then sit in the chair opposite grandma with my head down.

Grandpa Ronnie smiles. 'Now then Caroline. What have they been saying at school?'

My lip starts to quiver and I sob a little.

'Oh, come on girl...' starts grandma but Grandpa Ronnie hold his hand up for her to stop. Grandma sits back.

Grandpa Ronnie continues. 'It is school holidays soon so your grandma and me have been talking and think it is a good idea that you stay off school until after the holidays. I'm sure Tootsie will be glad as well!'

I start to smile a bit but Grandpa Ronnie holds his hands up again and continues. 'You have to help your grandma around the place and do some studies at home but I... we can't have you treated like that Caroline.'

'Your grandpa's right. We need time also to try and get you to stick up for yourself a bit more!'

I stare at grandma. 'But they keep teasing me about mum,' I say between sobs. 'How can I stand up for myself when they are doing that?'

Grandpa Ronnie frowns. 'Why don't you leave the girl alone Pearl!

Grandma frowns. 'Don't you talk to me like that Ronnie! I...'

Grandma stops as she sees me running upstairs crying.

'Now see what you have done Pearl,' says Grandpa Ronnie shaking his head.

I lie on my bed and cry, Tootsie lies with me. I am so upset that I cry myself to sleep.

The next day grandma shouts upstairs.

'Come on Caroline! We have to go and do some shopping for a couple of the ladies. Then we have to clean here a bit.'

I trudge downstairs and into the house where grandma has put a drink on the table with some porridge. Tootsie follows me and lies at my feet. I start to eat the porridge and take a few sips of my drink.

I look up and my eyes are watery. 'Why did mum have to go grandma?'

Grandma straightens up. 'She was very poorly Caroline and in pain. She may have not wanted to be in pain.'

'But the doctors could have made her better grandma.'

Grandma shakes her head. 'No they couldn't. The doctors had done all they could. You know, she was special to me as well Caroline! Now, I promised your mum I would take care of you for life and that is what I am going to do.'

I sob and then carry on with my porridge.

'I have made arrangements for you to see a special doctor in a couple of weeks. You are not taking your mum going very well and I need you to speak to him.'

I stare at grandma. 'A doctor? What kind of doctor?'

'A special doctor that will try and help with your upsets and moods. We can't have you moping and crying forever!'

'Grandma. Why do I have to see a doctor? I am just upset.'

'Well, I think you need one!' answers grandma. 'Now, no arguments Caroline!'

'Can Grandpa Ronnie come as well?'

Grandma shakes her head. 'Grandpa Ronnie is too busy and he is not so well with his leg. I think he will be okay with it though. He is worried about you too.' Grandma smiles. 'Now, come on and lets do that shopping.'

I nod my head and, after giving Tootsie her breakfast, get my coat and grandma and I go shopping.

'The doctor was a flipping psychiatrist!' Grandpa Ronnie is not happy! 'Our Caroline doesn't need a psychiatrist. She needs flipping love and a mother!'

'Don't you lecture me Ronnie!' shouts Pearl scowling. 'Do you want her to be affected by bullying *all* her life?'

Ronnie sighs. 'No, of course not! But she isn't going mad! Ten is very young to lose your mother Pearl! She is still affected by that.'

'Don't you think I know that? I am the one picking up the pieces, not you, so it is difficult for me as well!'

'Hey, you have brought one girl up Pearl – Sandy. Don't forget that! Just do the same with Caroline.'

'A different thing Ronnie. Caroline is my granddaughter, not my daughter! It is a different relationship altogether!'

Ronnie gets up and limps over to get his coat. 'I have heard enough for one day Pearl. Just you mind that you give that girl a good life and bring her up well.'

'Huh?' says Pearl. 'Why wouldn't I? I will *always* be there for her. I promised, don't forget!'

'Do it for love Pearl, not just promises!' Grandpa Ronnie opens the door and looks back at grandma.

'I will see you in a couple of days.'

Pearl nods. 'I might bring Caroline up to the guest house for a change. It will do her good.'

Ronnie nods. 'Okay then. See you.'

As the door shuts I hug Tootsie and I know that they were talking about me but I don't know what they are saying.

'Caroline,' shouts grandma. 'Come down for your drink. I am making tea now so it wont be long. Have half done the stew.'

When I don't answer grandma goes into the kitchen and makes the stew.

***

'Why do I have to go to a different school grandma?'

I am twelve now and getting the usual young woman problems, which I must admit grandma has taught me well about, so I am not scared really. I have just learned that I am going to a new school though.

'Because at the new school you wont get picked on and bullied. Besides, the nuns will teach you better probably.'

'Nuns? I am going to a school run by nuns?'

Grandma nods. 'You will go there on a Sunday evening and come back on Friday afternoon.'

I stare in disbelief. 'I have to stay there all week and... not come home every day? Why grandma?'

Grandma sighs. 'Because... it will be good for you.'

'How will being away from home be good for me? Grandma, do you not want me any more?'

'Don't be silly!' retorts grandma. 'Of course I do.'

'Then why are you sending me away? How could you!'

Grandma frowns. 'Now, don't you take that tone with me young lady! Listen to me. I am telling you that it will get you to learn better! Now, no more back chat! You start there week after next.'

I sigh. 'Where is it grandma?'

'In Prestwich, near Manchester. I have arranged for a lady from Social Services to take you first day. Then you will catch the bus.'

'You mean... you will not be taking me first day? That's horrible grandma!'

'Don't you *dare* talk to me like that!'

I start to go watery eyed a little. 'What is going to happen to Tootsie?'

'Tootsie will stay here. This is her home,'

I hug Tootsie. 'I will miss her grandma.'

'She'll be okay. Now, no more to be said about it.'

'Does grandpa Ronnie know?' And what about grandpa Harry?'

'Now don't you go bothering grandpa Harry about this. Grandpa Ronnie does know. Now, lets get tea on.'

Grandma goes into the kitchen and I start to cry silently.

School Days

The knock on the door makes my tummy jump and then my grandma shouts upstairs.

'Caroline, The lady from Social Services is here to take you to school. Hurry up!'

'Coming!' I shout back. 'Won't be a minute.'

I am carefully rolling up my posters of John Travolta and David Cassidy and putting them in my bag. The poster of Donny Osmond and the smaller one of John Travolta can stay here for weekends. When I finally get downstairs the Social lady is having a cup of tea.

'This is Mrs Smith. She is going to take you to Prestwich to start at Tower Grange. Sister Margaret is expecting you.'

Mrs Smith smiles She has a couple of teeth missing and her skirt is very long but she smiles nice and has a kindly manner. 'Hello Caroline. Don't worry about a thing. Your grandma is a little busy to take you but I will make sure that you get there okay.'

I frown. 'Grandma isn't busy Mrs Smith. She just doesn't care!'

'Now, just a minute young lady...' starts grandma but she is stopped by Mrs Smith holding her hand up.

'I can understand Caroline being upset and so should you,' says Mrs Smith.' She turns to me. 'I'm sure that your grandma does care.'

I shrug my shoulders and then get my coat. 'I'm ready when you are Mrs Smith.'

I go over to grandma and she lightly hugs me but not very tight, really.

'By grandma,' I say. 'I love you.'

Grandma pats my shoulder. 'Bye Caroline. Take care. See you on Friday. Love you too.'

I grab my bag and stand waiting for Mrs Smith. She finishes her tea and stands.

'Come on Caroline,' she says. 'There won't be much traffic at this time on a Sunday.'

We go out to the car and I look back to see grandma standing at the door. Is that watering I see in her eyes? I can't tell but at least she didn't just go in. As we drive away grandma waves and I wave back.

Mrs Smith smiles. 'It'll be okay Caroline. I know this school and the nuns are very nice. They will look after you.'

'Will I have my own room Mrs Smith?'

Mrs Smith shakes her head. 'I don't know. I don't think so but you will have to wait and see.'

The rest of the journey is in silence and then we are pulling into the driveway of a big house up a lane lined with trees. As we pulled up in front of the house a couple of nuns come out of the house and walk up to the car. As I get out they smile and one of them holds out her hand.

'Hello Caroline, welcome to Tower Grange. I am Sister Margaret and this is Sister Gabrielle. We will show you to your room and then you can join us for dinner.' She looks at my one bag. 'Is this the only luggage you have?'

I nod and shake the sister's hand. 'Yes Sister Margaret. I have folded my clothes up nice in here.'

Sister Margaret turns to Sister Gabrielle. 'Please take Caroline's bag up to dormitory two. The girls are expecting her.' She turns to Mrs Smith. 'Thank you for bringing Caroline but where is her grandma?

Mrs Smith clears her throat a bit. 'Grandma is a warden for a number of elderly people so she is busy today. I said I would bring Caroline.'

Sister Margaret nods. 'Well, thank you Mrs Smith.'

'Yes, thank you Mrs Smith for bringing me.'

'That's okay Caroline,' answers Mrs Smith. 'I will call back to see your grandma on my way home and tell her you got here okay.'

Sister Margaret puts her hand on my shoulder and guides me towards the entrance. 'Come on. Let's get you settled.'

I wave at Mrs Smith and then go into the school with Sister Margaret.

The inside of the house is fabulous and I gasp a little bit!

Sister Margaret smiles. 'Do you like our school Caroline?'

'Its lovely!' I answer looking around.

'I think you will like it here,' continues Sister Margaret.

We carry on up a flight of stairs and then walk along a corridor. Sister Margaret opens a door and indicates for me to go in. There are five girls all look up at the same time and stare at me. I slink back to slightly behind Sister Margaret as I remember what those horrible girls did to me at the other school.

Sister Margaret puts her hand on my shoulder again and guides me round. 'Girls, this is Caroline. She is coming to join us here so I would like you to show her the ropes, so to speak!' She indicates to the spare bed. 'That's yours Caroline. Make yourself at home and then dinner is in about half-an-hour. I think it is chicken dinner tonight!'

One of the girls laughs. 'Yeah, with Mrs Priestman's lumpy gravy!'

'Now now Jenny. You know Mrs Priestman does very good gravy!'

She turns to go out of the room and I go and sit on my bed. My posters have slid out of my bag slightly and I pull them out and unroll the John Travolta. As I'm looking at I sense someone and I look up to see two of the girls standing in front of me. I quickly push back to the back of my bed and put the poster up on front of me.

One of the girls frown and looks at the other and they both shrug their shoulders.

'What's the matter with her?' asks one of them.

'Don't know. Only wanted to look at who was on her poster!'

I slowly turn the poster around and the second girl gasps. 'Ooh, John Travolta! He *is* a dish!'

'Dead right!' says the first girl. 'Are you going to put it up then Caroline?'

'Put it up near me please!' says the first girl.

'You have enough posters up already Sally!' says the girl Jenny from across the room.

'Who's on the other one?' asks the first girl.'

'Do you not have enough with John Travolta, Jessica?' asks Sally. She laughs. 'Go on then Caroline. Who is on the other one?'

I reach into my bag and pull the other poster out. Unrolling it I smile.

'Ah, it's David Cassidy! Another dish!' says Jessica.

'You do have taste, don't you Caroline!' says Sally.

'I've left Donny Osmond at home!' I say, wondering if I should speak at all.'

'Donny Osmond?' says a new girl. 'Why didn't you bring him as well?'

Sally throws her head in the air. 'Don't listen to Ursula! She likes *all* the Osmonds!'

A loud bell rings and all the girls go towards the door.

'Come on Caroline,' says Jenny. 'Let's go and eat Mrs Priestman's lumpy gravy!'

I smile as I follow the others to the dining room.

Actually, Jenny is wrong about the gravy! It tastes yummy and so does the whole dinner. I tuck into it and when nearly finished I see Sister Margaret looking over and smiling.

Sally leans over to me. 'So, why did your mum and dad send you here then?'

I look at her and my eyes start to water. Sally frowns and Sister Margaret nods her head.

'What's the matter Caroline?' asks Jessica.

I stand up and then run out of the dining room, straight upstairs and then into my room, sobbing.

I feel a hand on my shoulder and I jerk further up the bed.

'It's okay Caroline. I know about what has happened,' I hear the voice of Sister Margaret say.'

I turn round and sit on the bed, looking at her through tear soaked eyes. Sister Margaret has a kind face and her short stocky frame belies her fitness. The calmness around her is nice.

'Everything will be okay. We will tell the girls all about it at the right time but for now please come and finish your dinner. It's jam sponge and custard!'

'I'm not hungry now Sister,' I say between sobs.

'Are you all right Caroline?' asks Sally as she sits on the bed next to Sister Margaret.

'Do you want to tell her?' asks the sister.

I look up at Sally. 'My dad went when I was about four and my mum died three years ago,' I say sobbing.

'Oh,' says Sally. 'I'm sorry. So who has sent you here then?'

'My grandma.' I wipe my eyes. 'She promised my mum she would look after me and bring me up.'

'Huh!' says Sally. 'A fine grandma she is then! Sending you away.' She smiles. 'Anyway, we'll look after you!'

'We all look after each other here, don't we Sister Margaret?' Jenny says as she comes into the room.

Sister Margaret nods. 'Well, you seem to do Jenny.'

'Come on Caroline,' says Sally getting up. 'Mrs Priestman's jam sponge is very nice!'

'Custard's a bit lumpy though!' says Jenny.

'*Everything* is lumpy to you!' says Sally.

I laugh and then everyone laughs. We go back down to the dining room for our sweet.

After dinner the girls and I are in the dormitory putting up my posters and they are helping me settle in. Posters safely up I start to unpack my clothes and the others leave me alone for a while.

After a about quarter of an hour Jessica comes and sits on my bed. 'I am sorry to hear about your mum. I haven't seen my dad for a few years now.' She smiles. 'Anyhow, things could be a lot worse. One of the other girls next door has a poster of Gary Newman up – and the Jackson Five! I feel sorry for her!'

We both laugh and then all the others laugh as well.

'Thank you all,' I say. Thank you for helping me settle in.'

'It's okay,' says Sally.

'Come on,' says Jenny. 'Supper time is soon. Let's go and watch telly for a bit!'

We all run off down to the telly room.

'Now girls, come on. Settle down!'

The man at the front of the class looks down the room over the top of his glasses. Then he looks at me and I sort of smile a bit and then just look back.

'So, we have a new girl here. You must be Caroline.'

I nod and say, 'Yes, Sir.'

My name is Mr Vernon and I teach Maths and a bit of English and Science. How are you with those?'

I shrug my shoulders. 'I suppose I'm okay Mr Vernon. I didn't do as well as I should because I didn't have a good time at my last school.'

Mr Vernon smiles. 'Well, Caroline, you will learn a lot more here!'

'Are you sure she will?' asks Jessica. 'We haven't!'

The class laughs and Mr Vernon frowns. 'Very funny Jessica! See me afterwards.'

Jessica frowns. 'Aww!' But then she can see Mr Vernon smiling.

The lesson goes okay and after lunch we go back into class and Sister Katrina is waiting. I have not met her before but she seems very nice like all the others.

'Now, girls. Today we are going to learn about some social aspects of being young ladies and how you should be to fit in with life.'

Sally grins. 'We know all that Sister Katrina from watching Happy Days!'

Sister Katrina tuts and shakes her head, 'Well, Sally. There are no 'Fonzie's' here! I suppose you'll have to listen to me!' She sits down. 'Now, who can start me off?'

'You should always say please and thank you,' I say, wondering if I should have done.

Sister Katrina nods. 'Very good Caroline. Anybody else?'

'Never pump in the dining room?' says Sally laughing.

The class erupts into laughter and Sister Katrina shakes her head again. 'True that may be but it is not something I was thinking of!'

'Always respect your elders and listen to what they have to say,' says Angela, one of the girls I haven't spoken to yet.

As Sister Katrina and a few of the other girls nod in approval I am left to think quite how I could apply that to my grandma.

After classes we go back to the dormitory to do some English homework that Mr Vernon has set and then the bell goes for dinner. It is sausage, mash and beans today with onions and gravy and apple pie and custard for afters. When dinner is over we go straight into the telly room and watch the rest of the news, because Mr Vernon said that we could probably learn a thing or two! After Coronation Street and On The Buses it is supper time and then we sidle off back to the dormitory. After a face wash and teeth clean I am lay in bed, quietly reading my last week's copy of 'Jackie', when Sally and Jenny come and sit on the bed with me.

'Any nice posters in there?' asks Sally.

I shake my head. 'Not this week, only Johnny Rotton and The Jam!'

'The Jam?' shouts Lisa from her bed. 'Paul Weller isn't half bad!'

Jenny shakes her head. 'Next you'll be saying Tom Jones is nice Lisa!'

'Ha, ha. Very funny!' retorts Lisa.

Sally shrugs her shoulders. 'Well, Angela likes Elvis. She's mad on him!'

Sister Katrina pops her head round the door. 'Come on girls, it's Ten o'clock. Lights out!'

We all get back to our beds and put the lights out. There is still some light from the corridor outside so it isn't pitch black.

'You do know Caroline,' whispers Sally, 'that on Sunday nights when we come back we all bring something to eat. Midnight snacks!'

'I smile to myself. 'Ace! I like that. Butties and crisps okay?'

'Yep!' says Jenny. 'cans of coke as well!'

Then soon after there is no sound as we all fall asleep.

The next day we are waiting in class but no teacher has arrived yet. Eventually, a lady comes bursting into the room and, after putting her things down and taking her coat off, sits down and seems to be catching her breath for a few minutes.

'Good morning girls. Sorry I am late.'

I look at Sally who just shrugs. 'She has to come a long way!'

'Yes, thank you for that Sally!' says the Lady. She looks at me. 'You must be Caroline. I am Barbara and I will be teaching English and Biology. Later we will throw in a bit of Drama because I want to do a little play around Christmas time for the sisters and we need to make a start.'

Jenny leans over to me. 'That'll suit Jessica. She is a bit of a drama queen!'

'Hey, I heard that!' says Jessica.

There is some laughing and then Barbara clears her throat. 'Let's make a start then girls. We are going to kick off with some advanced punctuation in English verse.'

We all open our books and the lesson gets started.

After lunch we are in the big hall, a wonderful room with a large fireplace and some wood panelling and we are sat on the floor in an arc shape looking at Barbara.

'Now then Caroline,' says Barbara. 'Have you done any drama before?'

I shake my head. 'Not much miss. Sorry.'

'No need to be sorry,' says Barbara. 'Just start us off with anything you can. A verse, a bit of acting you have seen on the telly. Anything.'

Barbara indicates to the floor in front of her and I stand up.

I look around at the sea of faces and then I clear my throat. I start to get a bit sad and then my eyes start to water a little. All the other girls frown a bit but Barbara holds her hand up and indicates for me to start.

I clear my throat again. 'To lose a life is to lose a light. To lose someone special is to lose a soul.' I sit cross-legged in front of the others and bow my head. 'And to lose your mum is to lose it all!'I start to sob and then Barbara helps me up and sits me down on a chair. Sally and Jenny come and sit with me.

'That was great acting Caroline!' says Jenny.

I look at the two girls with watery eyes. 'I... wasn't acting. It's how I feel.'

Sally puts her arm around me. 'Don't be sad Caroline. We will have lots of fun and lots of snacks

so you won't have time to be sad!'

'Thank you,' I say between little sobs.

After class we all go back to the dormitory and I lie on my bed for a little while. Then, the bell sounds for dinner and we all go down to dinner, egg and chips with peas!

'At least Mrs Priestman can't make the egg lumpy Jenny!' says Lisa.

'Oh, very funny!' says Jenny.

After egg and chips we have a red, creamy pudding put in front of us.

I push my spoon in and it seems sloppy. 'What is it?' I ask looking at Sally.

'Jelly made with evaporated milk, whisked up! Try it, it's very nice!'

'Lisa laughs. 'And it's okay if it's lumpy, so even Jenny can't complain!'

Jenny scowls and then we all tuck into the pudding, smiling. Mmm! It does taste good!

After dinner we watch telly again and then at lights out Jessica quickly comes over to me.

'I am really sorry about how you were feeling earlier Caroline. Sally is right, we *will* make it a happy place here! Promise!'

The rest of the week goes much the same and the highlight is Thursday night when we all watch Top Of The Pops! On the Friday I am standing in the car park of the school and watching most of the other girls being picked up by someone from their family – mums, dads, grandparents! I say goodbye to my friends and then pick up my bag and start to walk down to the gate.

'Caroline!'

I hear Sister Margaret shouting after me. I stop and turn to see her catch up with me.

'Have you enjoyed your first week here Caroline?' she asks.

I nod. 'Yes, Sister Margaret. I have. Thank you.'

'I know it has been a hard time but I want you to know that you will be okay with us.'

I smile a little. 'Thank you.'

'Now,' continues Sister Margaret, 'are you going to be okay going home?'

'Yes thank you Sister,' I say, picking up my bag. 'I know which buses to catch and my grandma should be at the other end.'

'Very well,' says Sister Margaret. 'See you Sunday.'

'Bye,' I say.

As I am travelling on the bus I am thinking what a lovely place the school is! I have made some new nice friends and the food is very good and, best of all, I have not been bullied! As I reach the other end I can see my grandma waiting. I get off the bus and smile at grandma.

'Hello grandma!'

'Hello Caroline,' says grandma with no real expression on her face. 'How was school?'

I smile. 'It was nice grandma! The nuns are really nice, and so are the teachers, and I have made some nice new friends...'

I look at grandma and see that she is not really interested. My face goes sad and stays that way for much of the weekend, only smiling when I am listening to the radio or playing with Tootsie, who never leaves me alone!

Sunday comes and I am quite excited about going back. I have told my grandma that we have been asked to take sandwiches, crisps, cakes and a drink as the cook is not in until the Monday. It is a white lie as I need to take them for our midnight snack! I say goodbye to Tootsie and then grandma and Grandpa Ronnie, who had come at lunchtime to see how I was doing. He had a lot more interest in what school was like for me and as I hugged him tight I can see grandma frowning a little. Then I go and hug grandma and she sighs.

'Now, think on,' says grandma as I pick my bag up. 'Take care on the buses and make sure you learn useful things.'

'Oh, can't you just say goodbye nicely Pearl?' says Grandpa Ronnie. 'It's bad enough the girl has to make her way there without you making her feel unhappy.'

'Unhappy?' says grandma sternly. 'She says she likes it there. And don't you tell me off again, Ronnie!'

I can see grandpa sigh and then wince in pain a little as he turns round. I am worried for grandpa Ronnie.

By the time I get back to school virtually everyone else is there but I am welcomed by my friends and then we go into the telly room where we are brought tea and biscuits.

'Ah, Caroline,' says Sister Katrina as she sets the biscuits down on the table. 'Was your journey okay? Have you managed the buses all right?'

I nod and smile. 'Yes thank you Sister Katrina. I am glad to be back here safe!'

After lights out we all lie on our beds and then some while later, when there is no noise from outside the dormitory, a lot of giggling starts and then some low lights start to go on.

'Not so open with the torches!' says Sally. 'We don't want sister to know we're still up!'

'Caroline?' I hear Jenny say. 'Have you got your goodies?'

'Yes I have!' I answer excitedly. 'I told my grandma the cook was off until tomorrow so she made me lots of butties and gave me a box of cakes!'

'Any pop?' asks Jessica.

'Coke and lemonade!' I answer.

'Great!' says Sally. 'Let's get going then!'

For the next half-hour all you can hear the most is munching of food and burping after the coke!

We are in the next door dormitory and it is nearly dinner time. I am sat to one side on one of the beds but some of the girls are comforting Angela. She is crying a little bit and we can understand why but Sister Gabrielle can't!

'I cannot understand why someone would cry so much over someone that is not part of the family!' says Sister Gabrielle.

Sally looks at her and sighs. 'Sister Gabrielle. When the pop star you like dies it is like losing part of the family! Do you not know that? Anyway, it is tragic that Elvis has died!'

'I know. I know,' says Sister Gabrielle. 'It is tragic but Angela is taking it a bit far!'

'So you don't know how it works then Sister Gabrielle!' says Jenny smiling.

'The girls are correct!' says Sister Margaret as she comes into the dormitory. 'Now, come on Angela. I know this has affected you like all the rest of the world but we need to talk and try and help you.' She looks around the room. 'Girls, go back to your dormitories and wait for dinner. Sister Gabrielle and I will look after Angela.'

We all give Angela a little squeeze on the arm and then we sidle back to our room.

'It is a bit bad, Elvis dying,' says Jessica.

'He wasn't very old, was he?' I say with slightly wet eyes. I am remembering my mum dying young and it is bringing it back a bit.

'Are you okay Caroline?' asks Sally.

I nod my head. 'I'm fine. I'm just thinking about mum with Elvis dying.'

Sally puts her arm around me. 'Don't worry Caroline. Mrs Priestman's beefburger and chips will put it right!

I smile and then the bell goes for dinner. We all dash off to the dining room, all except Angela and the sisters. Strangely, I know how she feels.

The next day we have breakfast and then we have to get a packed lunch each from Mrs Priestman as we are going on a trip for the day to a Roman museum in Chester. Barbara thinks it would be a good idea to see how people lived in old times so we know how lucky we are to live now! Sally thinks it is just so she doesn't have to sit in a classroom all day again! Never mind, we are all looking forward to it and soon the coach comes to take us. Once we are on board and Barbara has counted us the coach sets off and we all sit back.

'Can we have the radio on please Barbara?' asks Sally.

Barbara sighs and looks to the driver. 'Can we?'

The driver nods and smiles as he puts a load of classical rubbish on' He laughs as the resounding 'aww!' cuts in over the music and then he winks at Barbara and puts some decent pop music on!

The journey takes about an hour and then we all sidle off the coach with our bags and then we go into the museum. The tour and talk takes about an hour and then we are having our packed lunch on the banks of the river. A Punch and Judy show can be heard in the background and the weather is quite nice.

'A bit boring that museum,' says Lisa, 'but at least we got out.'

'I thought it was quite interesting,' I say taking a much on my cheese sandwich.

Lisa raises her eyebrow. 'Have you not been on many trips Caroline?'

'No,' I answer. 'My grandma never took me anywhere really. Miserable she is!'

Jenny takes hold of my hand. 'You are going to like the holiday in a few weeks then Caroline! We are going to stay in a convent in Llandudno for a week!'

'You are going to need your grandma to agree for you to go,' continues Sally. 'Do you think she will?'

I sigh and take on a sad look. 'I don;t think she will bother where I go during the week really,' I answer.

'Good!' says Sally. 'Then we will all have a good time!'

'Hurry up girls!' shouts Barbara. 'Coach leaves in fifteen minutes and we have got to get back to where it is parked.'

We have had some free time to look around the shops and, as you would think, we were in a record shop! We all groan a bit and then follow Barbara to the coach. Some of us fall asleep on the way home and then we have arrived back at the school, just in time for dinner!

'Come on, chop chop girls!' says Sister Margaret. Mrs Priestman has made a nice potato hash!'

'Urgh!' says Jenny. 'I hate red cabbage!'

'At least the gravy in the hash is smooth Jenny!' teases Jessica.

Jenny actually laughs.

After dinner it is Top Of The Pops again and the show is dedicated to Elvis, which makes Angela cry a little again!

Friday's lessons with Sister Margaret are quite boring, even though she is nice, and later I say goodbye to my friends and then get the bus home. Grandma is waiting for me as I get off the bus but I don't say much this time. When we get home Tootsie runs to me and licks my face! I cuddle her and then she follows me upstairs as I take my things up to my room.

Over supper I smile at grandma. 'We went to Chester yesterday grandma and saw the Roman museum!'

'Oh, very nice,' says grandma.

'Isn't it sad about Elvis grandma?'

'It is sad really,' says grandma. 'It is a shame. Your mother used to like Elvis, you know.'

I look sad a little and then grandma continues.

'Tomorrow Caroline I am taking you to stay with Grandpa Harry for the day. I am very busy and he wants to take you out into town. I think he is buying you some jumpers and shoes for school.'

I smile. 'Oh, it will be nice to see Grandpa Harry grandma.' I think for a moment. 'It is nice to see you as well grandma.'

'Hmm, that's as maybe,' says grandma, 'but I am very busy tomorrow. We'll spend some time Sunday until you have to go and get the bus.'

'Grandma?' I ask. 'In a couple of weeks we are going to stay in a convent in Llandudno. Is it okay if I go? You need to sign a form if it is.'

'That will be nice for you,' says grandma. 'I will sign it before you go back tomorrow.'

'Thanks grandma!' I give her a little hug. 'Goodnight.'

Grandma hugs me. 'Goodnight.'

'Come on Tootsie!' I say. 'let's go to bed.

Tootsie still beats me upstairs!

Grandpa and I have been shopping and we are back at his cottage having fish and peas!

'I am going to Llandudno for a little holiday in a few weeks. We are staying in a convent there!'

'That will be nice Caroline!' says Grandpa Harry, 'Llandudno is a nice place. You'll like it there.'

'All my friends are going so it should be a good time grandpa.'

'So your friends are nice then?' asks grandpa.

I nod and smile. 'They are lovely girls grandpa. We get on well.'

'That's good,' says Grandpa. 'You seem happy there then.'

I sigh. 'But I still am away from home in the week grandpa.'

Grandpa Harry smiles. 'It seems like it is a home from home anyway Caroline.'

I take a sip of my drink and put my plate to one side. 'The nuns are really nice grandpa. The teachers are okay as well.'

'Teachers?' asks Grandpa Harry.

'Yes. We have Mr Vernon and a lady called Barbara. The nuns teach things about life and God and everything.'

The knock on the door interrupts us and Grandpa Harry lets grandma in.

'Hello Pearl. Caroline has been telling me all about this wonderful school she has gone to. It sounds really nice, doesn't it?'

Grandma frowns. 'I don't really know a lot about it Harry.'

'Has she not told you much?' asks Grandpa Harry.

'I haven't had much time to listen if she had!'

'I have tried grandpa but grandma has been busy.'

'Oh, Pearl!' exclaims Grandpa Harry.

'Come on Caroline. Get your coat!' says grandma standing in front of the door.

I put on my coat and then hug Grandpa Harry. 'Thank you for my shoes and clothes grandpa, and for tea.' I hold my shoes up to grandma. 'Aren't they nice grandma?'

'Very nice,' says grandma.

I wave as we go out of the door. 'Bye grandpa. See you soon.'

'Bye.' says grandpa.

'It is a nice school grandma,' I say as we are walking for the bus. 'My friends are nice.'

'At least they don't bully you like the other place!' says grandma.

I stay in bed a bit for a lie in Sunday morning and then grandma shouts that breakfast will be ready in a while and I can suddenly smell the bacon! So can Tootsie and she runs downstairs as I get my dressing gown on.

'I have made a sausage for Tootsie as well.' says grandma. 'She can have it when it cools down.'

I sit down to egg, bacon, sausage and beans and when my grandma isn't looking I craftily give Tootsie some!

Later I get dressed and then go down with Tootsie and my grandma is packing my bag.

'I have put you some ham sandwiches and bacon crisps in Caroline,' says grandma with a frown. 'Just in case the cook isn't in again! Oh, and your signed form for Llandudno is in as well.'

'Thanks grandma.' I look at her for a few moments. 'We do get very good meals grandma.'

'I should think you do!' says grandma.

Then it is time to get my coat on and go back to school.

I give grandma a hug and then pick up my bag. 'Bye grandma. See you Friday!'

Grandma gives me a hug and pats my shoulder. 'Bye Caroline. Have a good week.'

The journey is the same as usual and when I get to school I meet up with Jessica and we go to the dormitory together. Later, after Sunday roast chicken dinner and treacle sponge and custard we go up to the room and put the radio on for the Top twenty! As we expected, Elvis is at number one with 'The Wonder Of You' and we can hear Angela weeping a little again!

After Sister Gabrielle has ordered lights out we are having our midnight feast.

'Have you got your form signed Caroline?' asks Sally.

'Oh yes!' I answer. 'it's going to be fun, isn't it!'

The other girls agree and then we have finished and it is torches out as well!

The next morning it is prayers as usual before breakfast and, as Jenny has suggested, the porridge *is* lumpy! She is right for once!

Once breakfast is over we get our things and then go to class, where Mr Vernon is waiting for us. He looks at us all over his spectacles and as we settle he clears his throat.

'Now,' he says, 'we are going to cover Maths this morning.'

The rest of the morning I struggle and although Mr Vernon recognises this he carries on as he can see I am doing the best I can. In the afternoon Sister Margaret takes us for Social Behaviour and she also takes our signed forms off us for the week in Llandudno.

'She smiles when I give her mine. 'Glad you are coming Caroline!'

'Yeah' says Jenny. 'We're going to have a great time!'

After dinner we watch some telly and then lights out comes.

The next morning I am looking in the mirror and frown. 'Not another one!'

Jessica turns to look at me. 'Another what?'

'Spot!' I answer, mauling with my face. 'I am getting covered in spots!'

'Don't worry about it!' shouts Lisa from across the bathroom. 'I have been getting them for weeks!'

'I think we all have them at the moment!' says Sally.

The next few weeks are much the same, general school work and fun at school and going home at weekends to my moping grandma and sometimes seeing my grandpas, which makes me smile. Tootsie also makes me smile and she and me are inseparable all weekend. I am glad grandma doesn't know I feed Tootsie scraps from the table! She would go mad!

The weeks go by and then it is the Sunday evening before we go to Llandudno.

Grandpa Harry is at our house. 'Have a good time Caroline! The weather is going to be okay so it'll be nice in Llandudno.'

'I will Grandpa Harry. The girls reckon we are going to have a really fun time!'

'Well, mind your manners and don't get into any bother!'

'There you go again Pearl! Always thinking about manners and behaving. Why not tell Caroline to have a good time?'

Grandma sighs. 'I know.' She turns to me. 'Have a good time Caroline. Er, stay safe.'

I give grandma a hug. 'Thanks grandma. Do you want me to bring a stick of rock back for you?'

Grandma nods. 'That would be nice!' She lets go of me and reaches into her handbag. 'Here you are

Caroline. A little bit of money to get by on your trip.'

'Thanks grandma,' I say again.

Then I hug Grandpa Harry. 'Bye grandpa! See you next week.'

'Bye Caroline,' says Grandpa Harry. 'Keep safe and enjoy it. Now, don't dawdle because you know the state of those blinking buses! Especially on a Sunday!'

I give Tootsie an extra special and long hug and she licks my face, making me giggle!

Then I get my bag and I am out of the door for the bus.

When I get to school my friends greet me and we are all laughing and then Sister Margaret shouts for us to listen.

'Now, after a snack from Mrs Priestman the coach will be here to take you all to Llandudno. I have just come off the telephone to Sister Francesca and she has nice rooms for you all. Sister Katrina and Sister Louie will be going with you for the week so make sure you give a good account of yourselves!' She bows her head. 'I know you will! Now, go on girls and have a great time and, don't forget your prayers!'

We all laugh a bit and then go inside for our snack.

A little later we are on the coach and Sister Louie has started a sing-song! It passes the time well as before we know it we have reached Llandudno and then it doesn't take long to find the convent we are staying at, Gogarth Abbey on the side of the Great Orme. Once we are settled into our rooms – there are only three of us to a room and I am sharing with Sally and Jessica – we go to the dining room for a supper of thick soup and bread. The convent is a big house with high ceilings and the dining room is wood-panelled. After supper we are sat in the prayer hall and Sister Francesca is addressing us. She is a tall, sharp-featured lady but with a kind face and a dignified manner.

'Welcome to Gogarth Abbey ladies. Here we spend a lot of time going into the community so you will all have plenty of time to be near the sea front! We learn a lot as well so, even though it is a holiday for you, it is a working holiday also.' She stops and looks around at our saddening faces and then smiles. 'Though, not too much work! You are here to enjoy yourselves!'

We start to smile and Sister Francesca continues. 'One of the days we are going up the Great Orme on the rail carriage and another we are going to look at Conway Castle. So, plenty to do!'

After this great news we go to our rooms and settle down to some serious chatter until lights out.

The next day we have prayers and then breakfast and then we are taken out on a general walkabout in Llandudno. It is a nice day and the sun is shining between the clouds. The morning is spent chatting to people and seeing if the place is tidy. We stop for our picnic lunch on the pier about midday and then we have ice cream. In the afternoon we go back to the convent for free time and then dinner is about six o'clock. Then we are in the main telly room.

'Are you enjoying it Caroline?' asks Sally.

I nod and smile. 'It's great isn't it! I can't wait to go up the Great Orme!'

'It looks high up though!' says Sally. 'It will probably be very windy!'

'Well, *I* am looking forward to the castle!' chips in Jenny.

Sister Louie comes into the room. 'Come on girls, Time to turn in. Lights out is in fifteen minutes.'

'Is it *that* late already? I ask.

'Come on. Let's get going then!' says Sally.

We go up to bed and wait for the next exciting day.

Day two and after morning prayers – we don't get away from that! – we eat a nice breakfast and then we are told we are walking around the Great Orme to get to the tramcar station to go up it. It is very windy when we get to the top and all our skirts are blowing! Sister Louie is pointing towards the cafe, trying to stop her nun's habit blowing all over the place and we follow her to the comfort of indoors.

'Phew!' says Sally. 'It *is* windy up here!'

I nod. 'You were right Sally, about the wind! Still, it's not that cold really.'

'Well, *I* am quite chilly!' says Lisa.

'You are always chilly Lisa!' says Jessica. 'She once put on the fire in the dormitory in summer!'

'I wasn't well!' retorts Lisa with a frown. 'I had a bad cold and chesty cough!'

'Okay, I suppose you did,' says Jessica begrudgingly.

We go back down for another walkabout in the afternoon and then we have an hour looking round the shops on the pier, and an ice cream!

Later there is some study to do and then dinner is announced by a bell, the same as Tower Grange, but the food isn't quite as good here. After dinner some of us watch telly and a couple of the girls play draughts and then it is supper and lights out. Sally and I talk for a while and then we drift off to sleep.

The next day we assemble in the car park after prayers and breakfast we get the coach and it takes us over the water to Conway. It is sunny and as we pull into the car park at the castle I stare a little at its beauty.

Jenny whistles. 'It *is* wonderful! I've been looking forward to this!'

We are taken on a tour and in the shop there is a little note pad with the castle on so I buy it for grandma. A few of the girls buy other things and then we walk down to the little harbour. We get fish and chips, bought by the sisters, and then we have a little bit of free time so Sally, Jenny and I are sitting on a bench looking at the boats.

'I would like a boat one day,' says Jenny.

'I would just like to come to places like this more often,' I say getting hold of Jenny's and Sally's hands, 'with good friends like you two!'

We all smile at each other and then look at the boats again for a while.

Then we are collected along with the others and taken back to Gogarth Abbey. The rest of the afternoon is taken up with a couple of short lessons from Sister Louie and Sister Francesca. After dinner – steak pie and chips – we watch telly again and then have a little chat in bed before lights out.

It is Thursday today and we are going to the Welsh Mountain Zoo. We have a great time and the sisters buy us burger and chips from the cafe! Jenny pulls faces at the monkeys, who seem to pull faces back! I like the monkeys though and Sally likes the tigers. After the zoo we go back into Llandudno and have some free time shopping. Sally and I go with Sister Louie and find out she likes looking in antique shops for small things, like plates and kettles! I see a little plate for fifty pence that my grandma would like so I get that for her, to go with the note book from Conway Castle. In the evening we have a sing-song after dinner and Sister Francesca leads prayer and then we are off to bed as the next day we are studying. We are all sad though that we've missed Top Of The Pops!

Friday morning comes and we have prayer and then a nice breakfast of bacon, egg, toast and some pancakes and then it is off to Llandudno again for a last walkabout and look around before we go back and get our things together. About two o'clock the coach is loaded up ready to take us back to Manchester.

'Thank you for your hospitality and a lovely time Sister Francesca,' says Sister Katrina. 'I know the girls have had a great time here, haven't you girls!'

'Yes Sister!' we all shout in unison.

Sister Francesca smiles. 'We have enjoyed you all being here. I hope that we have shown you enough of the area to make you want to come back!'

'Yes, Sister Francesca,' we all say together again.

Then we all get on the coach and wave goodbye as it pulls out of the car park. The journey home is good as the coach driver has a decent radio station on again and the sisters doze a bit. They don't really like the music!

About two hours later we are back at Tower Grange and I quickly get off the coach and run upstairs to get my other things as I need to catch my bus home.

Sister Margaret comes into the dormitory and smiles. 'Caroline, it is quite late today so Sister Katrina is going to take you home this evening. It will save you worrying about the bus.'

'Thank you Sister Margaret,' I smile and take my time a bit. 'Is there time for me to have a drink before we go?'

Sister Margaret nods. 'I think so Caroline.'

I go downstairs for my drink and then Sister Katrina and I are in the car and on the way home. We talk about the trip to Llandudno so the journey doesn't seem so log. At the other end my grandma is putting something in the bin as we pull up outside the house.

Grandma comes to the car as I am getting my bag out.

'We didn't get back from Llandudno until quite late so I have brought Caroline home,' says Sister Katrina to my grandma. She holds her hand out which grandma shakes. 'I am Sister Katrina.'

'Thank you Sister Katrina,' says grandma.

'I had a great time grandma!

'That's nice Caroline,' says grandma. 'Now, go inside as Tootsie is waiting.'

'Thank you Sister Katrina,' I say waving. 'See you on Sunday.'

'Good bye.' says the sister to grandma. I see grandma look strange at Sister Katrina as she drives off but I don't know why. Tootsie is all over me as grandma comes into the house.

'Sister Katrina is nice grandma, they all are.'

'Of course she is nice!' says grandma. 'She is a nun! Now, take your bag upstairs and I will get hot chocolate on.'

I go upstairs and think that I want it to be Sunday again so I can go back to my friends!

It is now year two and I am enjoying school – in fact, I have now got to the stage where I can't wait to get to school! Oh, except for Tootsie who I miss so much when I am not at home! I asked Sister Margaret if I could bring Tootsie with me, as a joke, but she said no!

It is quite exciting this week as I am due to start work experience in a chemists in Broughton. I am really looking forward to this and then the day is here and I am taken to my job! Once I am shown some basic things, like stacking some shelves and talking to some customers I get on with it okay, which seems to please the pharmacist Mr Isaacson. On my third day Mr Isaacson lets me serve a few customers as he thinks that I am friendly and very good with people! I am also checking prescriptions and giving them to him and I am really enjoying it. Every so often I had to clear the shelves and clean them and they were always spotless!

Most evenings Mr Isaacson takes me back to the school and I talk about the day's work with my friends at dinner. In fact, we swap stories as Sally has gone to work in a doctors surgery and Jenny works in a kennels with the dogs, which she likes very much! At dinner Sister Margaret tells us that next week we are going to see a Jewish Synagogue and Mrs Priestman will be getting a day off as they are laying on a buffet in the hall next door to it.

I am telling Mr Isaacson the next day and he tells me that I will really enjoy it and that the food will be tasty! I am serving more now and I have been allowed to stock some of the medicines on the shelves -well, I have cleaned them okay! A couple of the regular customers have got to know me now and I talk to them when they come in. One of them is an elderly Jewish lady called Mrs Abraham and I always ask her to sit down whilst we get her medicines. She always says I am very polite and a lovely young lady, which has Mr Isaacson smiling every time!

When it comes to Friday I don't really want to go home as I will want to tell grandma about the chemists but I know she won't be interested. However, when I get off the bus in Bolton it is Grandpa Ronnie that meets me and I have a big smile on my face!

I run to hug him. 'Grandpa, grandpa! I have been working in a chemist all week and it's brill!'

'Oh, great!' says grandpa Ronnie. 'I bet that was interesting! You can tell me all about it when we get home.'

'Is grandma okay?' I ask

'She's fine,' answers Grandpa Ronnie. 'She's just a bit busy this afternoon.'

We get home and grandma looks like she has just come in as she has still got her coat on.

'Hi grandma!'

'Oh, hello Caroline.' Grandma gives me a little hug and pats my shoulder. 'Have you had a good week?'

'Oh, yes grandma!' I answer excitedly. 'I have been working in a chemists shop! The owner, Mr Isaacson, is very nice!'

'Oh, a Jewish chemists!' says grandma. 'Have they looked after you?'

I frown. 'Yes, why do you ask like that?'

'Don't you be so lippy with me young lady!' says grandma. 'I am your grandma and don't you forget it!'

'Oh, leave her alone Pearl! She was only asking because it sounded like you didn't like the fact it was Jewish! You don't see her all week and then you are not nice when she has something exciting to tell you.'

Grandma scowls. 'If you can't say anything nice to me Ronnie then go home!'

Grandpa Ronnie goes right up to grandma. 'And don't you talk to me like that either Pearl!'

I run upstairs with watery eyes and Tootsie goes with me. I throw my bag on the floor and lie on my bed, sobbing. Tootsie lies with me and we stay there until grandma calls us for supper. Why does grandma not like me?

***

Sally and I have left little bits of food on plates all over the room as we try bits of the Jewish buffet and then if we don't like it we put it down with a quiet 'urgh!'. The small service in the synagogue was quite nice and the lady from the shop, Mrs Abraham, is there. I take Sally and Jenny over to talk to her and they say that she is a very nice lady. There is some Jewish music going at the buffet and some of the people are doing a traditional dance. Sisters Margaret and Gabrielle have come with us and they seem to be enjoying it as well. Sister Margaret has got talking to Mrs Abraham and another lady and the three of them seen to be laughing and getting on well.

'So, Caroline serves you in the shop then Mrs Abraham?' asks Sister Margaret.

'Oh yes dear,' answers Mrs Abraham. 'She always makes sure I have a seat and she is very polite. I always ask for her to serve me now!'

I am standing in the corner with Sally and we are eating Jewish apple cake, which we both like.

We see the Rabbi come over to us and we brush the crumbs off our clothes.

Rabbi Cohen smiles at me. 'Mrs Abraham tells me you look after her in the chemists.'

I nod and smile. 'That's right Rabbi. I make sure there's a chair free for her.'

'That's very kind young lady!' says the Rabbi. He turns to Sally. 'So, where is your work experience then?'

Sally clears her throat slightly. 'Oh, I work in a doctors surgery Sir.'

Rabbi Cohen smiles. 'Ah, yes. Doctor Grossman's surgery. I have it on good authority that you are doing okay too!'

Sister Margaret comes over. She bows slightly to Rabbi Cohen. 'I'm sorry Rabbi but I have to take the girls back now. Mrs Priestman will never forgive us if we miss supper!'

Sally and I look at each other and wonder how we are going to eat supper after all this food!

Rabbi Cohen laughs. 'Okay Sister Margaret. It has been lovely having you all. Have you enjoyed your time with us?'

Sister Margaret nods. 'We have had a lovely time! Thank you for having us.'

'Any time,' says Rabbi Cohen. He smiles at Sally and me. 'Keep up the good work girls and it was lovely to talk to you.'

We say our goodbyes, especially to Mrs Abraham, and then we get the coach back to school.

We actually manage to have some supper, mainly so as not to upset Mrs Priestman, and then we are lay on our beds having a chat.

'I like working for the doctors Caroline,' says Sally.

'The chemists is good too,' I answer. 'Jenny,' I call out. 'How do you like the kennels?'

'Oh, I love it!' says Jenny. 'Tomorrow I am going into the puppy house and giving some little puppies milk!'

'Aww, that'll be wonderful!' I say.

Sister Katrina pops her head round the door for lights out and we are quickly asleep after the busy day.

The next day I am back in the chemists and Mr Isaacson is talking to a customer about the buffet the night before. I am smiling and Mr Isaacson sees this.

He indicates towards me. 'Caroline here went, didn't you?'

I nod.

'It was a nice evening wasn't it?' asks Mr Isaacson of me.

'It was a lovely evening, Mr Isaacson,' I answer. 'The food was very nice and I had a little dance. It was good.'

'I'm glad to hear it!' says Mr Isaacson.

The rest of the morning I work hard cleaning the shelves and then stocking them and after lunch I am sat at the back of the shop finishing off my drink. I hear a familiar voice and I spring up and then dash to pick a chair up and take it into the shop area. I smile at Mrs Abraham as she sits down.

'Thank you young lady,' says Mrs Abraham. 'Did you enjoy the party last night?'

I nod. 'Yes, I enjoyed it very much thank you Mrs Abraham. Did you?'

Mrs Abraham laughs. 'Yes I did, thank you!' She thinks for a moment and grins. 'Although I didn't do much dancing!'

'I should hope not!' cuts in Mr Isaacson. 'Not with all the medicines we give you!'

The rest of the day is pretty mundane and then it is time for Mr Isaacson to run me back to school. When re reach Tower Grange Sister Margaret is looking at the gardens next to the car park. She spies the car pulling up and comes over.

'Good evening Mr Isaacson,' says Sister Margaret. 'Have you had a good day?'

'It's been quite good, thank you. The doctors was open later last night so there were a lot of prescriptions this morning.'

'And how is Caroline doing?' asks the sister.

'She is a great help!' says Mr Isaacson smiling at me. 'She keeps the place spotless and the shelves well stocked. I will miss her when her time is ended! Tell me, Sister Margaret. How much longer is Caroline spending with me?'

Sister Margaret drops her head slightly and I see a slight smile on her lips. 'Oh, I think we can spare her for next week as well!'

I spring up and clap my hands lightly. 'Oh, good! Thank you Sister Margaret!'

'Yes, thank you!' says Mr Isaacson.

I go home at weekend happy and spend some time with Grandpa Harry but, as usual, grandma is still too busy to bother much with me. Tootsie is glad to see me and I get to spend a little more time with her, even taking her for a couple of walks.

The next week at school I spend at Mr Isaacson's chemist and then my time there has come to an end. A happy thing happens, though, as the nuns arrange a surprise party for my fifteenth birthday and made me a lovely card! My friends gave me cards as well and we have a little buffet laid on by Mrs Priestman.

On the Thursday we are on our weekly visit to the baths and, as usual, I stand in the shallow end and splashed about as I can't swim.

The nights are great as the girls and I have become very good at dodging the sisters after lights out and our ever-increasing hoard of biscuits and chocolate has not been found yet, which is a good thing as we have heard that Sister Katrina has a very sweet tooth!

In the summer grandma and Grandpa Harry take me to Bournemouth for a week and the weather is lovely! The guest house is very nice and we have dinner there as well. In the evening there is entertainment but while grandma and Grandpa Harry have a little dance I sit in the corner and sip my lemonade!

The next day grandma and Grandpa hurry me up to get ready as the are taking me to the Isle of Wight on the ferry! I like it there and we go to a bay where there are different coloured sands. We have a really nice day on the island with a lunch of fish and chips of course! When we get back in the evening I am tired out and have a little something to eat and then I go to bed. In the morning we have breakfast and then we go and visit a model village, We feel like giants instead of the little people!

After the holiday I have a week at home and then it is back to school. My friends are all waiting and they tell me that they have been away as well. Sally has been to France and Jenny has been to Wales again, but this time to Tenby as it was warmer there! I tell them about Bournemouth and especially the Isle of Wight and they say that it must have been exciting!

'So was it okay with your grandma then?' asks Sally.

'It was okay really,' I answer. 'Grandpa Harry was there as well so it was quite good!

'That's all right then,' says Jenny.

At dinner Sister Margaret is also pleased that I had a good holiday. I tell her that I really enjoyed the Isle of Wight and then Sister Katrina says she has been there and she really enjoyed it!

After lights out we get the torches out – and the butties and crisps! Jessica has managed to get some big bottles of lemonade in so we have a really good midnight picnic.

Sally laughs. 'Jessica has got a boyfriend, haven't you Jessica?'

'Oh, shut up! He's just a friend from up the street!' retorts Jessica.

'Hah!' says Jenny, 'a likely story!'

We laugh that much that someone must have heard us and we hear the floor creaking down the corridor! Quickly, we hide all the evidence – we have been practising! – and put the torches out. When Sister Gabrielle puts her head round the door everything is quiet and we see her shake her head and then she goes. We giggle but afterwards go to sleep as we know we won't get away with it again tonight!

It is now Christmas and I am home with grandma for the week, going back to school the day after New Years Day. I am worried about Grandpa Ronnie as he seems to be limping very badly and often looks in a lot of pain! I ask him about it and he just smiles and says that his foot is hurting but it will get better soon. I don't believe him though. I am getting different presents now and one off my grandma is a personal cassette player and some David Cassidy and Osmonds tapes. I have to read some school books ready for the next year at school. Tootsie is, as ever, always by my side and although it is cold and frosty I don't mind wrapping up warm and taking her out. Luckily, Grandpa Harry has bought me a lovely new jumper for Christmas so I am nice and warm!

Christmas dinner is lovely and grandma has cooked the turkey very nicely again!

'So, what's happening in your last year at school Caroline?' asks Grandpa Ronnie.

'I swallow my mouthful of food. 'I go on another work experience this year. I think I am going into a nursery!'

'Huh!' says grandma. 'Better you than me! Wouldn't want all those screaming kids all day! Give me old folk any day!'

Grandpa Ronnie frowns. 'Oy, Pearl! Don't you go pouring scorn on Caroline's schooling! I think she will enjoy herself in a nursery. She is very good and friendly!'

'I suppose so.' mutters grandma. 'I hope you enjoy it Caroline.'

'Oh, I know I will grandma.'

'Have you any idea where the nursery is?' asks Grandpa Ronnie.

'I think Sister Margaret said something about it's in Oldham.'

'Oldham? Oldham?' says grandma sternly. 'That's a long way from Prestwich! What are those nuns playing at? They should know better!'

'I'm sure they know what they are doing Pearl,' says Grandpa Ronnie. He turns to me. 'Do you want any Christmas Pudding Caroline?'

I nod. 'Yes please grandpa!' I answer with a smile.

After dinner I help grandma wash the pots and Grandpa Ronnie snoozes in the chair.

'Grandma. What should I do when I finish school?' I ask.

'Well, I suppose you should get a job!' answers grandma. 'I could do with a little help with money around here. Anyway, it will do you good. No need to put all this work experience to waste.'

I frown and when I have finished I go upstairs with Tootsie, who is full from all the scraps of turkey! I wonder to myself why grandma has to be so horrible!

It is the day after New Years Day and I am on my way back to school on the bus. It is freezing! There is a bit of a frost forming this afternoon and by the time I get to Tower Grange the frost is quite thick. My friends and I are glad to see each other and later on we have our usual midnight feast after lights out! The talk is about what we got for Christmas and some of the girls are quite envious of the fact I have cassettes!

'You have to play David Cassidy first!' says Lisa.

'Especially 'Could It Be Forever'!' chips in Sally.

The next morning we have prayers and then a lovely breakfast of pancakes, orange juice and lots of tea – Mrs Priestman's pancakes are delicious! After breakfast Sister Margaret calls me over.

'I have just come off the phone with Mrs Jones, the head of the nursery. She is expecting you week after next and she is looking forward to you going!'

'Great! Thank you Sister Margaret.' I think for a moment. 'Is it the one in Oldham?'

Sister Margaret nods. 'Yes, but don't worry about getting there and back. Sister Katrina will take you in the morning and Mrs Jones will bring you back at night. She lives in Middleton so it isn't too far for her to go home after.'

'It works very well then, doesn't it Sister Margaret.'

'Indeed it does!' answers Sister Margaret. 'Now, off to class as Mr Vernon is waiting to start.'

I run off to class thinking about the nursery and looking forward to it!

From now on lessons get a bit mundane as I want the weeks to go by so I can go to the nursery. Then, the week comes to go and all weekend I am really not bothered about what grandma thinks! Besides, she will only have a go at me for working with children! Grandpa Ronnie is looking forward to me going though and is giving me pointers all weekend, in his own way!

Sunday evening comes and I can't wait to get going to school as tomorrow morning I am going to the nursery! Grandma can't understand it, the fact that I am not complaining at her lack of love towards me.

'You really are looking forward to this nursery, aren't you?' says grandma with eyebrows raised.

I nod and smile. 'I can't wait grandma! Mrs Jones the headmistress is looking forward to me going as well!'

'I am sure she will change her mind when you get there!'

I frown. 'Grandma! Why do you say that?'

'Well, you have no experience with children!'

I can feel myself getting quite mad. 'That's the idea grandma! I will get the experience by working there. Don't you know that?'

Grandma points to me. 'Don't you speak to me like that young lady! Don't forget, I am your grandma!

I shrug and then say no more, as I need grandma to carry on giving me spending money! I pick up my bag, give grandma a hug and kiss on the cheek and then I am off to get the bus.

At school I say the usual 'hellos and then put my things in the dormitory and went to watch telly with the others, whilst waiting for Mrs Priestman's Sunday roast! After lights out we are munching on our midnight snack, torches set so that the light could not be seen from the door.

'So, where is your work experience Sally?' I ask.

'I am going to work in C & A in the centre of Manchester, in the clothes section!'

Jenny laughs. 'That's good for you! You will probably get to try on the clothes!'

'Hah, I hope so!' says Sally.

'And where are you working Jenny?' I ask.

'Well, I am going back to the kennels as I want to see the tiny puppies through okay, They have got to know me according to the kennels! Where are you going Caroline?'

'To a nursery in Oldham. Can't wait!'

'Ugh! Not for me!' says Jenny. 'I can't even stand my little brother!'

A creak from the corridor causes us to turn the torches out quick but no-one comes in. Still, we need our sleep for starting work experience tomorrow.

The next day I am dropped off at the nursery, Corpus Christie, by Sister Katrina and Mrs Jones thanks the sister and then shows me inside. She is a nice lady, a bit stocky and about forty years old, but she has a nice smile and seems to be lovely with the children. I am shown to the very small children's class and get straight into helping put the toys out! As the day goes on I am really enjoying it, doing some painting with the older children and then we all have a sing-song in the main hall. At the end of the day Mrs Jones gets me into her car and we go back to Tower Grange.

'So, have you enjoyed it today Caroline?' she asks.

'Yes, thank you Mrs Jones. The children are lovely!'

Mrs Jones smiles. 'Tomorrow you can read some stories to the children. They like the stories, especially the 'Little Red Hen' and 'Rupert the Bear'!'

I thank Mrs Jones for bringing me back and after dinner my friends and I skip telly and go into our room to swap stories of the day.

The next day I am painting again and there are some lovely pictures of farm animals, the theme of the day. Then, later in the afternoon, as Mrs Jones had promised, I am reading stories to the little children. We start off with 'Twinkle' and then a couple of Rupert stories, in fact more than a couple as *I* like Rupert as well! After school Mrs Jones takes me back to school again and again, after dinner, the girls and me talk about our day. Sally says that she can have some clothes for nothing at the end of her work experience and Lisa calls her a jammy cow! Jenny has been told she can have a puppy of she wants but she says her mum won't let her. I say dogs are great and how much Tootsie loves me and Jenny scowls with a bit of jealousy!

'So, Caroline. What can you bring home after your work experience?' asks Lisa.

'A little kid!' says Sally laughing!

'Er, NO!' I say sternly. 'Definitely not!'

We laugh together until Sister Gabrielle pops her head round the door to announce lights out.

At the weekends grandma is not interested at all but I am getting to the stage where I don't really care, as I am really enjoying myself. At school, though, I am really happy and my time in the nursery lasts for another two weeks. When I have to finish it I am a bit miserable but Mrs Jones says that I can go back any time and help out and she gives me a brand new set of Rupert stories in a smart case. My eyes water a bit as I say thank you and then I give Mrs Jones, and a few of the children, a hug before Sister Katrina and I get in the car to go back to the school, as was arranged for the last day.

Sister Katrina sees me deep in thought as we drive along. 'What's wrong Caroline?'

I look her in the eyes. 'Oh, I am so happy at school, Sister Katrina, but I am wondering what will happen to me when I leave. My grandma isn't very loving or nice.'

'Oh, I'm sure she will be okay Caroline. You are sixteen now – it was my birthday last week – and quite a grown up young lady.'

My eyes water a little, 'But you don't know my grandma, Sister Katrina.'

Sister Katrina frowns and can see I'm upset but nothing else is said for the rest of the journey. When we reach school Sister Katrina goes off to see Sister Margaret and I see Sally in the entrance, Sally looking concerned when she sees my watery eyes.

'What's wrong Caroline?' asks Sally putting her arm around my shoulder.

'You and the others will have happy settled lives when you leave school but I have to put up with a life of my grandma moaning at me!'

Sally smiles. 'Why don't you stay and become a nun?'

I start to smile. 'I don't think things will be *that* bad!'

The rest of the year is spent doing normal lessons mixed in with some very good life lessons with the sisters. Mr Vernon and Barbara say they have enjoyed working with our year and I have to say that I like them a lot – better then the rubbishy teachers at the other school! It doesn't seem long though until it is the last week and I am starting to feel a bit glum at school finishing. Even though I am now sixteen and at the age for a lot more things I still get a lot of hassle from my grandma and just about no respect at all! As the weeks have gone on Sister Margaret and the other nuns can see my increasing sadness and a few times I have been asked if I am all right. I always answer that I am okay but I think they can tell otherwise. My friends can also see I am a little miserable and they try their hardest to make me laugh and keep me happier. Most of the time they succeed!

It is now the Friday before the last week and I say goodbye to my friends and then I am on the bus going home. A few tears have come into my eyes, which get a few worrying looks from people, but thankfully nobody approaches me as I just want to be left alone. At the other end grandma is waiting for me and she actually has a concerned look on her face.

'What's wrong grandma?' I ask as we walk home.

Grandma sighs. 'Your Grandpa Ronnie has a really bad foot and it is making him very ill. It is a little infected but I'm sure it will be okay.'

'How's it got like that?' I ask.

'I don't really know,' answers grandma. 'He mentioned something about trapping it and it hurting after that. Other than that I don't know really. Anyway, we are going to the guest house instead of home. You can stay with your grandpa as I am going out with a lady I have met, Mary.'

I frown. 'Who's Mary?'

'Oh, I went with Rene to the Clarence the other night and I got talking to Mary. She is on my wavelength and a very nice woman.'

I shrug. 'Oh, nice.'

When we get to Grandpa Ronnie's guest house I hug grandpa and then Tootsie come running up to me and licks me all over my face! I see that he is in a bit of pain.

'How have you hurt your foot grandpa?' I ask with a bit of a concerned look.

Grandpa Ronnie sits me down and tuns to grandma. 'Get the kettle on Pearl!' He laughs a bit as he sees grandma scowl. 'I am okay Caroline. Just a bit of a sore foot but nothing serious. Now, tell me a bit more about this nursery you worked in!'

'The children were lovely grandpa,' I say smiling. 'Mrs Jones the head let me read stories to them in the end so I loved it!'

'Good!' says Grandpa Ronnie. 'Now, let's get a drink and then you can tell me more.'

The evening goes well and then I am sat with Tootsie lying at my feet drinking my tea. Grandma is cooking some dinner, roast beef with potatoes, and Grandpa Ronnie is dozing in the chair.

Grandma comes in. 'Can you help me finish dinner a bit Caroline please? I am going out with Mary and Rene tonight playing bingo and I have to get ready as well. I will leave the washing up for you.'

I blow out through my cheeks and go with grandma into the kitchen, closely followed by Tootsie who is obviously after the scraps!

After dinner I am washing up, with Tootsie sat looking up at me, and Grandpa Ronnie hobbles in.

I smile. 'Did you enjoy your dinner grandpa?'

'Oh, it was lovely Caroline,' answers grandpa. 'I will say that you grandma can still cook!'

Grandpa Ronnie sits down on a stool. 'Right, Caroline. I have a new guest coming to stay next week so can you clean and get room twelve ready for me please?'

'No problem grandpa. Who is it who's coming?'

A man called Bill. He is moving into Bolton because of work so he will be staying for a while. A nice little earner for me anyway!'

I laugh. 'You are sounding like the man off 'Minder' grandpa! Okay, the room will be spotless and fit for a prince!'

Grandpa Ronnie smiles. 'Thank you Caroline. I knew I could count on you!'

Sunday dinner is really tasty – grandma has cooked it again – and then it is late afternoon and I am getting ready to go back to school. It will be the last week and I am still quite sad, but, I am not so worried now as I know I can spend more time with my grandpas. I have also been told by Grandpa Ronnie that I can do some more at the guest house which is good because I like it there. But, grandma puts the dampeners on it again by saying that I should get a job and earn my keep. If only I could get a job like at the guest house!

As grandma waves me off I think about what Sally said about becoming a nun. Is this what I would have to do to escape my grandma? I reach school and greet Jenny as she arrives at the same time. We go in together and meet Sally coming down the stairs.

'Hurry up you two!' says Sally. 'We're having a lovely joint of roast beef !'

I gulp a little. 'I've already had a roast dinner at Grandpa Ronnie's guest house! I'm full to the brim but I can't insult Mrs Priestman by not having any!'

Jenny thinks for a minute. 'Maybe you can make yourself sick and then claim that you're ill!'

'Not a bad idea,' says Sally nodding her head a bit.

'Hmm,' I say. 'I think I will just go and lie down and get my eyes to water a bit, claim I am really upset!'

I rush off upstairs to the girls shaking their heads and lay on my bed for a bit. After about half-an-hour there's a knock on the door and then Sister Gabrielle comes in and then sits on my bed.

'Are you all right Caroline?' asks Sister Gabrielle holding my hand.

I sit up and she can see my eyes are red. 'I'm fine,' I say in between sniffs.

I am not acting after all as when I got in the room I looked around and thought how much I will miss this place.

'I am just a bit upset that school is finishing Sister. I have really enjoyed it here. Everyone is so nice.'

Sister Gabrielle smiles and pats my hand. 'You are a nice person Caroline, very kind and considerate, and whatever happens from now on, whatever your grandma is like you, will find happiness in your life.'

I smile. 'I suppose I will but it might come too late.'

'It is *never* too late!' exclaims Sister Gabrielle as she gets up. Now, let's go and eat some treacle sponge and custard!'

I jump up and follow the sister downstairs.

The week is taken up with a bit of teaching, although not much and mostly from the sisters in preparing us for the world outside! A couple of times we have gone into Manchester for a bit of shopping and the nights have been a bit easier on us and less strict with lights out! On the Thursday night there is a big party with a buffet laid on by Mrs Priestman. There is a bit of music from a folk duo that Sister Margaret knows and everyone is happy and dancing! Sally, Jenny and me are sat in a corner drinking and munching on some crisps.

'Do you think we will see each other again after tomorrow?' asks Jenny.

Sally and I shrug our shoulders. 'Don't know,' says Sally.

I smile. 'I hope so. You girls have been great friends. Thank you!'

The evening draws to a close and then we have a bit of a chat after lights out, mainly about what we will do when we have left school. Sally says she wouldn't mind working in the doctors again and thinks she might go and learn some secretary skills. Jenny says she is going to ask if she can carry on at the kennels.

'What about you Caroline?' asks Sally.

'Oh, I think I want to be a nurse. I don't know how I go about it yet but I'm sure Grandpa Ronnie will know!'

The next day is Friday and the last day of school. We have breakfast after prayers and then most of the morning is taken up cleaning our space and packing. After lunch we get our bags downstairs and then all go into the main room as Sister Margaret wants to talk to us.

Sister Margaret clears her throat. 'I want you all to know that you have been a great set of girls and it has been a pleasure to work with you!' She indicates to the other sisters. 'Myself and the other sisters want to wish you all good luck and happiness and hope that you will come and visit us.'

A resounding cry of 'Thank you Sister Margaret!' comes from us all and then we give all the sisters a round of applause! After we are left to say our own goodbyes. The others go outside, though, and I stay a bit and collar Sister Margaret when she is on her own.

'Thank you Sister Margaret for helping me,' I say with a slight tear in my eye. 'I was really sad when my grandma sent me here but I have had a really nice and happy four years here. Thank you.'

Sister Margaret grabs me into a hug and then steps back and smiles. 'It has been a pleasure Caroline. I hope that you find your happiness in life.'

'Sister Gabrielle says I will,' I answer.

'Then I'm sure you will!' says Sister Margaret. 'Now go and say your goodbyes.'

I go into the hallway and take a last look at the splendid staircase and panelled walls. Then I go outside and Sally and Jenny come running up and the three of us go into a group hug. We are joined by Lisa and Jessica and then it is time for everyone to go.

'Bye Caroline,' says Sally. 'Make sure you don't take any nonsense from your grandma!'

'That's right!' says Jenny. 'Stay happy and keep grandpa on your side!'

'Oh, I will keep both of them on my side, and Tootsie!' I say back. I smile at my two closest friends. 'Thank you for being my friends.'

Everyone starts to sidle away and, after saying goodbye to the sisters and Mrs Priestman, I trudge out of the gates for my bus. I start to cry a little and then I am on the bus and on the way home, sobbing.

Loosing My Friends

Since I left school, some two weeks ago, I have been constantly barracked by my grandma to get a job! I knew it would happen eventually but I didn't think it would happen so soon! The thing that is worrying though is that Grandpa Ronnie is very poorly and his foot seems to be quite infected. He has been to the doctors a couple of times and I am not very happy because grandma doesn't seem to be bothered. Actually, grandma isn't helping much at all as her friend Mary is doing all the cooking for the guest house. Surely grandma should be doing it! There is little bit of happiness though! The man that has come to stay at the guest house, Bill, is a nice man and although he is quite a bit older than me I can tell that he likes me. After a few days we go out for a drink and we seem to get on very well. We go out a few times and then we seem to be an item!

Grandpa Ronnie, however, gets so bad and he has to go into hospital. Grandma says it is just a precaution but I think that it is a bit more serious. Grandma spends too much time going out with her friends to care, it seems, and then it becomes terrible as she tells me one day that she has met some bloke called Frank!

'How can you get friendly with another man when Grandpa Ronnie is so bad?' I ask grandma.

'Listen, I am not married to your grandpa so don't you tell me what to do! If I want to go out with another man I will and it is none of your business! Besides, you can talk!'

'And what's that supposed to mean grandma?'

'Well, this guy Bill. Fancy! How old is he? You're the one that's daft!'

I scowl. 'Well, Grandpa Ronnie thinks he is okay and he is!'

'Huh!' says grandma. 'I think the illness has got to your grandpa's head!'

'That's nasty!' I say to grandma and then I go quickly before she has a chance to say anything back. Tootsie follows me upstairs and I sit on the bed and scuffle her fur as I wonder what kind of woman my grandma is to say the things she does.

Later on I am getting ready to go and meet Bill and my grandma comes into the room. I nod slightly and grandma sits down.

'You do know that it's no good you seeing this Bill,' says grandma. 'He is too old and he is no good! If you see him I will fall out with you! I will!'

'Grandma. How do you know he is no good? I could say the same – how do you know this Frank is any good?'

'Oh, sixteen now and you think you know it all? Let me tell you young lady, I have done it and you are just a young girl. Don't you tell me about men!'

'How's Grandpa Ronnie?' I ask changing the subject. 'What's the doctor said?'

Grandma frowns. 'His foot is really bad. Anyway, I need to go and tend to a couple of the elderly ladies, Then I am going to the pub to meet Mary and Frank. Just think on what I have said

Caroline.'

As grandma turns and goes out of the room I make a scowl face and pull my tongue out at her. I look at Tootsie and indicate to her a witch sign and point to grandma!

Later on I am speaking to Bill about it.

'It isn't nice really,' says Bill, 'saying I'm bad. But, maybe she is trying to look after you in her own way.'

I shake my head. 'Not grandma! She is only interested in herself!'

Bill nods. 'I never see her in the guest house helping out. Ronnie is quite poorly and she should be helping him.'

'I know,' I answer. 'She's even got this new friend Mary roped in to do the work! And this new man of hers, Frank!'

'What's the matter with him?' asks Bill.

I shrug my shoulders. 'Oh, I don't know really. It's just that Grandpa Ronnie is very ill.' I sigh. 'She isn't being very fair to him.'

'What's she said about that?' Bill asks, getting hold of my hand.

'She just says that she isn't married to him any more.'

Bill smiles. 'Are we going out tomorrow?'

I nod. 'Yes, we can do.'

He leans over to kiss me.'Good! Another drink?'

The next day I see grandma looking really saddened and jerking around as she gets on with breakfast.

'What;s wrong grandma?' I ask as I nick a piece of toast.

'Your Grandpa Ronnie is very sick Caroline. In fact, his foot is so infected that he will have to have it cut off.'

I gaze at grandma for a while and then tears start to well up in my eyes. 'What's going to happen grandma?'

Grandma shakes her head. 'I don't know.' She straightens up a bit. 'Anyway. I have heard through a woman at the pub about a job. The sewing place on Marsden Road is looking for trainee machinists, if you're interested. It will be the chance to earn some money. Not ideal, but money all the same.'

'Hmm, okay grandma. I'll think about it.' I get my things together. 'Are you going to see Grandpa Ronnie?'

'I probably will later on, after I have sorted out my residents. He needs some support.'

'Can I go and see him grandma? It's awful that he has to lose his foot.' I start to go watery eyed again.

'I would keep away for now,' answers grandma. 'Not very nice, someone losing their foot.'

'But, he's my grandpa...'

'Not another word about it!' exclaims grandma. 'I will go and see him. Now, you go and sort out that job. Get some money earned!'

As grandma goes out to do her job I scowl a little and then decide to go and see about the job. I am worried and upset about Grandpa Ronnie though.

Later in the day I go to the guest house and, guess what, Mary is there again cooking dinner with grandma nowhere to be seen! I wait and talk to Mary for a bit – she seems really nice, a small stout lady with long black hair and very jolly – and then Bill comes down and after kissing we go out.

'How's Ronnie?' asks Bill.

'I don't know,' I say with slightly watery eyes. 'He has to have his foot taken off. That's all I know. Grandma wont even let me go and see him.'

Bill puts his arm around me and I cuddle in. 'That's up to you whether you go or not. You're not a baby!'

'I know,' I say, 'but it might upset me anyway. I will go and see him after his operation, cheer him up a bit!'

'We'll both go,' says Bill smiling.

When we get back to the guest house Mary and grandma are talking over a cup of tea.

'How's Grandpa Ronnie?' I ask.

'Okay really. He has his operation tomorrow so he may be better after that.'

I raise my eyebrows. 'What? When he has had a foot removed? How's that better?'

Bill smiles a bit. 'Oh, you know Ronnie. Week after next he'll be in Jean's bookies putting a bet on!'

I laugh a bit. 'Yeah, you're probably right! Anyway are we having a cup of tea Bill?'

'That'll do for starters!' laughs Bill.

We go off into the kitchen and leave grandma and Mary to it.

The next morning I go into the kitchen at the guest house and Mary is making breakfast.

'I frown. 'Where's grandma? You shouldn't be here doing the meals all the time.'

'Pearl is tending to her elderly people,' answers Mary. 'Anyway, what are you doing here so early Caroline?'

I put my head down a bit and smile. 'It got a bit late to go home last night so I stayed.'

Mary raises her eyebrows. 'Does your grandma know?'

'She will do!' I answer with a bigger smile. 'She will have noticed that I didn't go home!'

Mary shrugs her shoulders. 'Well, you are sixteen so she will have to realise you have grown up. Anyway, she's more interested in this Frank she's with!'

I laugh a bit and then I start to get a little sad.

'What's wrong?' asks Mary.

'Grandpa Ronnie is having his operation today. I hope he's all right.'

'I'm sure he'll be fine,' says Mary, putting her hand on my shoulder.

I nod and then put some toast in.

Bill comes down and gives me a kiss. 'Any for me?'

I sigh. 'Here, take this. You need to get to work.'

Bill takes a munch of his toast. 'What are you doing today?'

'I am going to see about a job, in the sewing factory on Marsden Road. Grandma says they are taking on.'

Mary nods. 'That's right. Betty in the pub works there and she told us. You'll be okay there. Not bad money.

'Great!' says Bill. 'Good luck!'

As Bill goes out to work Mary puts her hand on my shoulder again. 'You get off to find out about that job. Your grandpa will be okay and if your grandma asks where you were I won't say anything.'

I smile. 'Thanks Mary. Don't work too hard!'

I get my jacket and head out to see about the job.

Later in the day I go home and grandma is making a cup of tea. I have a little smile on my face and grandma frowns.

'What are you smiling about?' asks grandma.

'I got a job at that sewing place grandma! I start on Monday. Betty knew who I was and put a good word in.'

'Good! Says grandma. 'Now you can do something in life and earn some money as well.'

I scowl. 'Is that *all* you can think about? Money?'

'Well,' retorts grandma, 'at least now you can help out with paying for things!'

'Argh!' I say bending down to stroke Tootsie. 'I might as well go and live in the guest house for all you care!'

Grandma scowls and points her finger. 'Don't you talk to me like that! Don't forget I'm your grandma! Anyway, I know you spent last night there. I bet you were with that Bill! Do you not know better?'

'Well, what about you going out with that Frank while Grandpa Ronnie is suffering! I *am* sixteen grandma, I know what I'm doing!'

Grandma starts to shout. 'I am not married to Ronnie now! At least I have gone to see him!'

'Yes,' I say with some tears, 'and you told me not to go. How dare you throw that one at me!'

'Yes, I know I told you not to go...'

'How do you think I feel grandma about Grandpa Ronnie being in such a state? I am so upset and I can't see him!' I wipe my eyes. 'In fact, tomorrow I am going to see him, Bill and I both are.'

'Bill? Bill?' screams grandma. 'What has Bill got to do with it?'

'Have you forgotten Grandpa Ronnie took him in long term and helped him out? Bill wants to go because he is worried about him.'

'Well!' says grandma. 'Bill needs to be more concerned with what he does with you!'

'Bill is nice!' I say with a raised voice. 'At least he cares about me!'

'And what does that mean young lady? Asks grandma. 'You are getting very lippy girl!'

I throw my hands into the air. 'I'm going. I am going to the guest house and helping Mary a bit with the meals, something *you* should be doing anyway! I can also wait for Bill coming home.'

'Listen lady!' says grandma. 'I have enough to do here without cooking at the guest house!'

I shrug my shoulders. 'Okay grandma. Whatever. I'll see you later.'

With that, I take some cake and go out of the door to get the bus to Deane.

Mary is hard at work cutting up vegetables when I get to the guest house.

'Hi Mary,' I say as I make myself a drink. 'I tried to get grandma to help out here but she says she is too busy with her own job. Sorry Mary. I did try!'

Mary sighs. 'Its all right Caroline. I really don't mind doing this.'

I hear the door g and it is Bill. I smile as he comes into the kitchen and I hug him as he gets to me. 'Good day at work Bill?'

'Yep, not bad,' answers Bill nodding. 'What's for tea Mary?'

'Chicken pie with chips, sausage and mash or stew and dumplings.'

I smile. 'Oh, nice! Your stew is lovely Mary.'

'Go on with you!' says Mary with a grin. 'Go and get a drink for Bill and wait for tea!'

After stew and dumplings Bill and I are relaxing in the residents lounge. I have my head down a bit and I have a bit of a sad face.

'What's the matter?' asks Bill.

'I'm worried about Grandpa Ronnie,' I answer. 'I hope he's okay. Grandma isn't telling me much.'

Bill puts his arm around my shoulder. 'Your grandma doesn't tell anybody much! Ronnie will be okay. Do you think he wants to be kept away from the bookies for long?'

That makes me smile a little. 'No, you're right!'

'Where is your grandma now?' asks Bill.

I shrug my shoulders. 'She's at home working, or so she says! I told her off for not helping around here and leaving it all to Mary. Grandma says she is too busy with her own work!'

Bill sighs. 'Have you thought she might be right? She does have a job to do and she is going seeing Ronnie in between. Besides, Mary says she likes it here.'

I let out a big sigh. 'I know Bill, I know.'

Bill gives me a kiss on the cheek. 'What time are you going home?'

'I'll have some supper and then get off. I don't really want to be on the last bus as all the drunks and idiots are on so I won't be too late.'

'You could always stay again!' says Bill grinning.

'I don't know Bill. I want to but I want to be around grandma in case she has any news of Grandpa Ronnie.'

Bill raises his eyebrows. 'Hah, you want to be around your grandma? *That's* a first!'

I slap him on the arm. 'Don't be so cheeky!'

'Cup of tea anyone?' says Mary popping her head into the lounge.

One or two of the other residents nod their heads along with Bill and me. Soon after we get tea and Angel Cake and then it is soon time for me to go. I get my coat, say goodbye to Mary and the other residents and then give Bill a kiss and we arrange to meet tomorrow evening.

When I get in grandma is making a drink. 'Oh, you do come home then!'

Tootsie is all over me and licks my face. 'Of course grandma. I live here! Anyway, any news on Grandpa Ronnie?'

'He's still asleep and stable but not really doing fantastic.'

'Oh, grandma, he'll be okay. Like Bill says, he won't be out of the bookies for long.'

'Huh, Bill has no right to say anything!'

I frown. 'Why not? He is a resident and they are all worried about Grandpa Ronnie.' I turn to Tootsie. 'Come on, let's go to bed. I have to catch up on sleep ready for my job on Monday.'

With that, Tootsie and I go upstairs – she still beats me despite being seventeen – and then its teeth clean and bed.

Monday comes and I walk into my job for the first time. I look around and see rows of sewing machines, empty at the moment but soon they will be making a collective noise – and making garments as well! A small lady sees me and walks over with a slight side-to-side motion. I smile at her and she smiles back.

'Caroline, is it?' asks the lady. 'I am Mrs Harris, the supervisor. I will sit you with Anne for a while and you can see what it is we do here. Then, this afternoon you can go on a machine and sew something. Do you think that would be okay?'

I nod. 'Any way I can learn quickly would be good Mrs Harris. I want to get sewing as soon as I can!'

'Good!' says Mrs Harris with a smile. 'Let's go and find Anne.'

The rest of the morning is taken up with watching Anne, a sharp-featured thin woman who really doesn't look as though she wants me sat there! So, I say nothing and just watch what she does. She is very good though so I know I will learn a lot from her! After lunch Mrs Harris has a quick word with Anne and then she comes over to me.

'Anne says you paid very good attention, although you didn't say much, but never mind!' says Mrs Harris with a slight smile. 'Let's get you on a machine and give you a few garments to sew.'

So, I am put on a machine and it seems to go very well! The end of the day comes quite quickly and as I gather up my things to go Mrs Harris calls me over to a desk in the corner, her 'office'!

'Not bad Caroline,' says Mrs Harris. 'I think you'll be okay here. See you in the morning.'

I smile. 'Thank you Mrs Harris. See you tomorrow.'

When I get home grandma is in the kitchen and I dash through smiling. 'Hi grandma! Guess what? I've had a good day at work...' I cut it short as I see grandma with tears in her eyes. 'What's wrong grandma?'

Grandma looks at me and suddenly I get a shocked look on my face. 'It's Grandpa Ronnie isn't it? Is he okay?'

Grandma shakes her head. 'He's... had a heart attack Caroline!' Grandma sobs. 'The operation to remove his foot was too much and... he's died.'

I start to sob uncontrollably and grandma actually hugs me. Tootsie is jumping up at us and whimpering slightly and I release from grandma and pick her up. I cuddle Tootsie and I am making her wet with tears. Grandma and I can't say much and just sit quiet and have a drink.

'Grandma coughs a bit. 'He was very poorly Caroline and in great pain. You must have seen he couldn't walk!'

I say nothing but just nod a bit and keep on cuddling Tootsie, tears in my eyes. I sit like this for ages and then I put Tootsie down and go up to my room. I sit on my bed and sob some more. I can't believe my Grandpa Ronnie has gone. I lie down and must have cried myself to sleep.

The next morning I go downstairs and grandma is making some toast.

'I have to sort out some shopping for a couple of the ladies and then I have to go to the hospital to sort things out,' says grandma, looking a bit sad but not as much as yesterday. 'Are you going to work? You need to get on with it really!'

I look at grandma and frown. 'That's not very nice grandma!' I start to go watery eyed. 'You were like this when my mum passed away! You might be able to get on with it but I can't.'

Grandma sighs. 'I know you are upset Caroline but you have only just started this job.'

'Don't you think I know that grandma?' I sob a little. 'I am going to work but I am going straight from work to the guest house. I want to see Bill.'

Grandma ignores me and I grab some toast, say goodbye to Tootsie with a cuddle and then give grandma a curt glance as I go out of the door. I do not have a good day at work and everyone is very sympathetic to me. I do okay and after work I get the bus straight up to Deane to the guest house. When I get there Bill grabs me and hugs me for a while.

'Are you okay?' asks Bill. 'The hospital has rung here and told us what has happened. I am so sorry Caroline.'

I start to break down again and then look around at everyone. They are all sad looking but they all say they are sorry.

'I'll be okay Bill,' I say still hugging him. I look at everyone else and nod. 'Thank you everyone.'

Mary has been helping out again and has her coat on for going. 'How's Pearl?'

'Grandma? Oh, she's as uncaring as usual! She is going to the hospital afterwards.'

Mary shrugs. 'I suppose she can't be that uncaring if she's going to see him.'

'Hmm!' I say. 'She's only doing it because there is no-one else to go!'

'Well, I will be seeing her tonight Caroline so I will see how she is.' She thinks a while. 'Doesn't he have a son?'

I nod. 'Yes. I think his son will be sorting out the main arrangements.'

Everyone says goodbye as Mary goes out of the door and then I turn to Bill and he smiles.

'Do you want any tea?' asks Bill.

I shake my head. 'I might have a buttie later. I don't feel very hungry.' I smile back a bit. 'I think I will stay here tonight. I don't want to be on my own and grandma is obviously going out with Mary and the others.'

'Come on,' says Bill smiling. 'Let's get you a drink.'

It is a few days later now but I still don't feel like much breakfast and after a quick cup of tea and a piece of toast I'm off to work. It is Friday and work is okay now and Mrs Harris is very glad I'm getting into it. A few of the women keep saying how sorry they are about grandpa , including Anne who seems to like me now! Maybe its because I don't sit with her any more! I keep thinking about Grandpa Ronnie and how he suffered and really how little grandma thought of him. I shrug. Maybe the shock is too much for grandma too. But, I need to do this sewing properly so I get on with concentrating on my work and soon it is time for going home. I have got my first wage today so I decide to go to the old pasty shop and take some pasties home for tea. There is a bit of a queue in the shop so I am home a little later than usual.

'Oh, she gets home at last!' says grandma with a sarcastic tone.

I frown. 'Well, I got paid today so I went for pasties! Thought it would make a change for tea.'

As grandma takes the pasties I give her five pounds and she frowns a bit but takes the money.

'I'm getting good now grandma,' I say, putting the kettle on. 'I'm told my sewing is getting to a very good standard!'

'Good,' says grandma. 'The quicker you learn the quicker you will be on full money!'

I sigh. 'There you go again grandma. Thinking of money!'

'Well!' says grandma. 'What can you do without money, eh? Can't use buttons for food.'

'A lot of good it did Grandpa Ronnie in the end!' I sit down with my pasty and drink. 'He has a guest house and it didn't save him.'

'He's not even got that now!' says grandma.

I raise my eyebrows. 'What do you mean?'

Grandma takes a bite of her pasty and clears her throat. 'When he finds a buyer Ronnie's son is selling the guest house.'

I look horrified. 'He... he can't do that! That was Grandpa Ronnie's. He can't!'

'Caroline,' says grandma leaning forward. 'Your grandpa Ronnie gambled his money away in the betting shop so his son *has* to sell the place.'

My eyes start to water. 'What a shame. Oh, Grandpa Ronnie must be crying in his grave. What's going to happen to the people there?'

'Well, they'll have to find somewhere else to live and stay!' Grandma laughs sarcastically. 'Huh, including your older man Bill!'

I narrow my eyes. 'Oh, you would love that grandma, wouldn't you!'

'Don't you talk to me like that young lady! Remember, I am your grandma!'

I get up and give my last piece of pasty to Tootsie. 'I am going to get changed and then go to the guest house.'

'Well, don't be late!'

'Why grandma? It *is* Saturday tomorrow so I don't have to go to work.'

'Well, make sure you have your key. I am meeting Mary and Frank in the Clarence.'

I nod. 'Okay grandma. I will take Tootsie out before I get changed.'

As I am walking with Tootsie she seems to be not a lively as usual but I suppose even dogs can have an off day. However, she seems to be very quiet as I go out so I tell grandma I am not going to be too late.'

'Sell the guest house?' Bill shakes his head and takes a sip of his pint. 'How could Ronnie be daft enough to get into so much debt? I bet Jean been rubbing her hands!'

I sigh and take quite a gulp of my lager, which causes me to cough a little. As Bill slaps me on the back lightly I look around the pub and peer through the smoke, no real reason other than trying to find some comfort from the other people.

'Are you okay now?' asks Bill.

I nod. 'Yep, thanks. I don't know why Grandpa Ronnie got like that. It's just so sad that he was in pain and his foot was going bad and now his life work has gone bad as well. It's not fair!'

Bill takes a sup of his pint. 'Life isn't fair Caroline. Life isn't fair.'

We have a couple more drinks and then Bill walks me to the bus stop. We have a kiss and cuddle whilst waiting for the bus and eventually the bus comes.

'I still think you are going home a bit early,' says Bill.

I nod. 'I know, I'm sorry. It's just that Tootsie isn't very well and I want to check on her.'

Bill nods as the bus pulls up. 'Okay then. See you tomorrow.'

I give bill a kiss. 'I'll get to the guest house about dinner time. What are we doing?'

Bill shrugs his shoulders. 'Don't know yet. Should we decide tomorrow?'

'Okay then Bill. Nite.'

'Nite,' says Bill as the bus doors shut.'

The next morning grandma looks as miserable as usual and she is totally engrossed in making a cup of tea and breakfast.

'Morning grandma!'

Tootsie barks a little and grandma jumps. 'Oh! You pair of daft ones! Are you trying to give me a heart attack?'

It is quite warm this morning so the window is open a little and the noise of the traffic seems to be troubling Tootsie a bit.

'Where are you off to today?' asks grandma.

'Bill and I are not sure what we are going to do yet.'

'Huh!' says grandma.

I frown and give Tootsie a piece of toast. 'I am going to the guest house in a bit and we'll decide then. Anyway, what have you got against Bill?'

'I've told you before, he is too old and you are going to get yourself hurt!'

My frown turns into a scowl and I give Tootsie some more toast. 'He is a nice man grandma! You always try and see the bad in people!'

'I'll have you know young lady that I make sure I judge people very well! Anyway, you are only young so how can you tell me.'

I look at Tootsie and change the subject a bit. 'I think there is something wrong with Tootsie grandma. She isn't herself and she has never refused toast before. Plus, she doesn't usually get troubled by the traffic.'

Grandma sighs. 'She is getting old Caroline. Maybe it is old age.'

I shrug. 'I suppose so.' I give Tootsie a cuddle and then get my coat. 'I won't be late grandma.'

'It doesn't really matter,' says grandma. 'You're obviously old enough to know when to come home. I'll keep my eye on Tootsie. Don't worry.'

'Thanks grandma,' I say, giving her a small hug. 'I'll see you later.' I look at Tootsie again and shake my head. I hope she's okay.

Bill and I decide to go to Southport. As we are walking down Lord Street with an ice cream Bill can see I'm not very happy.

'What's wrong Caroline?'

'It's Tootsie Bill.' I take a bite of my cone. 'She's not looking very well. I'm worried about her.'

'How old is she now?' asks Bill.

'Seventeen. I know she's a good age but she seems to have gone strange all of a sudden.'

Bill shrugs. 'It could be her age you know. You can't rule that out.'

I finish my cone and wipe my mouth. 'That's what grandma said but I know her better. She's not right.'

Bill puts his arm around me. 'Do you want to go home and see if she's all right?'

'No, no its okay,' I say shaking my head. 'We'll go home when we said. About another hour or so. Grandma said she'll keep her eye on Tootsie.'

The rest of the afternoon and evening is great and as we are getting on the train to go home it is just starting to go cool and get a little darker. We don't talk much until we get to Bolton and then we decide to go for a few drinks. We eventually go back to the guest house for a nightcap and then I am ordering a taxi to go home.

'Do you not want to stay?' asks Bill.

'I give him a kiss on the cheek. 'I would love to but I want to check on Tootsie. Sorry.'

'I understand,' says Bill a little sadly. 'Are you coming round tomorrow?'

I grin. 'Probably later on. It *is* Sunday and I *am* having a lie in!'

Bill grins. 'Me too!' His face goes straight. 'Listen. I might need your help in looking for somewhere to live, now that the guest house is being sold.'

'I don't think it will be sold that quick Bill!' The taxi sounds its horn and I give Bill a kiss. 'Let's talk about it tomorrow. Goodnight!'

'Bill waves me off. 'Goodnight. See you tomorrow.'

Sunday is very quiet as always and grandma is just sitting and reading a magazine. I am sat stroking Tootsie and still haven't got dressed yet!

Grandma looks at me and frowns. 'Are you staying like that all day?'

'Nope.' I say shaking my head. 'I am going to get dressed in a minute and then go to see Bill.'

'He is no good you know!' says grandma. 'I can tell he's no good but you won't listen to me.'

'Why is he no good grandma? You keep saying this and you don't even know him!'

'Huh, I know his kind Caroline and I tell you he's no good!'

I jump up and head for the stairs with Tootsie ambling after me. 'Well, he's okay with me so I am going to get dressed and set off to the guest house. At least I can talk to people without them getting at someone!'

'Don't you speak to me like that! I am not getting at anyone, I just know his kind. Your mother would never speak to me like that!'

I look at her frowning and then run upstairs. Tootsie keeps up with me but doesn't beat me any more so I still know something is wrong.

When I get to Laurel Bank Bill his making a cup of tea – for everyone! I get a cup and stand grinning next to him, holding the cup out.

'Hi Bill. Don't forget me darling!'

'Smelled the kettle did you?' asks Bill grinning.

We go into the residents lounge and sit down.

'Where are you looking for a house?' I ask Bill.

'I don't know.' He sighs. 'I wouldn't mind staying round here. I like it round here.'

'It's not bad really,' I say. 'Up round our way, Morris Green isn't bad either.'

'Bill smiles. 'What are the pubs like?'

'There's only one,' I say shrugging my shoulders. 'The Morris Dancers.'

Bill grins. 'You see, that's a problem then! There are five round here!' He thinks for a moment. 'Actually, six if you count the Rumworth and want to walk home!'

I slap him on the arm. 'Is *that* all you can think about when choosing a place to live – how many pubs there are?'

Bill nods. 'It is an important factor!'

'Typical man!' I frown a little.

'What's wrong?' asks Bill.

'Tootsie is still not looking well. I am very worried about her. She's my little love.'

'She'll be all right,' says Bill with a comforting hand on my shoulder.

A voice sounds from the hallway. 'Afternoon everyone. What do we all want for dinner?'

I smile as Mary pops her head around the door. 'Hello Mary. Sunday roast?'

Mary's smile is pearly white against her black hair and I think what a lovely lady she is, always dressed neat but traditional lady like.

'Is that okay for everyone?' asks Mary.

Everybody nods and I get up. 'Can I help with the vegetables Mary?'

Mary nods. 'Please Caroline. What's your grandma up to today?'

I shrug my shoulders. 'I don't know. She was complaining at me and doing nothing much else when I left!'

'Complaining about what?' asks Bill.

I turn to him and frown. 'You, actually. She says she knows your type and you are no good.'

Bill scowls. 'Oh, she did, did she? Well, what do you think?'

I give him a pack on the cheek. 'I told her you were always okay with me and a lovely man so that was that!'

With that, I follow Mary into the kitchen.

The rest of Sunday is wonderful and so is Mary's Sunday roast! After dinner everyone relaxes, in spite of knowing that time in the guest house is running out. Sunday night television is much the same, which makes Bill and I get closer and do more close things together! But, tomorrow is Monday and I have to go to work so around ten o'clock I get my coat and Bill walks me to the bus stop.

'We didn't do much thinking on where you're going to live!' I say to Bill sighing.

'I know,' answers Bill, 'but I don't think it is going to be sold any time soon. I think we still have a bit of time!'

The bus pulls up and I give Bill a kiss. 'See you tomorrow night.'

'Have a good day at work,' shouts Bill as the bus doors shut.

'You too!' I shout back.

The journey back home gives me time to think and I realise I am so worried about Tootsie. I get home and I run into the house and grandma looks startled.

'You frightened me to death!' says grandma.

'I give Tootsie a hug and she licks my face. 'Sorry grandma. I was just worried about Tootsie.'

'Huh!' Grandma frowns. 'If you were that worried why didn't you stay in?'

I take on a shocked expression, my mouth open slightly. 'That's not fair! That's horrible grandma!'

Grandma points her finger. 'Don't you talk to me like that, young lady! Just because I'm right!'

'Well, grandma. Why didn't you stay in when Grandpa Ronnie was so poorly then?'

Grandma leans forwards and jabs her finger towards me. 'I wasn't married to him any more Caroline, if you remember!'

I nod a little. 'But you still cared in a way, didn't you grandma?'

'In a way, yes,' answers grandma.

'So it proves that you can still care even if you're not there all the time!'

Grandma raises her head haughtily. 'You think you're *really* clever don't you girl?'

I shake my head. 'No grandma. Just making a point, that's all.'

Nothing else is said and then after supper its time for me to get to bed. I give grandma a hug and then Tootsie and I slip up to bed. Tootsie, though, still doesn't seem herself and I lie awake for ages stroking her and worrying.

Monday morning is, well, Monday morning at work but I am getting very good now and getting on with everyone so it's good to me! However, my spirits are soon dampened when I get home as grandma is looking very glum and Tootsie is lying behind the chair, not looking good at all.

'What's wrong grandma?' I ask.

Grandma points to Tootsie.

I look more worried. 'What's happened grandma?'

'Tootsie ran out of the house today and ran away.'

I put my hand over my mouth and grandma continues. 'I got a phone call from Laurel Bank to say that she had turned up there.'

I look dismayed. 'At the guest house? How did she get there?'

'I have no idea,' says grandma shaking her head. 'Trouble is, she isn't so well. I might have to take her to the vets tomorrow.'

I go and sit on the floor next to Tootsie. 'What have you been doing little girl?' I ask. 'You dafty! You might have got killed.' I look up at grandma. 'She is a clever dog though for finding her way back to the guest house!'

'I suppose so,' answers grandma. 'Anyway, I will ring the vets in the morning and take her, just to be on the safe side.'

I nod. 'I need to come with you.'

Grandma shakes her head. 'You have to work Caroline. I'll take her. Now, that's that!'

I shrug my shoulders and realise that it is no use arguing. 'Okay grandma. Thanks.'

The rest of the evening and night Tootsie and I are inseparable and I even hug her as we go to sleep.

The next day I do not want to go to work at all but grandma makes me and says that everything will be okay. I cuddle Tootsie all the time, or so it seems, and I am watery eyed and sobbing as I go for my bus. All day at work I seem to be picked up for little bits of mistakes and everyone can see that I am not myself at all. I tell Mrs Harris what is wrong and she tells me that she's sure that it'll be okay. When home time comes I rush for the bus and then keep telling the bus driver in my head to hurry up.

When I get home I burst in the door and call out. 'Tootsie? Where are you?'

Tootsie doesn't come and I reckon that she is lay down in the kitchen or something. I go into the kitchen and grandma is there looking quite unhappy.

'Where's Tootsie grandma?'

'Er, she was very poorly when we got to the vets. The journey yesterday to the guest house caused her a great deal of stress.

'I sigh. 'So, has the vet kept her in then? When can she come home?'

Grandma just stares at me and I start to go watery eyed. 'Grandma?' I start to sob. 'Oh, no! No!'

I start to cry and grandma sighs. Putting her arm around me I bury my head into her shoulder and cry my eyes out. Grandma pats me on the head and then I just hug into her for a while.

'She had a heart attack Caroline,' says grandma with some sympathy in her voice. 'I'm so sorry Caroline.'

I sit down and just stare at the fireplace for what seems like ages and ages. I am brought out of my thoughts by grandma putting a cup of tea in front of me. I take a few swigs of the tea. 'Thanks grandma.'

'She was seventeen,' says grandma. 'At least you gave her great love and friendship.'

I nod. 'She was my friend grandma. She was a little love.'

'Do you want some tea?' asks grandma. 'I've made burger and chips for me.'

I shake my head. 'No thanks. I'm not very hungry. I'm going to finish my drink and then go to the guest house. I bet they don't know.'

Grandma nods. 'Okay, but don't go all night without anything to eat.'

'I won't grandma.'

When I get to the guest house everyone is really sorry and Bill hugs me for ages.

'I've lost my lovely friend Bill,' I say between sobs. 'I've lost my grandpa and now my little friend!' I start to cry.

Bill gives me a sympathetic smile. 'I'm sorry too. We'll get over it together Caroline. It'll be fine.'

Mary comes and sits down with us. 'Look at me. I'm still cooking here knowing that my efforts will be unrewarded in the end!'

Bill grins. 'Well, we all appreciate you, especially your roast dinners!'

Mary slaps Bill on the arm. 'Is that all?'

I try and smile but I just feel so sad and I want Tootsie back, grandpa as well!

I lean into Bill. 'I'm sick of feeling upset. The worst thing is grandma doesn't seem to care about anything that goes wrong for me.'

Mary listens in but says nothing.

The rest of the week gets better as it goes along and by Friday morning I am starting to get over Tootsie going a little bit. At least she is with Grandpa Ronnie and running around sprightly again! Bill and I seem to be very close now and grandma really doesn't like it! We are developing a great relationship and I don't care if grandma thinks he is a bad one because he is lovely with me and she is wrong about him! As the weeks go on we spend more and more time together and we become a really close couple. Grandma is really down about our relationship but there is nothing new there then!

***

A couple of months later I am starting to have a few problems every morning when I get up. I keep feeling very tired and I am usually sick in the morning, especially after I have a drink or some breakfast! Grandma thinks I am overdoing it a bit with working and going to the guest house to see Bill every night.

'See,' says grandma one morning, 'I told you he was a bad one! He's keeping you up 'till late and expecting you to still work hard! You want to start doing what is good for *you* young lady!'

I sit down and blow out my cheeks hard. 'Bill is good for me grandma. He's kind and we have a lot of fun. I can't work and not play all the time!' I sigh. 'Anyway, I've got to go to work now.'

Grandma frowns. 'Huh, where are you going after work? To the guest house I suppose.'

I nod my head. 'Your friend Mary is cooking tea again so I am going straight there from work.'

'Oh? My teas are not good enough any more?' says grandma curtly.

I get up and get my coat. 'Of course not grandma! You have been very busy lately and I am just going there tonight. That's all.' I give grandma a kiss on the cheek. 'See you later.'

That evening Mary, Bill and I are having a talk together but I keep yawning and have run to the loo once or twice more than usual.

'Is everything all right love?' asks Bill. He looks into my eyes. 'You look really tired.'

I raise my eyebrows. 'Oh, thanks!'

'Maybe you should have an early night love,' continues Bill.

I shrug my shoulders. 'Maybe you're right.'

'You know that your grandma will have a nice cup of hot chocolate and a biscuit on the go,' says Mary, 'so go on! Get off with you!'

I gulp and choke a little at the mention of chocolate and biscuits, causing Mary and Bill to frown at each other.

'Come on,' says Bill. 'I'll walk you to the bus stop.'

Motherhood

'You are what?' Grandma scowls and her face takes on an annoyed look. 'How can you be so stupid?'

'You mean you're not pleased grandma? You'll be a great grandma now!'

This morning the reason for my apparent ill feelings and sickness became clear – I was expecting a baby! I can only think it is a good job it is a Saturday when I've found out!

'Pleased? Pleased? Why would I be pleased? You silly girl!'

I frown. 'Why am I silly? I'm happy! It's great grandma!'

'I suppose that waste of space Bill is the father? I told you he was no good!'

'Well of course he's the father!' I put my hands on my hips. 'Who else would it be?'

'That makes you even more stupid!' says grandma angrily. 'Does he know?'

'No,' I say with a smile. 'I'm going now to tell him!'

Grandma gets her coat and throws it around her. 'Well, you tell him from me that he will have *me* to answer to now!'

With that, grandma storms out of the house.

As I run into the grounds of Laurel Bank and up the side steps to go in Bill is just coming out. I throw my arms around his neck and he raises his eyebrows.

'What's wrong with you?' asks Bill.

'Nothing!' I say with a grin. 'Nothing at all!' I grab his hand and turn him around. 'Let's go back inside!'

Bill follows me in but with a slight frown. 'What's going on love? Have you drunk happy juice?'

I drag him into the lounge and put his hand on my tummy. 'We are going to have a baby!'

Bill's eyes widen and his mouth drops open. 'What? Wh... when did you find out?'

'This morning,' I answer grinning. 'I found out this morning. Are you not happy?'

'Happy? I think it's great!' Bill grabs me into a hug. 'Come here you!'

Mary comes dashing into the room. 'I heard some commotion. What's going on?'

I am still grinning. 'I'm going to have a baby Mary.' I point at Bill. '*We're* going to have a baby!'

Mary hugs us both. 'Oh, that's great! Congratulations!'

Bill looks me in the eyes. 'Does your grandma know?'

I look sheepish. 'Sorry, she does. She was in the house when I did the test. I had to tell her. I'm sorry.'

Bill smiles. 'It's okay. What did she say?'

'She said I was stupid and that it proves you are no good!'

'Huh!' says Bill. 'There's a surprise!'

I look at him and smile. 'We're not stupid! I think it's great, don't you?'

'I think it's wonderful!' says Bill.

'Don't mind your grandma,' says Mary, 'she'll come round.'

I shake my head a little. 'You don't know her properly Mary. I don't think she will!'

'Well, never mind her!' Bill smiles. 'We're happy so that's all that matters!'

'I know, I know,' I say with a little trepidation in my voice, 'but she is my grandma and the nearest I have to a mum. She should be happy!'

'From what you say she is *never* happy!' says Bill sarcastically.

We all start to laugh and then Mary turns to go out of the room. 'I'm going to put the kettle on and start the dinner.'

'I'll help,' I offer. 'Where were you going Bill?'

'To get the papers,' answers Bill heading out the door. 'I won't be long.'

Mary and I go into the kitchen and I start to chop some vegetables.

'I can understand what your grandma means Caroline,' says Mary. 'You are having a baby with a man much older than you who has children from being married before. I think she is trying to look out for you.'

I shrug my shoulders and carry on chopping carrots. 'Maybe, but we'll see.'

The next few weeks I am still being sick every morning but Bill and I are very happy. Bill is still looking for somewhere to live and he has seen a couple of houses not far from the guest house. Mary just carries on with the cooking, in between going out with grandma and her new man Paddy, who Mary says is a typical Irishman but she adores him! Grandma is still seeing her fella Frank but he seems to be drinking a lot, which grandma certainly does not condone!

It is now a few weeks on and grandma is looking at me one morning.

'What are you going to do Caroline?' asks grandma.

I frown. 'What do you mean?'

'Well, with this baby. What are you going to do about this baby?'

'I'm going to have it in about seven months grandma, that's what!'

Grandma scowls. 'Don't get flippant with me, young lady! You can't have it, can you? You need to get rid of it!'

I stare open mouthed. 'What? You want me to get rid of it? Why? That's awful!'

'It's not awful!' retorts grandma. 'You are very young and he is a lot older. You have only just got your first job and, really, you are not mature enough!'

'Grandma, how could you! You are being horrible! I am mature enough to work and know what I'm doing so how can you say that?'

'Well, I'm not supporting you! You can't live here if you have a baby.'

'Are you telling me to go grandma?' My eyes start to water a little. 'How can you be so nasty?'

'I'm telling you, young lady,' continues grandma, 'you can't live here if you have a baby! You have to get rid of it if you want to stay.'

I get my coat on to go out and start to cry. 'You are nasty and awful, grandma! I am *not* getting rid of my baby! Bill and I are really happy!'

Grandma purses her lips together. 'That's it then! You need to get somewhere else to live.'

'You are throwing me out when I'm pregnant! You can go to hell grandma!'

I storm out of the door and head for the bus stop crying. I get the bus to Grandpa Harry's and when he answers the door I am sobbing like mad.

'What's wrong Caroline?' Grandpa Harry puts his arm around me and we go inside. 'Sit down poppet and tell me what's wrong.'

I try to tell Grandpa Harry in between sobs. 'Oh, grandpa. I am having a baby with Bill and that heartless grandma of mine wants me to get rid of it!'

Grandpa raises his eyebrows. 'A baby? That's great poppet! I'm really pleased.'

'I am so happy grandpa but grandma says if I don't get rid of it she will throw me out! Grandpa, I don't want to get rid of it.'

'She's just being her usual nasty self is Pearl!' Grandpa Harry smiles. 'You can move in here Caroline if you want.'

I throw my hands around grandpa's neck. 'Oh, thank you grandpa! I love you!'

Life at grandpa Harry's is great but I have never eaten so much fish! Still, the chippy three times a week is better than once and grandpa does make the point that I am now eating for two! I also like his Rich Tea biscuits with butter spread on them, especially with his cups of tea which he makes perfect! Bill is busy looking for a house and the residents seem to be happy at the moment as no-one seems to be interested in the guest house much at the moment. Mary still helps out but less and less but, alas, she is still going out with my grandma. I keep asking Mary if grandma asks about me but all she says is that she thinks I should get rid of the baby and that's that! Frank is also a big part of grandma and Mary says that grandma is taking him to Spain next week! In fact, grandma and Mary have booked to go as well in a couple of months.

About a couple of months after I moved into grandpa's I am looking a bit big now and Bill has found a nice house not far from Laurel Bank. Things seem to be looking up a bit but, as Grandpa Harry points out, grandma is not on the scene so they will run smooth! I have to laugh at this as I know grandpa is right! Work is going okay also and I am now one of the fastest machinists in the place! Mrs Harris puts it down to the fact that I can't move so much anyway so I can be still and sew better! I don't quite know how that works but I will take her word for it! Grandpa Harry is much more understanding about me going and seeing Bill and even is very concerned about me going on the bus in my advanced state!

'You mind those blasted buses!' he says to me one Friday evening.

'I'll be okay grandpa. Some of the usual drivers know me now so I'll be all right.'

'You make sure Bill is at the other end to meet you then,' says Grandpa Harry pointing his finger slightly.

I smile. 'Oh, he will be grandpa. He's very good like that.'

'So, where's this house he's found Caroline?' Grandpa gets the kettle on and I nod that I want one.

I get the biscuit tin from the cupboard. 'In Morris Green. A nicely kept terrace grandpa.'

Grandpa nods. 'Very nice. Not a bad area at all. Not very many pubs though.'

I throw my head up. 'Oh! You sound just like Bill!'

Grandpa grins. 'Man after my own heart!

'There is a nice butty and pie shop – and a good chippy,' I continue.

'Well, it's not all bad then!' says grandpa laughing. 'Isn't that pub the Morris Dancers the only one?'

I nod as I take a bite of my biscuit. 'Although, the Stags is only on the main road, about ten minutes walk.'

Grandpa raises his eyebrows. 'Ten minutes? Far too long to stagger home!'

Grandpa Harry and I have a good laugh together and then I am getting my coat on ready to go to the guest house. I don't move around as quick, of course, which makes grandpa laugh and make references to Weebles! I shake my head and give grandpa a hug before I go.

'You won't be late, will you?' asks grandpa.

'No, I won't be late,' I answer shaking my head. 'I'm usually tired by ten o'clock now! See you later.'

I look back and see grandpa shaking his head as I close the door. I know he will be okay – it's the pub and chippy for him!

As usual, Bill is waiting at the other end and he smiles as I get off the bus. I wave and then hug him, as close as I can given the circumstances!

'Everything okay?' asks Bill.

I nod. 'Yep! Grandpa will be going out to the pub but I've told him I won't be too late.'

'Quite right,' says Bill. He looks at me closely.

'What?' I ask.

'Oh, I'm just thinking how much happier you are living with your grandpa *and* with your grandma out of the way!'

I nod. 'Yeah, I think you're right. Grandpa Harry helps and he is kind.' I smile. 'He always asks after you!'

Bill nods. 'That's nice. Anyway, do you want to go and see the house? It's empty now and I have got the keys.'

I grin. 'That would be great! I have been waiting to see it for days!'

Bill frowns a bit. 'It needs a tidy up but it'll be okay for you to go in.'

'Come on then! Let's get going!' I start to walk past the bank but Bill gets hold of my arm.

'Not so fast!' says Bill. 'You can't go walking all that way. We'll get a taxi.'

I smile. 'Okay. Let's go and phone for one.'

I look around the living room and make little nods of approval. Then I wander into the kitchen and it looks very nice. Bill studies my face a bit, looking for any show of disapproval.

'Let's go upstairs and see the bedrooms.'

Bill grins. 'I thought you'd never ask!'

I slap him on the arm. 'That's what got me this way in the first place!'

'Do you like the place?' asks Bill. 'The rent is very reasonable and I like where it is.'

'I love it!' I answer. 'A very nice place! When do you move in?'

'I think I can move in next Wednesday,' answers Bill thoughtfully. 'You are going to come and stay, aren't you?'

I nod. 'So long as you have plenty of Vimto and Jaffa Cakes in! I can't seem to get enough of them!'

Bill shakes his head. 'Better than marmalade on kippers I suppose!'

After we have had some of Mary's wonderful vegetable soup and crusty bread Bill and I are sitting in the resident's lounge. The people are all asking me if I want anything doing but I politely decline. Bill notices some bulbs are out in the lamps and goes to get some more from the cupboard, as the light in the room is so much better with all the lamps on. There are two settees along the walls and five chairs positioned around the room, two more in the middle. Bill and I usually sit on the settee by the window and the only other regular place occupied is the chair by the fireplace, an elderly but sprightly lady called Ethel sits there! Ethel is lovely and is usually knitting something. In fact, she is very kindly knitting a cardigan and shawl for the baby, pale green of course as we don't know whether it is a boy or girl!

Bill comes back and soon all the lamps have new bulbs in. 'That's better!'

It is now about nine o'clock and I get up to get my coat. 'I'm sorry, I have to get back.' I yawn a bit. 'I promised grandpa I'd not be late and, as he puts is, those 'blasted buses' are not as frequent at night!'

'Well,' says Bill with a smile, 'if we order a taxi for you in about half-an-hour you can have a night cap before you go!'

I sigh and laugh. 'Okay, you win. Mary, have we got any Vimto?'

A laugh comes from the kitchen. 'Do you want it hot or cold Caroline?'

'Oh, hot I think,' I answer hugging back into Bill.

After my drink the taxi arrives and I am kissing Bill and then I'm on my way. It's Friday night and I know that Grandpa Harry will be coming home with fish and peas in a bit! I hope the taxi gets home in time but then I know it will – the pubs don't shut until eleven!

Another couple of months have passed and It's not far off the baby being born. I am looking very big now and grandpa says I really do look like a Weeble! I love living with Grandpa Harry but I know that when the baby is born it wouldn't be fair to have the baby living with him as well. I know he would let us live there as long as needs be but Bill has asked and it is okay for the three of us to live together when the baby is born so I think that is where I will go. There is still no contact from my grandma but Mary says that she is still insistent that I should have got rid of the baby. Grandpa Harry says I shouldn't worry as I am better off without her being around at this time. Mary also says that grandma is having more and more trouble with this man of hers Frank. Apparently he is drinking a lot and being quite nasty with grandma but I smile as I am thinking it is time grandma got some of her own medicine! Serves her right then!

As the days go by I get slightly slower when moving around but I can still sew with speed so everything seems okay there, as does everything with Bill's house. I have helped him as much as I can but it is looking really nice and he has managed to get a lovely suite, as well as a dining set for the kitchen. We are sitting having a cup of tea and have just finished our fish and chips – it is

Friday – but Bill can see that I am quite deep in thought.

'What's the matter Caroline? Are you not feeling well?'

I look up at him. 'Oh, yes. I'm fine. Just wondering if Grandpa Harry will be all right when the baby's born and I move out. He has been wonderful to me and I will be moving out.'

Bill smiles. 'I'm sure he will be the first to wish you well love.' He holds my hand. 'Anyway, you are not abandoning him altogether. You'll still see him.'

I sigh. 'You're right Bill. He is happy for me – us.'

Suddenly I hold my tunny and wince a little bit.

Bill leans forward. 'Are you okay?'

'Just a few pangs and kicks,' I answer nodding. 'Nothing serious, all natural!'

'That's okay then,' says Bill, getting up and clearing the cups away. 'I suppose we had better get you a taxi ordered. Harry will be wanting to know you are okay.'

I nod and then make my way slowly up the stairs to the toilet, something else I seem to be doing a lot of lately!'

Then the taxi beeps its horn and I get my coat on. 'Bye Bill. See you tomorrow darling.'

I give him a kiss and hug and then I am off back home to grandpa's, for the time being for I know that home is going to be where I have just driven from!

When I get home grandpa is still at the pub and when he gets home I am sat in the chair deep in thought.

'Hi, poppet,' says grandpa. 'Penny for them?'

'Are you going to be okay grandpa when I've had this baby?'

Grandpa Harry raises his eyebrows. 'Shouldn't I be asking you that?'

I laugh. 'No, I mean I will be moving out and you have been great letting me live here.'

Grandpa Harry holds my hand and smiles. 'Poppet, I have my pub, my chippy and my telly at night so I will be fine! Besides, you and the baby need to be with their father, the three of you together. Now, stop being so silly. I'm not your grandma!'

'Huh, thank God for that!' I say laughing.

Suddenly, I double over and cry out. 'Argh, oh no. I think I am getting more and more twinges.'

'Er, you're not starting yet, are you?' asks grandpa with a concerned tone.

'No, not yet I don't think.' I double up again. 'Actually, I think I am grandpa! Oh oh! Aargh!'

Grandpa dashes over to the phone and rings for an ambulance. When it's on its way grandpa rings Bill.

'Hi Bill,' says grandpa. 'It's Harry, Caroline's grandpa. I've just called for an ambulance – she's gone into labour!'

When grandpa has put the phone down he turns to me grinning. 'That's got him in a flap a bit! I've told him you are okay though so he will meet us at the hospital.'

I am sitting on the chair and trying to breathe. 'Thanks... grandpa. Oh, that's a big twinge!'

I know I am young and I know that worries grandpa but I smile and assure grandpa that I can cope. The ambulance arrives and grandpa sees that I get onto it okay.

'You are Caroline's guardian, right?' asks the ambulance man.

Grandpa shakes his head. 'No. I am her grandpa. She has been living here but she is going to live with the baby's father after it is born, he is meeting us at the hospital.'

The ambulance man nods. 'Okay. But you are coming with her now?'

'Of course,' answers Grandpa Harry.

Grandpa gets on board the ambulance and we are off to the hospital.

I smile and hold onto my baby girl! She's absolutely beautiful and I can see that Bill is very proud and very happy – and Grandpa Harry, well! I haven't seen him this happy since he found an extra loaf of bread in the cupboard! I am happy but I don't feel very well but I am smiling because I have a beautiful baby!

'Have you thought of a name yet?' asks Grandpa Harry.

'Yes,' I answer proudly. 'She's called Ann!'

'It's a lovely name, isn't it Harry?' asks Bill.

Grandpa Harry nods. 'Well, I like it very much but it's more important that you two like it!'

'Oh, we love it grandpa!' I say with a great big smile.

Grandpa Harry looks at Ann and smiles. 'Well, I'll have to cut down on the beer now! I am a great grandpa after all!'

Grandpa looks at me and frowns a little. 'Do you want me to tell your grandma?'

I shake my head. 'No, grandpa. She wanted me to get rid of it so why should she know?'

Grandpa Harry nods. 'Okay then. Let her find out through Mary.' Grandpa kisses Ann on the head and then me on the cheek. 'I'll see you tomorrow poppet.'

'Okay grandpa. Bye and, thanks!'

Bill sits on the bed and puts his arm around me. 'I love you Caroline,' he looks down at Ann. 'She's gorgeous, just like her mum!'

The nurse comes up to the bed and takes my temperature. 'Go on,' she says to Bill. 'Time for you to go home.'

Bill gives me a kiss. 'They're throwing me out now. I'll be back tomorrow lunchtime. I have got a few days holiday owing at work so I can decorate that last wall now I know which colour – pink!'

'Bye darling,' I say, blowing a kiss. 'We'll see you tomorrow.'

As Bill leaves the ward and the nurse finishes I put Ann in her cot and settle back for a snooze.'

Bill and Grandpa Harry come and go in the hospital for the next three days and then it is time for me to go home. The nurses have been keeping their eye on me as I haven't been feeling well but I am feeling great now as I am going home to be a family – Bill, Ann and me! The taxi pulls up at the door and then we are inside. I take Ann up to her room and show her around the rest of her new home. Then she needs a feed and a sleep and after Bill and I get some tea on.

'Grandma has been awful with me,' I say to Bill with some resignation, 'but I am really happy now!

Bill smiles as he peels potatoes. 'So am I. I have a beautiful partner and a beautiful daughter and things couldn't be better!' He looks at me and smiles. 'Should we invite Great Grandpa Harry for tea on Sunday?'

I grin. 'Oh, I'm sure he'll love that!'

Ann seems to be okay in the night and wakes up for a feed and some hefty burping after! Bill sleeps through, as men do, but I don't mind! In the morning it is Saturday and Bill goes out for a paper and some shopping. I get the bath and give Ann a nice wash down, after which I put some baby oil on and her new baby grow that Grandpa Harry has bought, together with the lovely cardigan that Ethel from the guest house has knitted! I am feeding Ann when Bill comes back in.

I look up and smile. 'She's got Ethel's cardigan on!'

Bill smiles. 'Aw, that looks nice. Do you want a pasty or a meat pie?'

'A meat pie please darling, though not yet. I'll have it with a tea in a minute. Got to finish feeding Anne and wind her yet.'

Bill holds his hands out. 'You put the kettle on and I'll get the wind up. Mine's the meat and potato!'

When I go back into the lounge I smile as Bill is cuddling Ann and I'm sure she is smiling but, of course, I know it is just wind! Bill, however, is looking at me strangely.

'What's the matter?' I ask.

'Are you all right love?'

I shrug a little. 'I'm fine. Why, do I not look it?'

Bill shakes his head and rocks Ann slightly as she starts to whimper. 'No, not really. You look pale and about to collapse.'

'I admit I do feel a little tired but I *have* just had a baby!' I offer, sighing.

Bill has managed to rock Ann to sleep. 'I suppose that'll be it then.' He gets up carefully with Ann. 'I'll just put her down and then we'll eat.'

After our pie I have a small doze and Bill has a read of the paper. The next thing I know Bill is shaking me and I stir, rubbing my eyes and then stretching.

'What's the matter darling?; I ask.

'I'm just a bit worried about you.' Bill looks me in the eyes. 'You look very pale and you keep mumbling and stirring.'

'I get up and stretch again. The room is going a bit darker and I realise I have been asleep for a good few hours. 'How's Ann? Is she okay?'

'She's fine,' says Bill nodding. 'She'll be waking up for a feed soon.'

'I'll get her,' I say with a smile and a slight yawn.

Bill nods and then disappears into the kitchen. When he comes back I am crouched in the corner, crying and Ann is still in her cot.

Bill runs over and grabs onto me. 'What's the matter Caroline?'

I don't answer at first and then slowly look up. 'What? Oh, where am I?'

'You're in the corner of the room,' answers Bill, 'crouching down in the corner of the room.'

Bill helps me up and I smile. 'How did I get here?'

'You were going to get Ann up and I found you in the corner.' Bill sits me down in the chair. 'Don't worry Caroline. I'll go and get Ann.'

I just sit in the chair and watch Bill with Anne, smiling at him sorting out her feed and I just feel happy.

In the night, however, I am aware of Bill shaking my shoulder and I look up to see the worried look on his face.

'Hmm, oh, what's wrong darling?' I ask.

Bill sighs. 'Why are you sitting in the bath?'

'Er I don't know. Am I?'

Actually, over the course of the next few days I keep doing some very odd things and sometimes Bill is quite worried about Ann. I would never do anything to hurt her and he knows this but I am really not myself at the moment. I am very tired a lot of the time and Bill suggested I go to the doctors and get some sort of a tonic. A day or two later I am not quite as tired but once or twice Bill has found me in odd places, including once at the bottom of the yard with a sandwich and a brew – it isn't really that warm! Grandpa Harry is here as well and he is also very worried. They take me inside and then Ann is crying for a feed so I sort that out and then am looking tired again, according to Bill. Grandpa Harry and Bill look after Ann and I sleep for the rest of the evening.

The next day, however, Bill sends for the doctor as I am rocking backwards and forwards in the chair and crying. The doctor confirms that I am not going mad but he is very concerned about the state I am in and sends for an ambulance. I resist and don't want to go at first but Bill says it will be okay and that he and Anne will be along in a little while.

The nurse brings me a drink and a biscuit and I smile and then settle back onto the bed. It is my second day in hospital and I am wondering why I am here. Nobody will give me a straight answer and all the nurses keep telling me that I need to speak to the doctor. But, whenever the doctors come to see me they only talk about medical things or to take my temperature. The night time comes again and Bill comes to visit with Ann and Grandpa Harry.

'Why am I in here?' I ask Bill as I am cuddling Ann.

Bill smiles. 'You have been acting very strange love. You are not very well at all and you need looking after.'

'Don't worry poppet,' says Grandpa Harry. 'You are just feeling a bit down so a few days in here and you will be as right as rain!'

'But, I need to be with Ann!' I hug her and go watery eyed. 'I need to be with her, she needs her mother!'

Bill strokes my hand. 'Ann is fine. You'll be out of here in no time and then we can be together as a family.'

I give a big sigh. 'Okay darling. I suppose you and grandpa are right.'

The nurse calls for end of visiting and grandpa and bill get up. I kiss Ann and give her a big hug and then I pass her to Bill and give him a kiss. 'Bye darling.'

Grandpa Harry leans down and gives me a hug and then the three of them go, leaving me to reflect on why I'm here and to cry slightly at not being able to be with Ann. Then the nurse in bringing me a cup of tea and biscuits.

It's day three in hospital and the nurses seem to be running around me a lot more. I don't feel right and I know there is something more wrong as I have had a couple of extra visits from the doctor. Afternoon visiting time arrives and when nobody comes to see me I start to get anxious and then cry a bit. I start to get frantic by the time visiting ends as neither Bill nor Grandpa Harry has been and I have not seen Ann. The sister comes and gives me an injection and after a while I settle down and then am asleep. I must have been asleep as then it is evening and I wake up to find I still feel drowsy and I still haven't had any visitors. I am so very upset and then I get some more medicine and eventually I drift off to sleep again.

The next morning I am brought some breakfast but I just push it to one side and start to get out of bed. I am still drowsy and the nurse goes to hold me up but I push her as well and start to get angry.

'Where is my daughter? Where is Ann? I want my baby!'

Two more nurses come to help and then after another injection I settle down.

Pearl, my grandma, is sitting in her usual chair, sipping a cup of tea and looking quizzically at the two women sitting opposite in the settee.

'The thing is,' began one of the women, 'Caroline is not very well at all. She is having serious post-natal problems and her doing strange things is a result of that. She has had to go into hospital and obviously she cannot have baby Ann in with her.'

Pearl sips her tea again. 'Huh! I said she should have got rid of it and now it seems I was right! I knew she wouldn't cope. She's far too young, silly girl!'

'Now, now Mrs Webb, that's not the kind of talk we want to hear!' says the second woman. 'It doesn't achieve anything.'

'Why are you here talking to me anyway?' asks grandma.

'We need someone to look after the baby while Caroline recovers.'

Grandma raises her eyebrows. 'Pah! *I'm* not looking after a baby! Why should I look after it?'

'Her!' says the first lady sternly. 'We *do not* refer to a lovely life like Ann in the way you did!'

'Anyway,' continues grandma, 'why can't the baby's father look after her?'

The second lady clears her throat. 'Ah, well, you see. We have quite a concern that he isn't really capable of looking after a new baby on his own.'

'What do you mean?' asks grandma. 'Surely a child's father is the best one? Is he such a lazy effort that he can't cope? I knew he was a bad one!'

'He hasn't refused as such,' says the first lady. 'We don't feel he can look after baby Ann properly on his own.'

Grandma shrugs and finishes her tea. 'Well, that's as maybe but I'm not looking after her. You'll have to find someone else! Now, I have work to do for my residents. Good day.'

The two women look at each other and then gather their things and make for the door.

'Are you sure you don't want to help Mrs Webb?'

'Definitely sure!' answers grandma. 'Now, good day!'

The two women leave and grandma mutters to herself 'of all the cheek!' as she closes the door.

I have had a bad night and the next day I have been doped a little. But, I can make out that the woman sat at the side of the bed is some sort of children specialist or, even worse, some sort of social worker! I can't figure out who the man in the suit is, though, but he must be very important as he has a very shiny briefcase.

'Caroline, are you okay to talk for a few minutes?' asks the woman.

I nod. 'Who... who are you and what do you want?' I turn and shout down the ward. 'Nurse, nurse!

Who are these people?'

I start to get very restless and the nurse comes and calms me down. She points to the two people. This lady is a social worker and the gentleman is... well, someone who looks after the legalities.'

I frown. 'Legalit... what?'

The woman leans forward. 'Caroline, you are very ill and whilst you are in here someone needs to look after Ann.'

'Why... why can't Bill look after her?' I say with a little bit of a wavering voice.

The woman looks down slightly and clears her throat. 'We don't think that it is a good idea for Ann's father to look after her.' She looks to the man and he smiles slightly and gives a little nod. 'We have arranged for Ann to go to a foster family until you are better.'

I stare open-mouthed and wide-eyed and my eyes start to water. 'What? Why can't he look after Ann? Where... where are you taking my baby?'

I start to get frantic and the sister comes over to give me some more medicine. I try to fend her off but in the end I sigh and settle down.

'I am so sorry Caroline,' says the woman. 'We went to ask your grandma if she would look after Ann but she refused. So, we have to send her elsewhere.'

The sister can see that I am getting really upset so she indicates for the man and woman to go, which they get up and do. When they have gone the sister and a nurse take me into an office at the end of the ward,

'I'm very sorry Caroline,' says the sister as we sit down. 'We'll get you better as quickly as possible and then you can have Ann back with you.' She takes my hand and smiles.

I stare at the wall. 'My grandma refused to look after Ann? Why is she so horrible?'

The sister pats my hand. 'Lots of older people don't want to look after babies.'

'She's not *that* old!' I retort frowning.

'Whatever the reason,' continues the sister, 'she refused so Ann has had to go to somebody else.'

The nurse smiles. 'I'll go and make you a cup of tea Caroline and bring the biscuits!'

As I nod and the nurse leaves the room the sister looks me in the eyes. 'We'll get you right and back with your baby in no time. Now, let's get tea and then you can have a rest.'

I go back to my bed and realise that there is no use bothering, for now.

The next day it sinks in a bit that my baby has been taken away and I have quite a bad morning. In the afternoon I frown deeply as I see my grandma coming down the ward. I get up to leave my bed to try and hide but I am still slightly woozy from medicine and eventually grandma pulls up a chair and sits by the bed.

'What are *you* doing here?' I ask quite angrily.

'Well, that's not a nice way to speak to your grandma when I have come to visit you!'

'You refused to look after Ann!' I throw my hand out and look away. 'Am I supposed to be pleased you're here?'

'Now, Caroline. I have come to see how you are. I heard you are not very well.' Grandma shuffles a little uncomfortably.

I raise my eyebrows and my voice. 'Not very well? I am quite poorly and have just been told that my baby is in foster care. How am I supposed to be well?' I shout for the nurse.

Grandma frowns and when the nurse comes she looks at grandma a little strangely.

'Will you please ask my grandma to leave?' I ask the nurse.

The nurse raises her eyebrows. 'Why do you want your grandma to leave? She has come to see you.'

'Well, I don't want to see her! She refused to take care of my baby! Now, will you please ask her to leave? Now!'

I start to get very restless and start to get out of bed. I go towards my grandma but the sister comes over and I stop.

'What's going on?' asks the sister.

'Caroline doesn't want this lady here...'

'I am her grandma, not just some lady!'

'I don't want her here!' I scowl and start to shout a bit. 'Now, can you please ask her to leave?'

The sister smiles at grandma. 'Can you just give us a minute?'

The sister takes me back into her office. 'Why do you want your grandma to go?'

I shake my head. 'She's not interested in *me*! She told me to get rid of the baby and now she refuses to look after her. What kind of person does that? She is a horrible, nasty woman and I don't want her here!'

I start to really cry now and the sister hugs onto me. We go back onto the ward and grandma frowns as she sees me.

'I think you had better leave Caroline alone,' says the sister to grandma. 'She is very poorly and her getting upset is not helping her at all.'

Grandma gets up and drags her bag off the bed. 'Huh, I come here to see how my granddaughter is and I get asked to leave.' She looks at me. 'I hope you are happy Caroline.'

'Now, I have told you she is very poorly!' The sister indicates to the door leading out of the ward. 'I would like you to leave now.'

As grandma starts to go out of the ward the nurse gets me back into bed and the sister catches up with grandma.

'Give her a few days and then try again,' says the sister smiling.

Grandma frowns and then storms out of the ward. I settle down and soon drift off to sleep.

By the end of the week Bill has visited every evening and Grandpa Harry has been a couple of times, not with any fish and peas though! It is now Saturday and Bill has been in the daytime as this evening he is going to a snooker competition. Grandma has come back this evening, though, and although I can't forgive what she's done I let her stay as she has calmed down and she does seem genuinely concerned. Grandma and I have a decent chat in the end and when visiting time is over and grandma has gone I relax back in bed and stare at the ward, not really looking at anything in particular.

The nurse comes to take my temperature and blood pressure and smiles. 'Did you have a better chat with your grandma?'

I nod. 'It wasn't bad. At least she seemed to be concerned this time!'

'I think she was concerned the other day,' says the nurse, taking the thing off my arm that takes the blood pressure. 'It's just that you were in a lot worse state then.'

I raise my eyes. 'So. Am I getting better then?'

The nurse smiles and nods. 'You are a lot better then you were a few days ago Caroline! Would you like some tea?'

I nod and smile. 'Please! That would be very nice!'

The next day Bill and I are talking and having a cup of tea in the lounge bit as I am feeling a bit better.

'I don't know why they wouldn't let me keep Ann with me,' says Bill. 'I have tried to get some answers but nobody will tell me anything or let me see her even.'

I smile. 'She is okay though. That social worker lady says that Ann is doing fine.'

Bill smiles and then thinks for a moment. 'When will you be coming out?'

'The doctors reckon it'll not be long now. Another few weeks of getting better like this and I should be coming home!'

'It's a house that's too quiet again!' says Bill. 'I want the life back in it!'

The bell goes for end of visiting and Bill leans in and gives me a peck. 'I'll see you tomorrow night. I have put in some overtime at work so I'm going looking at a few cars. Better than getting around on the bus!;

I smile. 'That's good! See you tomorrow then.'

After he has gone the nurse brings tea round. 'He's all right, isn't he?' asks the nurse of me.

'He's lovely!' I answer. 'I can't think why they wouldn't let him look after Ann.'

The nurse sighs and checks her pocket watch. 'My experience is they must have their reasons. Anyway, never mind. You might be out f here soon so you'll all be back together soon.'

The next few weeks seem to fly by and then it is on the Saturday about three-and-a-half months after I went in. I am really happy today as the doctor has been round and says I can go home tomorrow! My grandma has been to see me in the afternoon and now Bill and I are sitting in the lounge.

'Once we are settled back in we will contact the social services woman and she can bring Ann back to us!' I look at Bill and then at the nurse and she smiles.

'When we discharge you tomorrow Caroline,' says the nurse, 'the doctor will send a letter to social services and let them know you have gone home and you're okay.'

'Thank you,' I say smiling. 'What time can I go home?'

'The nurse pats my hand and smiles. 'When the doctor says you can! No, only joking! He will do his rounds about midday and then we should be able to discharge you about two o'clock.'

Bill nods. 'I'll be here around two then!'

'In a car?' I ask.

Bill nods. 'Yep! We've got a little car now.'

'See you at two then darling!' I give him a peck and he waves as he leaves the ward.

The next day I am dressed and when Bill arrives we get my things and then we are off home. I thank the sister and nurses as they have been my friends and then we are off! The car isn't bad and soon we are home and Bill is putting the kettle on.

Bill smiles as we sit with our brew, 'Tomorrow we will start the ball rolling to get Ann back.'

I take a sip of my tea and nod. 'Yes, first thing. Anyway, let's go to the chippy after. I am dying for a fish!

I have now been out of hospital for a week and there have been three previous visits from social services, after countless telephone calls to them, and now the two ladies that went to see my grandma are sat in our living room at home on the fourth visit. I am smiling as I am cuddling Ann and she is making little noises of contentment. Bill is looking through some paperwork with the lady that came into hospital.

'Everything seems okay,' says the lady. 'You seem a really happy family together, so, I think that we can be on our way.' She leans into Ann and me and smiles. 'Good bye little one.'

I look up at the lady and then down at Ann. 'Say bye to the nice lady!' I take hold of Ann's hand and 'wave' it for her!

Bill sees the ladies to the door and then sits back down with us. 'Happy?' Bill asks me.

I nod my head and grin. 'I am very happy! I feel fine now and Ann is back with us.'

'You've given everybody a scare,' says Bill, 'including Harry. He has been very worried.'

'Have you told him we're home?' I look down at Ann as she burps a little and I move her position to get her wind up.

'Yes, I've rung him and he says he'll come and see us in a couple of days.' Bill frowns a little. 'Are you tired?'

'A little,' I say nodding.

'Well, we can have a snooze when she's gone to sleep,' continues Bill.

'That would be nice!' I answer.

Families

Life is settling down nicely and Grandpa Harry comes to see us quite a lot. I think he wants to see Ann more than anyone! Bill is working hard, as I haven't gone back to work of course and it's a wonder that we have any time for each other at all! The guest house has now gone and I can't help feeling sad. Never mind – there is a lot to think about here and, actually, every one of the residents has found a new place to stay so that's okay. Besides, grandpa Ronnie is gone anyway so it really makes no difference now. It is four-and-a-half months since I came out of hospital and Ann is starting to develop a lovely little personality. My grandma is friends with me again and quite often I take Ann to see her, or we go out shopping. Grandma gets involved all the time and I wonder if she still thinks I should have had Ann taken away before she was born. Grandma has also been for tea at our house a few times but she obviously doesn't like Bill and I don't think he likes her either!

I am, however, drinking more and more Vimto again which is very familiar! I am feeling tired a lot more and in the mornings I am feeling a little bit sick!

It is a Thursday and Bill has come home from work to find me smiling a broad smile.

'What's up with you?' asks Bill.

'It's confirmed!' I say with a little laugh. 'We are going to have another baby!'

Bill raises his eyebrows and stares at me for a few moments.

'Well?' I ask. 'Are you okay?'

Bill hugs onto me and grins as well. 'That... is superb! Oh, I am so pleased!'

I nod and then my face goes a bit into thinking mode. 'I wonder how my grandma will take it? She's only just got over Ann and made friends with her again.'

Bill shakes his head. 'I have no idea what she'll think. I hope that she's okay with it. I don't want you being upset or poorly like last time. When are you going to tell her?'

'Well, we are going out shopping next Wednesday so I will probably tell her then.'

'Over a cup of coffee and a cake? Good idea!' muses Bill laughing.

Ann starts to cry a little and I pick her up. 'This little girl needs feeding!'

'Whoa! Be careful picking her up in your state!' says Bill.

I smile at him. 'I'll be fine! Anyway, you can make a cup of tea if you like!'

Grandma and I have had a good shop and Ann has been asleep for a lot of the time anyway. We are sat in Whiteheads cafe and grandma is making the usual silly noises at Ann and trying to give her a little bit of the froth off her coffee.

'She can't have that grandma!' I try to pull grandma's arm a little.

Grandma moves her arm back and carries on giving Ann some froth. 'Don't be so silly Caroline! It's only like giving her milk! It won't do her any harm.'

I sigh. 'Okay grandma, if you say so.' I grin and grandma looks. 'I just hope you are as good with the second one!'

Grandma frowns and then suddenly her eyes go wide. 'What did you say?'

I carry on grinning. 'I am going to have another baby! Isn't it great grandma?'

'What a fool you are!' Grandma sits up straight and scowls. 'Oh, you are a fool! What are you playing at? Are you totally stupid? You've only just got over the other one and now you're pregnant again. What kind of fool *are* you?'

'Why are you being so horrible grandma?' I lie Ann down a little and cover her up. Finishing my coffee I get up to go. 'We've sorted everything out grandma. The way you are with Ann I thought you would be pleased'

'Pleased? Pleased?' carries on grandma. 'I think you are a fool. And him! That man again! When are you going to learn about the bad ones like him?'

I wheel the pram between the tables and am aware of people looking at me. The thing is, they seem to be looking more kindly than my own grandma.

'If you walk away now you won't see me!' says grandma in a raised voice. 'Don't come crying back to me when you're ill!'

I lower my head a little as the other people look on. 'Bye grandma. I don't know why you are so horrible but we'll be fine with or without you.'

'Well, it'll have to be without then! Foolish girl!'

I am actually a little watery eyed as I can't believe that grandma can be so horrible again. When I get home Bill is still at work so I make myself a drink and reflect on how rotten my grandma is. When eventually Bill does get home Ann is having a sleep and he can see that I have been crying.

'What's the matter?' asks Bill sitting next to me and putting his arm around me.

'Why does grandma have to be so horrible?'

Bill sighs. 'I bet you mean about us having another baby.'

I nod. 'I told her in Whiteheads cafe. She started being really horrible and everyone was looking at us! It was awful!'

'Don't let her get you in a state. I don't want you to be ill love. Not this time.'

I sniff a bit and then force a little smile. 'Oh, I wont be ill darling. Don't worry, I'll be okay. I have Ann and you to get me through anything grandma throws at me! Besides, she doesn't want to see me again so she's not going to be a problem.'

'Look, you know what she's like so don't worry about it. We'll just get on with our lives and look forward to Ann's brother or sister!' Bill gets up and heads for the kitchen. 'Brew?'

I smile and nod. 'Please. What do you want for your tea?'

'Why don't we get a take away?' asks Bill. 'I don't want you cooking after you've been upset.'

'No need!' I say. 'I'm okay to cook something. We have some stuff in to make a stew. It won't take long.'

'Right,' says Bill. 'I'll have my brew and then go and get some beer.'

'Ah, we need some bread as well darling.' I get my purse out of my handbag.

The next few weeks I keep drinking more and more Vimto and my need to eat Jaffa Cakes has come back again! Nothing is seen or heard from my grandma and when I tell Grandpa Harry he isn't surprised at all.

'Well, that's your grandma for you!' says grandpa. 'You should know what she is like by now!'

I have taken Ann to see Grandpa Harry as it's his day off and Bill is at work.

'It was really upsetting though grandpa,' I say giving Ann her feed. 'Everyone around us was looking and staring. It wasn't nice.'

Grandpa Harry smiles. 'I'm sure they could see that it was your grandma being funny. Her problem is that you're not doing what she wants!'

'But I am a mother and old enough to make my own decisions!' I put Ann on my shoulder and get her wind up. 'She's no right to tell me off in front of a cafe full of people. You wouldn't have done that grandpa.'

I'm not your grandmother, thank God!' says grandpa with a wry smile.

I smile back. 'Yeah, I thank God you're not as well!'

We have a good laugh and I'm sure Ann is actually laughing as well. When it's time to go I am a little sad that I have to because it is lovely being with Grandpa Harry. But, Bill will be coming home from work in a bit so I want to get tea ready.

'Having something nice for tea?' asks grandpa as he helps me get Ann's coat on.

'Chicken and chips!' I put Ann in her pram and then kiss grandpa goodbye. 'What are you going to have grandpa?'

'I might have something at the pub. They do a nice chicken and chips in a basket. Or, maybe scampi!'

'Just make sure you get home safe grandpa. See you in a few days.'

'Bye Caroline,' says grandpa as we head for the bus stop.

In no time at all it is nearly time for our new baby to be born and I am feeling okay. Grandpa Harry has been very supportive and he tells me he has told grandma about my progress. She hasn't been interested, however, which is no surprise to any of us! It's also getting quite cold as it's coming into November in a couple of days and I make sure that Ann and me are always well wrapped up. It is Ann's First Birthday today and we are excited as we are having a little party for her. Grandpa Harry has just arrived and Mary has been here for an hour or so. Bill arrives home from work and the party can get started! Everybody loves how Ann has turned out, a lovely happy little girl, but as the night gets on Bill can see I am tired.

'Do you want them to leave love?' asks Bill.

I switch on the kettle and turn to him.

'No, I'm okay,' I answer giving him a kiss on the cheek. 'It's not hard having grandpa and Mary. I love having them here!'

Bill shrugs. 'Okay, just don't overdo it. We don't want you ill again.'

I smile. 'I'll be fine! Now, go and ask who wants tea!'

When everybody has gone Bill and I blow out our cheeks and then smile at each other. Then we both look at Ann, who has fallen asleep.

'She's beautiful,' I say. 'I hope the new baby will be as lovely!'

'I am sure he or she will be!' says Bill. 'We made them both so the new baby is bound to be beautiful!'

I yawn quite a long yawn and then close my eyes for a few seconds. 'I'm shattered!'

'Well, I have to be up anyway for work,' says Bill, 'so we can take a drink to bed if you like.'

I nod. 'That sounds like a good idea!'

The next day I am just pottering around the house and giving Ann attention whenever she needs it. I am very tired though and my need to sit down and doze off is getting more and more frequent! But, towards the end of the afternoon I am getting more and more twinges and, judging by last time, I know I will not be far off going into labour. When Bill gets home I am trying to do my breathing exercises and crying out every so often at the twinges, which are definitely getting stronger!

'Are you... getting ready to...?'

I nod and then take a couple of deep breaths.

'Er, I'll get your coat.'

'Ring... Grandpa Harry,' I say between gasps. 'He is... going to look after Ann.'

Grandpa Harry arrives as soon as he can and then we are getting into the car. When we reach the hospital it seems I am just in time! I go to the ward after checking in and then they are taking me down to give birth! A short time later and Bill and I are looking at our new baby girl and cuddling her! We have called her Louise and she *is* beautiful, just like Bill said she would be! I am told I need to stay in a couple of days so Bill says he will tell Grandpa Harry the good news.

'Will you bring Ann in to see her little sister?' I ask Bill.

Bill nods. 'I'll bring her tomorrow. She'll not know her very much!'

I smile. 'I know what you mean, but, I think she will in a way.'

Bill gives us a kiss and then I am on my own with our beautiful Louise.

The next day the four of us are in the lounge on the ward, the happy family. Ann does seem to be smiling at Louise but I am right when I say she won't know her much. Not yet anyway!

Then we are at home a few days later and Ann is toddling around, occasionally her face taking on a contorted look as she hears a little sound or cry from Louise. We settle into a nice life and Grandpa Harry is around quite a lot to see us and the girls. In fact, he has looked after them a couple of times, allowing Bill and I to go out together, which I'm quite impressed with! Mary has visited as well a couple of times but no grandma yet. Mary says she asks a little bit but only, it seems, out of duty.

As it gets a week away from Christmas there is a knock at the door one evening. I am just getting

Louise down for the night so Bill answers the door. I hear an exchange of words that don't make much sense but Bill does seem a bit confused. When I go into the living room grandma's bloke Frank is sitting in the chair looking a little uncomfortable, drink in his hand and attempting a smile at me.

'Hello Frank.' I say. 'What are you doing here?'

Frank clears his throat. 'Er, Pearl has sent some Christmas presents for the girls and a little something for you.'

I nod a little. 'Thank you Frank. Why didn't my grandma bring it herself? Oh, don't tell me – she is still fallen out with me! Silly when she is only down the road!'

Frank nods. 'Sorry, I have no idea. I'm just playing Santa today.'

I sigh. 'I suppose I can't blame you. Thank you for bringing them Frank.'

Bill reaches for the bottle of whisky again. 'Another drink for the road Frank?'

'I don't mind if I do thanks,' says Frank holding up his glass.

Frank actually seems quite a nice guy so the evening doesn't go too bad.

Christmas comes and goes and then the next year settles in. I am walking down the lane on my way to grandma's with the two girls. The double buggy is quite a maul but I have got used to it a little and have learned how to get the best out of making people move out of the way politely! I turn into the complex and then I am knocking on grandma's door. Grandma opens the door and raises her eyebrows.

'Hello grandma!' I smile at her surprised face. 'I thought I would bring the girls to see you. Can we come in?'

Grandma sighs and invites us in.

I get Louise out of the buggy first and then Ann, who totters around much to grandma's surprise. I sit down with Louise and take her coat off. Ann goes up to grandma and stands at the side of her chair, supporting herself with the arm.

'Thank you for the Christmas presents grandma. They were a lovely thought.'

'That's okay,' answers grandma. 'I'm glad you liked them.' She looks at Ann and smiles a little. 'Hello darling. Would you like grandma to get you some pop?'

I smile. 'Some juice would be nice grandma, wouldn't it Ann?'

A noise from Louise causes grandma to look over. Then she goes into the kitchen and comes back with a glass of orange juice.

'Now, sit down like a good girl then you don't spill it.' Grandma puts the pop down and lifts Ann onto the chair. Ann makes a funny face and noise but then holds her hand out and takes the pop.

'Can I hold her?' asks grandma looking at Louise and smiling.

'Of course grandma,' I say holding Louise out to her.

I don't know what is going through grandma's mind, especially knowing she advised to get rid of Anne, but she seems to be loving having the girls around. It all seems a bit strange at the moment but I suppose I would rather have grandma around and in the girls' lives than not. Actually, the afternoon seems to go very well and the girls do seem to have taken to grandma okay. By the time we are ready for going grandma seems a bit worn out and puffing a bit, which makes me smile and I am glad she knows what hard work it is having two little children!

I wheel the pram towards the door and grandma opens it. 'Thanks for having us grandma. It's been nice.'

Grandma nods. 'Yes, I've enjoyed it. Anyway, take care and see you soon.'

I wave goodbye for the girls and then head off home.

When Bill comes home I am feeding Louise and Ann is sitting watching telly.

'How did it go at your grandma's?' asks Bill.

I smile and give him a little kiss. 'It went okay actually! I can't believe how she took to them.'

Bill picks up Ann and gives her a big hug. 'I can't believe it either!'

I shrug my shoulders and then move Louise onto the left one to get her wind up. 'I'll get tea on when I've sorted Louise out. Do you want to put the kettle on?'

Bill puts Ann back down in front of the telly and nods. 'Okay. Tea?'

'Yes please,' I answer as Louise gives quite a big burp!

Another year goes and then, of course, Louise is the party girl on her first birthday! Ann is into everything, including Louise's cake and biscuits if she can, and actually the two girls get on very well. Ann is very protective of Louise and it is lovely watching how they play and get on together! Bill is doing okay at work and Grandpa Harry, well, he still baby sits from time-to-time! The biggest surprise is my grandma. She is all over the girls, which I can't quite believe, and she is always buying them little things and fussing over what they wear and eat. It is a far cry from her wanting me to get rid of Ann and falling out with me. Is it too much to hope that she is actually changing her ways?

Ann is now three and she is starting pre-school nursery today! I sigh a little sigh of relief in one sense as I will only have one little girl to bother about in the daytime, giving me some respite at least! Bill and I have been talking as well and have decided that we will get married. We love each other and it makes sense from the girls' point of view as well. I am meeting grandma today and she is picking Ann up from nursery with me. I think this is nice and grandma stays with Louise outside while I go in and get Ann. When we get outside Ann runs to grandma but I wonder if she is only running to Louise! Actually, when we go and see my grandma Ann always runs up to the window and shouts, 'Grandma! Grandma!' which is really sweet!

'Hello sweetheart!' says grandma. 'Have you enjoyed it at nursery?'

'Yes grandma,' says Ann waving a piece of paper. ' We've been drawing!'

Grandma takes the paper off Ann and looks. 'Well, that's nice!'

'I am smiling. 'What is it? I haven't seen it yet.'

'It's a cow mummy!' says Ann with her hand on her hip.'

Grandma and I laugh and then Louise makes a few noises, as if to say she's bored and wants to go. We are going back to grandma's for a drink and biscuits and I am dreading it a little as I know I have to tell her that Bill and I are getting married.

We get settled down at grandmas and I take the girls' coats off and, after giving Louise to grandma to hold, put them over the pram.

'Cup of tea grandma?' I ask as I make my way into the kitchen.

'That would be nice please?' answers grandma. Then she talks to Louise. 'How's the lovely Louise? Oh, she's such a pretty girl!' She looks at Ann. 'And you are too sweetheart.'

The girls are making happy noises and I am smiling because grandma seems to be quite happy with them. I go back into the living room with a couple of cups of tea and a beaker of orange juice for Ann. I then go and get a plate of cake and some biscuits.

'Bill and I have been talking grandma,' I say sitting down and taking Ann off grandma to give her a feed, 'and we have decided to get married. We think it will be the best for the girls.'

'You are doing what?' Grandma's face goes into a scowl. 'Are you mad? You are stark raving mad! What do you think...'

Grandma!' I interrupt. 'We *have* got two daughters and we *have* been living together for a year.'

Grandma gets up and goes over to the pram. 'I think you have said enough, young lady! Don't expect any support from me! Getting married! Stupid girl!'

I stare at grandma and my eyes start to water. 'But... you love the girls! Why are you being like this?'

'I said I think you have said enough! Now, I have some work to do so isn't it time you were getting home?

I put Louise's coat on as quick as I can and tell Ann to put hers on as well. Ann keeps asking why we are going from grandma's but I just say grandma's busy and we need to get home to get daddy's tea on.

I turn to look at grandma as I manoeuvre the buggy out of the front door. 'What is wrong with you grandma?'

'Me! What's wrong with me?' Grandma stares at me. 'Huh! It's you who are wrong! Getting married! You are a fool Caroline!'

I slam the door as I go off to get the bus.

When I get home there is the usual 'litter' of take-away leaflets behind the door but I step over them as I just want to get the girls' coats off and get a drink. I throw the coats onto the settee in anger, unusual for me, and then after I settle Louise in her bouncy chair I put the kettle on. What has happened suddenly hits me, though, and I slump into the chair and cry my eyes out. Ann comes over and puts her hand on mine. I look at her and cuddle her into me.

'Why are you crying mummy? Why was grandma shouting?'

I try and force a smile. 'She's busy darling and I am just tired.'

Then the door goes and Bill comes home. He sees my state and frowns.

'Had a good day at work darling?' I ask still forcing a smile.

Bill nods. 'What's the matter?'

My lip quivers a bit. 'I told grandma we were getting married. She flipped and fell out with me.'

'Mummy is upset daddy,' says Ann. 'Grandma wasn't nice!'

Bill shakes his head. 'I am not surprised! She's a horrible woman, upsetting you and the girls like that!' He comes and puts his arm around me and kisses me on the cheek. 'What's she said?'

I sigh a very big sigh. 'She said I was mad! I was a fool. I tried to say that we were a family and we know the girls will be better with us married but she wouldn't listen. Darling, we have two daughters. Why shouldn't we get married? We love each other.'

'She can't tell us what to do,' says Bill trying to comfort me. He picks Ann up and hugs her. 'I know it's hurtful but never mind. I'm looking forward to marrying you!

I smile and wipe my eyes. I look at Louise and she has dozed off in her bouncer. 'She's horrible! My grandma is the one who is supposed to be a mum to me and aren't mums supposed to be happy about their daughters getting married?'

'Not all mothers,' says Bill with resignation.

We both have a darn good sigh and then Louise is moaning a little so I take her out of the bouncer – she needs feeding, of course!

***

'You look beautiful!' I am proudly admiring my two girls as their pretty matching dresses make them look so beautiful.

It is the day of our wedding and we are getting towards going to the register office. Bill, of course, is already there and we are running around for the last bits and pieces while we wait for the car. Grandpa Harry is walking me 'down the aisle' so he is travelling with the girls and me. The car arrives and Ann is very excited.

'Car's here!' shouts Grandpa Harry.

Ann jumps up-and-down. 'Mummy, are we going now?'

I nod. 'Yes darling. Daddy will be waiting!'

The mood on the journey is really happy and when we get to the register office we are asked to go straight in as it's nearly our time.

'Nervous?' asks grandpa Harry.

'A little,' I say, 'but excited as well grandpa.'

Grandpa Harry regards me and smiles. 'You look beautiful, just like your mother did on her wedding day!'

I start to go watery eyed a little but then remember that my make-up will be spoiled so I turn my attention to the girls. 'Don't they look fantastic grandpa?'

'Beautiful, just like you!' replies Grandpa Harry.

Then the registrar asks us to go in and I enter the room to see Bill standing at the front. He looks back at me and smiles and the girls are looking very happy. The ceremony goes smoothly and then we are married and are a proper family at last! Grandpa Harry looks really proud and afterwards we have some photos done and then we are off to the restaurant for a meal. There are only a few friends, mostly Bill's friends, my grandpa and the girls and the meal is a lovely one, all-in-all a great way to start married life!

After, we go home and then we all get into relax gear and settle down.

'Are you happy?' asks Bill.

'I am very happy darling!' I answer giving Bill a kiss on the cheek. 'Thank you for marrying me!'

Ann comes up to us. 'Have I got a real mummy and daddy now?'

Bill and I look at each other and laugh! We are so glad that we have our girls!

We don't see Grandpa Harry for a few days and then he comes to tea. He plays with the girls and has a chat with Bill while I get the meal ready, a chicken dinner with my special roasters!

'So, have you heard from Caroline's grandma Harry?' asks Bill.

'She knows that you have got married,' answers grandpa, 'but she isn't interested at all!'

Bill sighs. 'There's no surprise in that! She really has been very horrible to Caroline.'

I walk in with a drink for everyone. 'Oh, let's not talk about her! It's been a happy few days and I don't want anything to spoil it!'

Ann looks up at Grandpa Harry. 'Why did grandma not come to mummy and daddy's wedding grandpa?'

'Er, well, she was very busy with some poorly people she looks after sweetheart.'

Ann folds her arms and scowls. 'Well she still should have come!'

'Sweetheart,' I interrupt, 'will you come and help mummy get the knives and forks?'

I go back into the kitchen with Ann in tow – it breaks up her thoughts and no more is said about grandma for a good while.

Life is pretty good over the next couple of years and the girls are growing up to be very beautiful. Ann is now four and just about to start school proper. Louise is now in the pre-school that Ann went to. My grandma has been in touch once or twice and now seems to accept that I'm married. Not that she can do anything about it anyway! I did take the girls down at Christmas and grandma did get them presents. She still doesn't want anything to do with Bill though and although Grandpa Harry has said he has told her that Bill is a good man she just refuses to believe it.

A few weeks after Christmas Bill is at work and I have taken Louise to see my grandma, as it is one of the days she isn't at pre-school. Ann is at school and grandma and I are having a cup of tea.

'I suppose I have to accept that you are married Caroline,' says grandma with her usual narky tone. 'But, I still don't have to like him. Not a nice man, I'm sure!

I shake my head a little bit. 'Grandma, how do you know he's not a nice man when you don't really know him?'

'Hm! I can tell a bad one when I see them! Grandma leans into Louise a little. 'We can can't we sweetheart! We can tell the bad ones, can't we?'

I scowl. 'Don't talk to her like that grandma! It's still her daddy and it's not fair that you say things like that to her!'

Grandma seems like she is smirking a little and I wonder how she can still be horrible like that.

It is now the middle of the afternoon and grandma and I are having somewhat of a decent conversation for once. Louise is on the floor playing and eating another biscuit and I am nice and relaxed in the chair, glancing at the telly now and then as the afternoon news is on. Suddenly there is a knock at the door and grandma sighs as she gets up to answer it.

I hear some voices at the door and at first grandma doesn't let them in.

'Who is it grandma?' I ask.

'Just a minute,' answers grandma.

Grandma asks the person at the door to wait a minute and then looks at me with a frown. 'It's Social Services. They've got Ann in the car...'

'Ann? How can they have Ann? She's at school...'

The woman at the door insists she comes in and I can see that there is a policeman with them.

'Mrs Caroline Ward? I am Mrs Black of Social Services. Can you please get your other daughter ready to go?'

I stare at the woman. 'Go? Go where?'

'I'm afraid that Ann and Louise have to come with me,' answers Mrs Black.

'Go with you... why?' I am now getting a bit upset and Louise is looking at me wondering what is going on.

Mrs Black from Social Services starts to put Louise's coat on. I go to stop her but the policeman comes in and stops me. I try to wrestle a little and Louise is pulling away from the woman and crying.

'What is happening?' I ask between pulling and tears. 'Why are you taking them away? I've done nothing wrong. What is going on?' I look at grandma. 'Grandma, tell them!'

After Mrs Black takes Louise kicking and screaming from the house I break free from the policeman and follow outside. Ann gets out of the car and runs to me shouting 'mummy!' I go to hug her and then she is being pulled from me and the two girls are put in the car, screaming and crying. I am crying myself and looking at my grandma for support.

I am taken back inside, sobbing my heart out and shaking. Grandma really is no use at all and just sits in the corner and looks at everyone in turn.

The social worker woman Mrs Black clears her throat. 'Mrs Ward. We have receive some disturbing information that has given us reason to believe that your children could be abused.'

I stare through red, swollen eyes. 'Abused? They haven't been abused. What... what are you talking about?'

'I've never seen anything to suggest they are abused, to be fair,' says grandma.

Mrs Black shakes her head and looks back to me. 'Your husband's children from his first marriage...'

'See! See!' says grandma. 'I told you he was a bad one...'

'Mrs Webb, please be quiet!' says Mrs Black. She continues talking to me. 'Your husband's children from his previous marriage have said that he used to abuse them. So, we have to take Ann and Louise away to protect them.'

I shake my head. 'But, he hasn't done anything to them! Neither have I. How can you take them away? Please! They're my girls. Please!'

'Nevertheless,' continues Mrs Black, 'we have to protect them so we are putting them into care for the time being.'

Mrs Black gets up to go. 'I suggest you talk to us tomorrow when we've all had chance to settle down.'

I try to stop her going but I am held back by the policeman and then they are gone. I stare at grandma and sob. 'Why did you let them go?'

'How could I stop them?' answers grandma. 'But I told you he was a bad one!'

'You don't know that grandma. We only have his other kids word.'

'Hmm!' says grandma.

As the weeks go on we have contacted a solicitor who has taken over the case. There have been many to-ings and fro-ings between Social Services, the solicitors office and the courts and we have made some progress in that the solicitor seems to think that I can get some sort of order to get my girls back. I am totally devastated and can't stop crying. Grandma is really not much help but actually is being supportive. I have told Bill to go and although he says he has no idea what they are on about I say I can't take the chance and I don't want anything to do with him. I am so upset and I can't even look at him in the end.

The solicitor is brilliant though and eventually I am able to see Ann and Louise. A short time after I get to see them a little bit more but I struggle to tell them what is going on.

I am really down and at my grandma's one day and we are having tea. 'Will I ever get them back grandma?' I am still very upset as I can't have my girls properly.

'I don't know,' answers grandma. 'I told you though that he was bad!'

'Please stop going on about that grandma.' I take a sip of my drink.

'They came and talked to me you know,' continues grandma. 'They were asking me what I knew.'

'What did you say to them?' I asked.

Grandma looks at me in her usual surly way. 'I told them I didn't really know much at all. I said that I hadn't really seen you much recently so I couldn't comment.'

I stare at her. 'Couldn't comment? That's not nice! You could have told them that I could never do anything like that.'

'You couldn't, that bad 'un could though!'

'We don't know that grandma.' I shake my head and sigh.

'Well, if you don't think he could why did you tell him to get lost?'

'Oh, you *would* say something like that!' I get up to go. 'You are not being fair at all!'

Grandma points at me. 'Now listen here young lady! Don't you speak to me like that!'

I get my coat on and pick up my bag. 'I have had my children taken away from me for no reason and all you can do is have a go at me! I'm going home.'

'Huh!' says grandma. 'Where's home? You can't go back to him! You can stay here if you like but you have to stop talking to your grandma like that!'

'Well, I can go and stay with Grandpa Harry if you like! He'll be nice to me!'

'Go and stay with him then! Says grandma.

I sigh. 'Look grandma. I don't want to argue or fall out but I haven't done anything wrong. They have taken the girls away and... oh, I don't know what to think.'

Grandma gets up and takes my coat off me. She hangs it up and then shakes her head a bit. 'Let's have a cup of tea.'

I slump down in the chair and then I am awoken from a doze by grandma with the cup of tea. I smile and drink my tea. Then Frank comes home and grandma ignores me then, preferring to interrogate him as to where he's been.

'I had a little bit of business with a mate,' says Frank. He looks at me and smiles. 'How are you bearing up love?'

'Oh, I suppose I will be okay,' I sigh as I settle back in the chair.

'We need to get going on some sort of court battle, or something, don't you think Pearl?' says Frank.

'Court battle?' says grandma sternly. 'Court battle? What are you talking about?'

Frank shrugs his shoulders. 'Well, you're not going to leave it, are you? Caroline has had her girls taken away and we have to get them back. She's done nothing wrong!'

'Well, I suppose we can go and see a solicitor,' says grandma with a little bit of resignation.

I look at them both in turn. 'It wouldn't do any harm to try. Please.'

Grandma throws her hands up, 'Okay. Tomorrow morning we can go and see a solicitor. See what we can do.'

I sigh and then start to smile a little bit.

The next few weeks we are scurrying backwards and forwards to the solicitors and the letters are starting to stack up! I am allowed to see the girls a little and am pleased at how they are growing and proud of how they are bearing up. I cannot take them out unsupervised but I get to spend a good few hours with them when I do see them. But, that's really no good at all. They are my girls and I can't be with them – where's the fairness in that? However, a couple of weeks further on and we have a date to go into court and find out what is going on. I am really quite hopeful as the solicitor is very good. But, I look at the faces of my grandma and Frank, even Grandpa Harry and I get the impression that they don't share my confidence.

The day of the hearing arrives and our solicitor is giving a very good account of himself. But, the Social Services solicitor is really very, very good. In fact, it doesn't look good at all really. The room in the court is very old and unwelcoming and quite sparse, save for the couple of tables and the rickety chairs we are sat on. Grandma is being really supportive but I can tell she is as troubled by the lack of light and the lack of getting anywhere as I am! When we finally get out nothing really has been achieved but our solicitor is confident that he can get me more access to see the girls so we go away a little happier than when we arrived at the court.

As the days go by it becomes more obvious that it isn't going well as the telephone calls and letters from our solicitor don't seem to be very positive. And then, things take a turn for the worst as our solicitor rings and tells us that I can't spend any more time with the girls.

I look despairingly at grandma. 'Why can I not be with them grandma? I haven't done anything wrong.'

'I suppose you did get in with a wrong one!' answers grandma.

I start to cry and Frank consoles me.

'You really are not very nice under the circumstances,' says Frank to grandma. 'You can't blame Caroline for this and, anyway, nobody has proved that Bill has done what he is being accused of.'

'Huh!' says grandma. 'There must be something as Social Services wouldn't have acted like they did! Anyway, when is it any of your business?'

Frank scowls. 'It is my business Pearl when I can see some injustice going on! Anyhow, why can't you be a lot more supportive? She is your granddaughter in a very great need of help.'

Grandma sighs. 'We'll talk to the solicitor again tomorrow, though what use that will be I don't know. If we don't get any joy we'll take it further.'

The fading afternoon light casts strange shadows on the walls and grandma puts the lamps on.

'Where can we take it to grandma?' I ask, sitting in the chair immediately under one of the lamps.

'Well, I suppose we can take it to the Europe Court,' answers grandma.

Frank brings drinks in from the kitchen. 'Don't you need special lawyers for that?'

Grandma nods. 'Probably. But if we do then we'll talk to one of them as well.'

I give grandma a small hug and she pats me on the shoulder. 'Thank you grandma.'

I am very despondent as it is now over six months since the girls were first taken from my grandma's. I am losing all hope of seeing them much ever again and although I do see them a little they are starting to be less and less loving as they really don't know me as well. Then, on a Thursday comes the knock on the door that no-one wanted. Mrs Black and the other lady from Social Services come into grandma's and sit down'

'Well?' I ask. 'What is happening with my girls?'

The two women look at each other and then I read their faces and know something is wrong.

'I'm really sorry to say that they are somebody else's girls now Caroline,' says Mrs Black. 'They have been separated into adopted families. I'm very sorry.'

I start to lash out and kick and cry. 'Ann! Louise! How can you take them away? I had those girls they, they are my girls. Please! How can you have them adopted without me saying?'

'Right!' says grandma. 'You people are all the same! We are going to the European Court and fighting this!'

Mrs black and the other woman get up to go. 'Well, good luck with that! Our decision is final and nothing can overturn it.'

Grandma is hugging me and trying to stop me sobbing as the two women go.

We are told by the solicitor that it is no use fighting in Europe so, that's it! I have lost my children and I have done nothing wrong. I will never recover from this.

Marriage

After the terrible heartbreak of losing Ann and Louise I divorced Bill and, although he protested his innocence, I could not bear to stay with him and I never saw him or the girls again. I am trying now to settle down into some sort of life but it is difficult with those sort of memories. I have taken a job as a cleaner and it is going really well! I am even being given some supervisory duties from time-to-time and I am really enjoying it. Grandma is trying to be supportive but she is having her own problems as well as Frank is drinking more and being quite abusive at times. In fact, once the police had to be called as he smashed all the windows at grandma's! She decided that it was better to tell him to go and I had to admit I agreed with her. Grandma, though, in her usual nasty fashion took out a court order to keep him away from her, which I must say I didn't agree with at all! He didn't deserve that! Grandpa Harry is still coming for his tea from time-to-time and at least he knows how upset I still am and he understands what I have been and still am going through.

I have the house to myself this week as grandma has gone on holiday to Spain with Mary. My job is going really well and I am now doing more supervising than just cleaning. I am even now the responsible key holder for the library! I have a reputation for always doing an excellent job and this gets me a great cleaning job at the Bolton Evening News, the local newspaper. It is here that my life takes a sudden change for the better, or at least one of the times when it seems to be getting better. I keep bumping into a man called Colin who is one of the printers. We always seem to have a good chat and a laugh and as the weeks go on we seem to be getting to know each other very well! Anyway, it is Friday afternoon and some of the staff at the newspaper knock off early so usually the place is quite empty. I am busy working away and then I sense that there is someone watching me and I look around, spying Colin by the door with a smile on his face. He still looks a very nice and decent man, although he is quite a bit older than me and we seem to get on very well and certainly don't look out of place together!

'Now I know why the place is spotless!' says Colin, nodding a little.

I stop polishing for a moment and put my hand on my hip. 'You'll get nothing but a great job with me!'

Colin frowns a little. 'The problem is, I mean I do my polishing at home and it always makes me incredibly thirsty!' He grins. 'Does it you?'

I raise my eyebrows and carry on with polishing the cabinet. 'Are you offering to make me a cup of tea, by any chance?'

Colin shakes his head. 'Nope. I'm wondering if you would prefer lager! So much more refreshing!'

I stop and look at him, smiling a bit. 'Are you asking me out?'

Colin grins again. 'I can wait around until you finish. Just a quick drink before we go home?'

'Okay. Go on then! It does sound good and it is Friday.'

Afterwards we are sat in the Boars Head and I have to say the lager *does* taste very good after a week of working!

'So, am I sat here with a single woman or do you hold a guilty secret?' says Colin with his eyebrows raised.

I sigh. 'You've no need to worry Colin. I am newly divorced so no secrets!'

'Good!' says Colin. 'We can do this again then!'

I nod and smile. 'I suppose so.'

'How's tomorrow night then?' continued Colin.

I put my hand on my lip and put my chin up in mock thought. 'Hmm! Well, I have to think if I'm washing my hair!'

'You could wash it and then go out with me!' Colin takes a sip of his drink. 'That will give you a reason to have nice hair!'

'You mean it isn't nice now?' I say with a frown and a slap on Colin's arm.

'Colin rubs his arm and winces in mock pain. 'Of course it is! The dusty look is very much in at the moment!'

'Cheeky beggar!' I say.

I am smiling very much inside though as Colin is a very nice guy and I like being in his company. I go home that night and grandma can see I am smiling.

'What's wrong with you?' asks grandma. 'have you had some praise for your polishing?'

'Actually I have!' I answer. 'One of the printers called Colin says I do a great job! I've also had a drink with him earlier and I am going out with him tomorrow night.'

'Huh! You've only just got divorced! What are you playing at?'

'There you go again grandma! He's actually very nice and I like him. So, I've said yes and we are going out tomorrow. Is that okay?'

'Well, I suppose so!' says grandma , putting the kettle on.

The next morning I get ready quite early and go shopping for something to wear tonight. I get a nice dress and then I am home, washing my hair and then making it nice and putting my slap on! I come downstairs and grandma actually smiles a bit.

'Well?' I ask grandma.

'You look really nice Caroline. This Colin should be well pleased he is out with you!'

'Thanks grandma!' I get my coat and briskly head out of the door. 'Bye grandma. Don't wait up!'

Colin and I have a really great time and by the time we are saying goodnight I am liking him a lot more! We make a date for Thursday night – he will wait around after work again as my cleaning finishes a little later on a Thursday – but as I am laying in bed that night I decide that I want to see him sooner! Grandma and I are eating Sunday breakfast and she can see that there is a twinkle in my eye!

'I see this Colin has really got you smiling again!' says grandma shaking her head a little. 'I suppose that can't be a bad thing.'

'The trouble is grandma,' I say taking a sip of my tea, 'that we are going out on Thursday.'

Grandma frowns. 'So why is that bad?'

I grin. 'Because I want to see him before then!'

'Oh, I don't know!' says grandma. 'Why don't you ring him up then and go out tomorrow or something! Anyway, you haven't told me what he's like.'

'Well,' I start to say, 'he's slim and quite small and he's ten years older than me!'

Grandma raises her eyebrows. 'Ten years older? Ten years? What are you thinking girl?'

I frown. 'What does it matter grandma? He's nice and we get on very well!'

'Hmm! So long as you know what you are doing! After the last older guy you need to!'

I shake my head. 'Oh, grandma! This is a totally different thing all together!'

The thing is, I actually am able to wait until Thursday and we have a great time again. I am telling Colin about my grandma's concerns over his age and he laughs.

'That's the problem with grandmas!' Colin takes a sip of his pint. 'They always think they know best for you!'

I swallow my drink. 'Actually, she is always falling out with me. She is very nasty to me sometimes and I never know whether she actually does care.'

Colin holds my hand and I must admit I really like it! 'I'm sure she does care at times.'

I look at him and shake my head. 'Wait until you meet her. You'll get a better idea of what I'm on about then! She's merciless!'

Colin and I have a real laugh and at the end of the evening we are very much starting to be a couple. We start to see each other most nights and then, after a couple of months, we are talking about me moving in with him as he has asked me! Grandma, of course, is totally against it as usual but I am not listening and soon I am packing my things up and waiting for the taxi to take me to my new home!

'Are you sure you know what you're doing?' asks grandma.

'Of course I'm sure grandma!' The taxi beeps outside and I pick up my case. 'That's me on the way!'

I give grandma a kiss and a hug. 'Thank you grandma.'

Grandma pats me on the back of the shoulder and then I am getting into the taxi and on my way to Colin.

When I arrive Colin helps me in with my things and then he has set the table with a nice rose, bottle of wine and has cooked a nice steak and chips!

'Just my way of saying I am so glad you're here!'

I give him a lovely kiss and then we are getting on with our new life together!

***

'I'm tired!' I slump into the chair and blow my cheeks out. 'Doing these extra bits because of holidays really get me tired.'

'Never mind' says Colin. 'You could always get another job!'

'How come? I've not long been in this one!'

I have not cleaned for a while now as I have taken a job in a care home, looking after elderly people and the job wears me out a lot quicker than flicking a duster and buffing floors! However, in a lot of ways it is a lot more rewarding of course! Being Senior Care Assistant I get to do a lot of work and, whilst I know Colin is only thinking of me when he worries, I am liking the job so it isn't really much of a problem.

'So, what would you suggest I do then?' I ask him through a mouthful of crisps.

'Er, I don't know! Maybe in a place where there are more staff to less people!'

'Possibly.' I smile at him. 'Maybe I could join the fire service!'

'Is that supposed to be funny?' asks Colin.

'Not really!' I answer. 'Besides, I like the job and working extra will help us save for holidays.'

'Ah, you're only saying that because your grandpa has gone to Yugoslavia!'

'Well, we could go somewhere nice like that later on in the year.'

Colin gets up to make a drink. 'I like Spain. I have been to Benidorm but I wouldn't mind going to one of the islands. Somewhere like Majorca.'

As Colin goes into the kitchen I shout after him. 'I quite fancy Greece, or maybe Cyprus.' I am smiling as I know that this relationship is a nice one as we seem to like the same things. I wonder if grandma will approve?

'Do you think your mum and dad will be in tomorrow?' I shout.

'I think so. Why?' shouts back Colin.

'Well, its my day off and I thought I'd go round and have a brew with them.'

Colin brings the drinks in. 'Why not? I think they'll be in.'

I take a sip of my drink. 'Good. Then in the evening we can go and see my grandma and find out if she's heard from Grandpa Harry.'

Colin frowns. 'Huh, from what you say about your grandma that'll be a bag of laughs!'

I have to laugh as he is right in a way but I suppose we have to give her a chance.

'I hope you get on with her,' I say with some trepidation.

Colin smiles. 'I usually get on with everybody so it won't be a problem!'

'She might snap though! She is having trouble finding somewhere to live and the council is being a bit slow.' I take another sip of my drink.

'Oh yes,' says Colin. 'She is retiring isn't she. Never mind. It will come to us all!'

We laugh the rest of the evening and then look forward to tomorrow.

I have had a really good day with Colin's parents and they seem to like me a lot, which is a good thing really! His sister and one of his nieces turned up and that was nice as I had a very good time and it was nice to meet them. We are on the way to grandma's and I can sense Colin's apprehension, which makes me smile a little! However, when we get to grandma's she is in a right state and clearly very upset.

I frown and put my arm around grandma's shoulder. 'Grandma, what's wrong?'

She looks at me and then nods at Colin. 'Hello Colin. Caroline, I don't know what to say to you. I... I'm really sorry!'

I raise my eyebrows. 'What is it grandma?' Tell me.'

'Your grandpa has died in Yugoslavia. He's had a heart attack.'

I stare at grandma and then turn to Colin. I start to cry and then he is hugging me, trying to stop me shaking.

Colin looks at grandma over my shoulder. 'However did you find out Pearl?'

'I've... had a call from his brother. It's... tragic.' She looks at my watery eyes and frowns. 'I really don't know what to say Caroline. I'm sorry.'

I nod slightly and then go over to hug grandma. She pats me on the back of the shoulder, as usual, and we actually have a nice moment for once.

'What's going to happen now?' asks Colin.

'Well, he is going to have to be brought back to England,' answers grandma. 'I suppose his brother will be making the arrangements.'

I cry a little bit. 'Poor Grandpa Harry. I loved him so much. He was always there for me.'

'I know,' says Colin.

Grandma frowns. 'Are you saying I wasn't?'

'Grandma,' I say, 'you know what Grandpa Harry did for me. He... he's gone grandma.'

'Huh! Says grandma going into the kitchen. 'If you two don't mind I have work to do and my tea to make! Goodbye.'

Colin and I look at each other and then shrug our shoulders. I shout 'goodbye' to grandma as we go out of the door and then we are soon in the pub.

'What was all that about?' asks Colin.

'Oh, grandma and me are always going through periods of not speaking, or falling out. She has thrown me out a few times and Grandpa Harry always let me move in with him.'

'Oh,' says Colin. 'Then you must really miss him.'

I nod. 'I do Colin, I do.'

Colin looks at my less than happy face. 'I am so sorry that your grandpa has gone Caroline.' Colin smiles at me and I raise my eyebrows. 'I can try and make you happier if you like.'

'Oh, and how do you propose to do that?' I ask in a cheeky way.

'Well, I could ask you if you wanted to get married!' Colin looks at my surprised face. 'Would you like to?'

I stay staring at him. 'Like to what? Like you to ask me?'

Colin throws his head up. 'No! Like to get married!'

I nod a little. 'I suppose it would be nice!'

Colin's mouth widens. 'Nice? So, would you then?' Would you like to get married to me?'

I smile and hug onto him. 'Go on then! Yes, I would like that very much!'

We leave it a couple of days to go and see grandma again and then we decide that we will go and tell her about getting married. When we get to grandma's she is just coming off the phone and by the conversation we guess she is onto Grandpa Harry's brother.

Grandma puts the phone down and looks at us. 'Hello you two. Sorry about that. I was just trying to help with bringing Harry back from Yugoslavia. I am so sorry Caroline.'

I smile and give grandma a hug. 'Oh, grandma, it's okay. I am very upset. Why did he have to go? Out of the country as well!'

'It isn't the best way,' answers grandma, 'but we all have to go when we have to.'

Nobody says anything for quite some time but we just look at each other. Grandma breaks the mood by making a cup of tea which we all drink before a word is said.

Colin finally breaks the silence. 'Why don't you make the mood lighter by telling Pearl our news?'

I sigh and then smile at grandma's bemused look. 'We have decided to get married grandma!'

Grandma frowns slightly and shakes her head.

'I take it you're not happy about it as usual!' I look at Colin and start to go watery-eyed a little.

Grandma looks at me and smiles a little. 'Actually, I'm okay Caroline. Colin. It is up to you two and I won't stand in your way.' grandma smiles. 'Congratulations!'

I wipe my eyes and give grandma a hug, smiling. Colin is also smiling because he obviously doesn't believe my grandma's reaction! But it seems I can actually do something nice and not have my grandma ignoring me or telling me to get away! Later in the evening Colin and I are at home, relaxing and making the first arrangements for our wedding. Is grandma going to come? I think so this time. Anyway, Colin's family will be there and I get on very well with them so I know it will be a happy occasion.

The next day grandma rings me and says that she would like to help with the arrangements and would I like to go in town. I am slightly shocked but hide this as I tell her I would love to. I meet grandma and we have a good shop, including looking at some wonderful outfits! After town we go up to see my grandma's sister and husband, Auntie Elsie and Uncle Bill. Martin, their son, is quite nice and he seems as pleased as them that I am getting married.

The wedding is fabulous and the nice thing is that grandma was actually there enjoying herself! The reception went full swing and the best man speech is very kind to me, so that makes my day as well! As the guests sidle away and we have done the obligatory rounds and chatted to everyone we have time to ourselves. Sat with a drink, we blow our cheeks and then smile at each other. The Park Hotel has probably never seen the likes of this kind of do in its history and the sight of Mary's bloke Paddy singing to all the guests with a pint of Guinness in his hand will probably go down in the pub's history! Auntie Elsie and Uncle Bill have gone some time earlier, having said that they have thoroughly enjoyed the wedding and wished us luck, and so too have their daughter Griselda and her husband Lionel. I am so glad as Griselda is a sneering, sanctimonious peevish woman and spent all the reception either grinning at Colin and me or saying not nice things to other people. She could have turned it nasty at one point as Paddy was near to knocking her head off and he would have done Mary not pulled him away, saying he had two pints on the table that he hadn't even touched! But, it all ended quite happily when she had gone and so here we are, Colin and me, sitting sipping our drinks and feeling very happy!

'Why don't we book a holiday?' asks Colin giving me a kiss on the cheek.

'I raise my eyebrows. 'That'd be nice! Where were you thinking of?'

Colin finishes his drink. 'Oh, I don't know. Somewhere quite a way from here!' He thinks for a moment and then smiles. 'How about Cyprus?'

I nod. 'Fantastic! When are we going?'

'Give it a few weeks,' says Colin, 'and then we'll go and look at some travel agents.'

Colin's mum comes up to us. 'What are you two talking about then?'

'Going on holiday mum,' says Colin. 'We're thinking of Cyprus. Get away from here, no disrespect mum!'

Colin's mother purses her lips. 'I don't blame you at all! I wish I could get away from here for a while.'

Colin frowns. 'What's the matter mum? This isn't like you.'

'Oh, I'm just having a bit of a moan.' Colin's mum looks at me. 'I'm sorry love but it's your grandma.'

I stare at her. 'Grandma? Why, what's she said?'

Colin's mum waves her hand dismissively. 'Oh, just that she keeps going on about how much I'm drinking. In fact, she is telling everybody about how much they are drinking!'

I sigh. 'That's not right at all. I'll go and have a word with her. I'm sorry.'

Colin's mum puts her hand on mine. 'Oh, don't do that, not on your wedding day. It's nothing really, just me being touchy.' She hugs onto Colin. 'I'm so happy for you Colin. You look so happy and I'm glad you've got a nice girl like Caroline!'

Colin looks at me as if to say 'help' but says nothing and just smiles.

When she has gone I shake my head. 'Grandma has no right to say that, to your mum or anybody! Just wait until I speak to her!'

Colin hugs me. 'Oh, leave it! Let's not spoil a perfect day.'

'You're right,' I say holding my glass up for another drink and grinning. 'I'll take this up with grandma later!'

'But grandma! You can't go around saying things like that to people!'

Grandma throws her hand up. 'Well, they were drinking enough to sink a ship! I didn't want it ruining your wedding.'

I sigh. 'It's a nice thought grandma, thanks, but people are allowed to drink what they want. Nothing was ruined.' I frown. 'Huh, at least they stayed till the end, not like your sister and her family!'

'That may be,' says grandma with a scowl, 'and don't you talk about them like that! You have no right to talk about them like that, especially as you have married into a family with the boozing in-laws!'

'I beg your pardon?' I take on a furious tone. 'And *you* have no right to say *that* about Colin's mum and dad! His dad is very poorly and his mum is very nice, especially to me!'

All grandma can do is take on a po face and things go silent.

'Anyway,' I continue, 'Colin and I are going to book a holiday to Cyprus. You know, get away from it all.'

'Huh, very nice,' says grandma with her face still contorted. 'When are you going?'

'In a couple of weeks,' I answer, getting up and retrieving my coat from the back of the chair. 'We haven't been to the travel agents yet but we are hoping to get a late booking.'

I give grandma a hug. 'Anyway, please don't be so nasty to Colin's parents.' I give grandma a kiss. 'Bye.'

'Grandma hugs me. 'Bye.'

As I leave I wonder why I thought that everything was going to be okay. Grandma is starting her tricks again!

When I get home I get tea on as Colin has been working but it is my day off. My new job in the rest home is really good but getting used to the shifts isn't! When Colin comes home I give him a peck on the cheek and then make a brew.

'So, how did it go with your grandma?'

I scowl a little. 'Don't ask! It ended up a heated exchange of words as usual but I did tell her not to say those kinds of things about your mum and dad.'

'Thanks love,' says Colin. 'I have to say though that I think my mum can take it!'

'But what about your dad?' I ask. 'He's not so well.'

Colin takes a drink of his tea. 'Oh, don't worry about that! Mum will screen him pretty well!'

'That's not the point Colin!' I get up to see to the tea. 'She shouldn't say things about them.'

Our holiday, or 'honeymoon', is very, very nice and it is a welcome break for us both. As we stand at the carousel waiting for our luggage we look at each other and shake our heads.

Colin sighs. 'Back to reality then.'

I nod as I spot one of our cases and point to it. 'Yep! A big reality! Back to grandma as well!'

'I think she'll be okay,' says Colin.

'You don't know her,' I answer as I get my case off the carousel. 'I have visions of her and your parents at war!'

Colin laughs. 'I don't think so. Your grandma wouldn't survive my mum!'

'I think she would!' I say with a big grin on my face. 'Grandma would put a spell on her!'

Colin's case isn't that far behind and, wonder of wonders, the taxi is waiting outside for us! When we get home we plonk our cases down and then plonk ourselves down. After we have gathered our thoughts I go into the kitchen to make a cup of tea and Colin goes to take the cases into the bedroom.

A minute later he comes into the kitchen carrying an envelope and a note. His face is looking very shocked and glum.

'What's the matter darling?' I ask frowning.

'We... need to go to mum's, now! Dad's in hospital. He... he's very ill.'

'Oh, I'm so sorry.' I get my coat again.'Come on, let's get going.'

When we get to Colin's parents his mum is in a right state, pacing up-and-down and looking a bit watery-eyed.

'Mum? Is dad okay?' Colin puts his hand on his mum's shoulder.

'Colin's mum shakes her head. 'We need to go back to the hospital Colin. He might not have long.'

'Can I ring my grandma?' I ask. 'I just want to let her know we're back okay.'

Colin nods. 'Yes, of course.'

Grandma is pleased we're back and actually seems quite concerned about Colin's dad. As we go to the hospital I can see Colin is quite worked up and I hold his hand, trying to give him a kindly look. When we see his dad he looks really very ill and I offer to go and get some coffees. The day seems long and after some time Colin says that I should go and see grandma. I nod and give him a kiss and then hug his mum and then I leave and get the bus to grandma's. We have a good chat about the holiday and a couple of cups of tea and then I get up to go back to the hospital.

I sigh and lower my head. 'Colin's dad is very poorly. They don't think he'll last much longer.'

'Well,' says grandma, 'you'd better go back to him then.'

I give grandma a hug and then am back off to the hospital. I notice grandma is looking a bit grumpy but she looks like that most of the time so I just shrug it off. When I get back to the hospital there is a flurry of activity and I see Colin and his mum looking very worked up.

'Has something happened?' I ask to as I get to Colin.

Colin shakes his head and hugs onto me. 'No, but he has deteriorated a lot. They don't think he'll last the night.'

The doctors are proved right, sadly, as Colin's dad passes away in the middle of the night. I spend ages consoling Colin as his sister and mum sort of console each other. As the morning draws close we all go and leave the staff to get on with what they have to do. After we have seen Colin's mum and sister home we head off home ourselves. When we get home Colin breaks down and gets very upset. We just sit and hug until we fall asleep.

The funeral is about a week after and I think it is nice that Colin asks my grandma to go. She does go but I get the impression that she doesn't really want to be there. There is a bit of a do afterwards and then everyone slopes off home.

Grandma comes up to us. 'Would you both like to come for tea tomorrow?'

I stare wide-eyed at her. 'Er, yes, of course. Thanks grandma.' I look at Colin. 'That's nice of grandma darling?'

Colin smiles. 'Thanks Pearl. That's lovely.'

Grandma smiles. 'I've asked Mary as well so we can have a good chat.'

'Right' I get my coat off the chair. 'Come on Colin. What time should we come grandma?'

'Get there about four o'clock if you like,' answers grandma.

The next day Colin has a lot of arranging to do and he also says that his mum needs him as she is very upset. I can understand so, as I am not back at work for a couple of days, I do a bit of shopping and then get home for about two o'clock. Colin comes in about an hour later and then we get ready and go to grandmas.

Mary smiles as we go in and then looks at Colin with a kindly smile. 'I am so sorry to hear about your father Colin.'

Colin smiles and nods in acknowledgement.

The tea of steak dinner is very tasty and after we have washed up we sit with a drink.

'Have you got everything sorted Colin?' asks grandma.

Colin nods. 'Pretty much thanks. Mum needs me a lot at the moment though. She's very upset and can't stop crying much.'

Grandma shakes her head. 'Well, she always did seem that she needed you close anyway.'

Colin widens his eyes. 'What's that supposed to mean Pearl?'

Grandma frowns. 'A fine way to talk to me! You are very close to her and she does still seem to have you on apron strings.'

I shake my head. 'Grandma!'

Colin scowls at grandma and then gets up. Grabbing his coat he looks at me. 'Are you coming?'

He breezes past grandma and I can see grandma with a shocked look on her face. Mary is also shocked and goes to get her coat as well.

'I can't believe you've said that grandma!' I scowl at her. 'He's only just lost his father!'

'Now, don't you talk to me in that tone lady!'

I dismiss her with a hand wave. 'You're horrible!'

As we are going out of the door grandma shouts. 'If you go like that you can stay away!'

Colin storms out of the door. 'Come on Caroline. I am not staying here a minute longer.'

A couple of days later I go back to see grandma and she lets me in whilst seeming to not really want me there.

I sit down in the chair. 'Colin is really upset grandma. You were horrible to him!'

Grandma's eyes go wide. 'Horrible to him? He was horrible to me! Oh, if I hadn't moved back he would have struck me! I was in fear! He is the horrible one! I never want to see him here again!'

'I think you've got that one wrong grandma! Colin would never hit you...'

'Oh yes he would!' said grandma. 'He almost struck me. Now, listen to me young lady. I am telling you that he is no good! You are never to bring him here again!'

I get up to go. 'Fine!'

As I am opening the door to go grandma carries on. 'If you go like this you'd better not come back!'

I slam the door behind me and go home to Colin.

As the weeks and months go on Colin seems more and more upset at his father going. He also spends a lot of time with his mum and I notice that he is bringing home more beer and stocking the fridge. Where we used to sit at home together and watch telly he now goes to the pub more and when I ask him about it he just says that he needs a drink and that's that.

I have been for an interview at the hospital today for a job as Auxiliary Nurse and I think it has gone pretty well! I get the feeling they like my experience in the care home so I am hoping I get the job as I really want it! When Colin comes in from work I tell him but he just says he is pleased and hopes that I get it. After tea he has a kip and then gets changed and gets his coat on.

'You're not going out again are you?' I shake my head a little.

'Yes,' answers Colin, 'just for a couple. You don't mind, do you?'

I sigh. 'Why don't you stay in darling? We can have a drink here together.'

'Tell you what,' says Colin. 'Why don't you come out with me? It won't be busy tonight.'

I shake my head. 'I don't really want to go out.'

Colin kisses me on the cheek. 'I won't be long then.'

As he closes the door I go into the kitchen to clean up, frowning and feeling a little unhappy.

Finally, after about nine months I have had enough and I start to question Colin more about his drinking. I go and see his mum who agrees with me that it isn't good that he drinks so much. She tries to tell him as well but he isn't listening to anyone. I have also been to see grandma a couple of times and she is quite nice to me and quite understanding about my not coping with Colin's drinking.

'I don't know what's happened to him grandma,' I say in between sips of tea. 'I feel sorry in a way because he might be suffering because of his father going.'

'Huh, I don't!' says grandma. 'You would do well to get rid of him! I didn't resort to drink when Harry died abroad. Anyway, after what he did to me it's clear he's no good!'

'Grandma! That's really unfair! He never went near you.'

'Have you come for a fight young lady? Because if you have you can get out right now!'

'I have come to you because I am a bit upset. Why are you having a go at me grandma?' I stare at her.

'I am not having a go at you Caroline, I am having a go at that drinking husband of yours! You need to get rid of him!'

I hold my hand out in an assertive gesture. 'People react differently grandma! Colin has just lost his father!'

'Yes, and you are trying to help him through but he keeps going out to have a drink!' interrupts grandma.'

I finish my tea and then take my cup in the kitchen. When I come back I get my coat on and grandma frowns.

'I have to get home and start some tea grandma.' Colin will be home soon.' I give grandma a hug.

'Had a good day with your grandma?' asks Colin. I smile at him.

'As good as possible,' I answer. 'Did you have a good day at work?'

Colin smiles. 'As good as possible! Had an extra print run today because of that road accident story. It'll sell more papers you see!'

'That's awful!' I start to dish tea out. 'Good stories should sell newspapers.'

'They never do,' says Colin, 'they never do.'

I lift my eyebrows between mouth-fulls. 'What are we doing tonight?'

'Well, I'm going to get changed and then go to the pub.'

'Oh, not the pub again!' I shake my head. 'Please don't go to the pub.'

Colin gets up. 'Why not? I want a drink and there isn't one in the house.' he goes upstairs. 'I'll just get changed then.'

As the next few months pass Colin's drinking gets worse and I am starting to get to the stage where I have had enough. I have had countless chats with his mum and my grandma and both of them say that they can't blame me for getting fed up, especially grandma who is loving it all! Colin's sister says it is totally out of character for him so I really don't know what's going on. I know that it can't go on though.

The bright side is that I think I have a very good chance of getting the job at the hospital and if so the wage and hours will be a lot better. Just in case I need an escape route!

Finally, after weeks of Colin almost going out every night I have had enough! I have been offered the job at the hospital so I know that I will be able to sort myself out. It is a Thursday and it is my day off so I go into town and look for any potential houses. I find two or three that I know I will be able to afford and when I get home I start to get a few things together. When Colin comes home I tell him that I have had enough and that he needs to stop drinking.

'I know you miss your dad,' I say with my hand on his cheek, 'but you don't need to drink like this! It's not fair that you are doing this and not spending time with me when I am helping.'

Colin brushes me aside. 'I am getting some things together and going to my mum's. She's upset as well and I need to be with her for a few days.'

I shake my head. 'I have been to see your mum and she agrees you shouldn't drink. Why don't...'

Colin carries on upstairs and then comes down with a bag with some things in.

'So you're going then?'

Colin nods. 'Yes! For a few days.'

'Well. Make it longer if you want!' My face is quite angry now. 'I have had enough!'

Colin walks out and the door bangs behind him. That's it then, I suppose.

The Boy Next Door

One of the houses I went to ask about is very nice, a lovely terraced house on the main bus route so I decide to take it. I move my things out and think that it is sad in a way but I have to move on with my life. It's quite a task trying to juggle settling in with starting a new job but I'll manage it. I get things as straight as I can and then I have to concentrate on the new job and settling in there. That is far more important now. After the first three days I have a couple of days off so I am able to get straight. The wallpaper is okay but not really to my taste, a light background with wide stripy pattern, but it'll do for now because I don't know when I'll have time to change it. I am really enjoying the job though and the people I am looking after are very nice people. There are a couple of staff that don't seem very nice though and there is one Sister that seems quite horrible actually but most of the nurses say she is horrible anyway. It doesn't help starting divorce proceedings against Colin and, although I have done the process before and it is different this time it's still not any easier. In fact, although it is quite a smooth divorce it is a little bit stressing all the same. I am also trying to get my house to my taste and although I have only had chance to do half it is looking okay.

I have been in my house about six months now and I still haven't got it finished. Work is quite hectic though so it is not surprising that there are still a couple of rooms that are far from done! It is the end of a couple of quite heavy shifts, mainly because of the aforementioned horrible Sister who does want to seem to make life difficult. I am trudging up my small front path when I notice a person coming out of the house next door. It is a man about the same age as me but I haven't really taken much notice as I don't ever really get friendly with neighbours.

'You look like you've had a hard day!'

I look up and smile at the man and he smiles back. 'I have a bit. It's been a long one anyway.' I sigh as I put my key in the lock.

'Daniel.' The man is holding his hand out.

I shake his hand. 'Nice to meet you Daniel. I'm Caroline.'

'Have you settled in then?' asks Daniel.

I nod. 'Just about. I've still got quite a bit to do to get the place to my taste but it's finding the time.'

'I know what you mean,' says Daniel. 'I've been here nearly twelve months and I'm still trying to get this place to my taste!' He indicates towards his house.

I sigh. 'Well there's no hope for me then!'

Daniel shuts his door and locks it. 'Listen,' he says. 'I have just got to go and do a couple of errands and then I'll be back. Do you fancy a brew and a chat later?'

I frown a little. 'Oh, I don't know. I've had a bit of hard day and am quite tired. Perhaps another time?'

Daniel nods. 'Okay. I'll see you around then!' He grins.

'Hard not to, seeing as we live next door to each other!' I say with a little laugh. 'See you then.'

'See you then,' says Daniel back. 'Bye.'

As the weeks go by my little house starts to take shape a bit more and Daniel seems quite a nice guy, so, after countless brief chats on the front path and the back yard I agree to have a drink with him. We haven't gone far – only up to the 'Top Bull' – and the night is really nice as we have a really good chat.

'I bet you have a really easy, no nonsense life,' I ask in between sips of lager.

'Daniel raises his eyes. 'Oh, what makes you think that?'

'You don't seem stressed,' I continue. 'Totally calm and cool.'

Daniel takes a long drink. 'I have my fair share of stress, believe me! Anyway, you look calm as well.'

'Huh, with my recent life. I'm hiding it well then.'

'Oh? That bad eh?' Colin finishes his drink. 'Another one?'

I finish mine and nod. 'Go on then please.'

'So tell me,' says Daniel when we have our drinks, 'what are you hiding well?'

'An overbearing grandma for one,' I answer. 'It's like being haunted at times!'

Daniel laughs a little. 'I think we have all had one of those at some time!'

I shake my head. 'Not like mine. She's totally horrible with me at times.'

Daniel nods. 'And what do your mum and dad say?'

'My dad left when I was a baby and my mum died when I was ten. My grandma has brought me up.'

Daniel looks at me sympathetically. 'I'm sorry.'

'It's okay,' I tell him. 'You weren't to know.'

Daniel nods again. 'Hence the overbearing grandma!'

I look at him and give a big smile. 'We should do this again.'

Daniel laughs. 'Well we don't have to go far to ask one another!'

We laugh for a while and then I realise that he *is* quite nice!

'My mum and dad are okay most of the time,' says Daniel, 'but I hardly ever see them. They are always with the caravan somewhere. I think they are in North Wales at the moment.'

'A caravan? That sounds nice,' I say.

'They've had it for a while,' continues Daniel. 'Sometimes they park it somewhere for me and I stay in it for a few days. Gets me out and about!'

'My grandma used to have three caravans at one time, large static caravans. My Grandpa Ronnie used to have a guest house.' I sigh. 'Both my grandpas are dead now. In fact, Grandpa Harry used to live up the road from here in Oakenbottom! I lived there for a while.'

Daniel nods and we finish our drinks. 'I like caravans!' He says. 'They are cheap, comfortable holidays and you meet lots of nice people.'

'Sounds good to me!' I answer. I met a lot of nice people at the guest house as well, including my first husband!'

Daniel raises his eyebrows. 'First husband? How many have you had?'

I slap his arm lightly. 'Nosey! Two actually!' I look at his face. 'Oh, don't get any ideas! I'm not Liz Taylor!'

Daniel laughs and points at the door. 'Shall we?'

The bus isn't too long in coming and when we get home we put our keys in the doors virtually in unison. Daniel leans over and gives me a kiss on the cheek. I smile, although slightly taken aback and then I give him a proper kiss.

'I've enjoyed tonight,' I say.

Daniel nods. 'Me too. Do you fancy a coffee? Pick a house!'

I smile but shake my head. 'No thanks. I have to go to work tomorrow lunchtime so I need to get to sleep.' I see his disappointed face. 'I am off on Saturday though so we can go out into town if you like.'

Daniel nods. 'Okay. See you around then for a couple of days!'

We go in and as I shut the door I am wearing a beaming smile. He is nice!

Daniel and I are seeing each other quite a bit now, I mean going out together, as it is pretty difficult *not* to see each other when we live next door! A couple of days ago we went to see his mum and dad, as they have come back from North Wales, and I must say they are very nice people! It is a bit difficult for me as I seem to like him very much and it isn't all that long since... well, since Colin. Apart from being a very nice lady Daniel's mum doesn't seem well and when I ask him he says that she has had some health problems recently.

'Her doctor has said it is something called a hiatus hernia, whatever that is,' says Daniel one night in the pub. 'She has terrible trouble eating and it makes her really sick sometimes.' He takes a drink. 'Apparently, dad and her have been talking about her having it operated on.'

I smile. 'I might see them then! I have to go by the theatres a lot.'

Daniel takes a sip of his drink. 'So, what has your grandma said about you and me?'

'Well, there's the strange thing,' I say. 'She hasn't said much really. She has been on a school reunion and met some bloke. She seems too occupied with him to care.'

Daniel laughs. 'From what you've said about her I have got off lightly then!'

'Probably!' I answer laughing.

'So, is it safe to invite her to my sister's birthday? We are having a meal and you can invite her and this bloke if you want. It might break the ice with our families.'

I raise my eyebrows. 'Break the ice? Are we a true item then?'

Daniel nods. 'Course we are! Didn't you know?'

I snuggle my head into his shoulder. 'I am so glad it didn't pass me!'

The next couple of weeks I am quite busy at work and Daniel and I go out as much as we can. I have also been to see grandma a couple of times and she is definitely into this new bloke. He seems okay and acts like a bit of a gentleman so I suppose I am pleased for grandma. She is also actually pleased for me.

'Bit of good luck, him living next door!' says grandma over a cup of coffee in Whitakers.

Grandma and I have gone into town to do a bit of shopping.

'So, what's this bloke of yours like?' I ask.

'Edgar! He is called Edgar,' says grandma sternly. 'He is really nice. He is actually seeing someone else but...'

'Someone else? Grandma! How can you see him then?'

Grandma frowns. 'He is going to tell her he has met me!'

I shake my head and shrug my shoulders. 'I would make sure he does grandma. Don't get hurt.'

'Huh! That's rich, coming from you young lady!' Grandma finishes her coffee. 'Not exactly the best to be giving advice, are you?'

I get up to go. 'That's not called for grandma! I'm only trying to look out for you.'

Grandma nods. 'Okay. You'll meet him at your Daniel's sister's meal.'

Grandma and I go for our separate buses and when I get home I knock on Daniel's door.

Daniel opens the door and smiles. 'Come in! Kettle's on.'

The day of the meal comes and I am talking to Daniel's dad when grandma and her bloke Edgar arrive. I go over to grandma and she introduces me. As I get talking to him he does seem a bit full of himself and I get the impression he thinks he is somebody! Daniel gets the same impression after he has spoken to him as well. The thing is, grandma actually thinks Daniel is okay so that's all I'm worried about! The meal goes okay and everyone speaks to everyone else at some point, even grandma and Edgar, but I get the impression that they don't really want to bother with Daniel's family. Must be something to do with how they have parked themselves in the corner with a drink each! Daniel's mum has gone over to them to talk to them but it seems it is too easy for them to hide in a corner of the pub.

'What's wrong with your grandma and Edgar?' asks Daniel.

I shake my head. 'I don't know really. They're just being miserable beggars, especially him! He really does think he is someone!'

'I agree there,' says Daniel nodding. 'When dad went to talk to him he sort of talked down, which isn't a good thing to do to dad really!'

I pull him over to the bar. 'Let's get us a drink and leave them to be miserable old folk!'

Daniel's sister is nice and I get on with her very well. She is a bit put out that grandma hasn't talked to her much but as the night went on Daniel's grandma and grandpa go and sit with grandma and Edgar and they seem to all talk okay. Daniel's brother-in-law is good fun and I get quite a few laughs talking to him. Grandma and Edgar are the first to go, of course, and seem to be saying goodbye to everyone out of politeness more than anything else.

Actually, everyone seems to be starting to slope off and very soon there's only Daniel, me, his sister and her husband left.

'I'm surprised mum has lasted so well with her eating and been out so long,' says Daniel.

His sister nods. 'She's done well.' She turns to me. 'Who was that man with your grandma?'

'Edgar, grandma's latest bloke,' I answer.

'He's a bit full of himself, isn't he?' continues Daniel's sister.

I laugh. 'You noticed as well then!' I turn to Daniel. 'Will your mum be okay then?'

'She'll be fine,' answers Daniel, 'I'll give her a call in the morning.'

I prod him in the chest and smile. 'You make sure you do, because I'll be working!'

Daniel's sister and her husband finish their drinks and then say goodbye. Then there is just Daniel and I.

'Shall I take you home?' asks Daniel laughing.

'Are you sure it's not out of your way?' I have a cheeky grin on my face.

'Ha, ha!' says Daniel. 'Come on then.'

Life settles down pretty much and Daniel and I start talking about getting a house together. Daniel works for the council and so he suggests that he make enquiries to see if there are any houses going that we can have. We find one towards the other side of town from where we are and after both of us have served the necessary notices on our current houses we move in together. I tell grandma and she seems slightly pleased, which I suppose is good enough, but really she is too much into Edgar to really be bothered about anything or anybody else! I am very settled with Daniel as we whip our new house into our taste, which is a feat in itself between work. However, after a couple of months we have it pretty much how we want it so we are now relaxing when we are at home together.

'This is nice,' I say one evening when I have done an early shift and we can actually be together in the evening.

Daniel nods. 'I am loving every minute! Shall we get married?'

I pull away and look at him with a surprised expression. 'Are you serious?'

Daniel mirrors my surprised expression. 'Why? Is it not a good idea? Do you... not like the idea?'

I sigh. 'Yes, well, I think we are good together, so, why not?'

'So is that a yes then?' asks Daniel. 'Are you going to marry me?'

I am smiling now. 'Yes!'

The next day I am on an early so when I finish work I go and see grandma. She is at Edgar's but he isn't there as grandma says he has gone telling this other woman that he is finished with her.

'Has he not told her yet? That's terrible grandma!'

'Now then, you listen to me young lady! Edgar will tell her when he is ready.'

I shrug. 'I'm only trying to protect you!'

When Edgar comes home grandma has made tea and then we sit down to eat. I decide that I am going to tell grandma about Daniel's proposal whilst she is with Edgar as it might be better. Halfway through tea the conversation is pretty general but suddenly I start to smile. Grandma and Edgar frown.

'Anyway, I have something to tell you. Daniel and I are very happy together, especially since we moved in together. So, we have decided to get married!'

Grandma frowns. 'What? Oh, no! Not again. You silly girl. When will you learn? You silly girl!'

I scowl. 'Why are you being like that grandma? Daniel is a nice man. Surely you can see that after meeting him?'

I look at Edgar and he is saying nothing but grandma nods. 'I know he seems a nice man Caroline but don't you think it's silly to get married?'

'No, I don't think so grandma!'

I look at Edgar and he frowns a bit and then goes into the kitchen. Then, after a few drinks, I get my coat on to go.

Grandma hugs me and pats me on the shoulder. 'Edgar and I are going away next week.'

I raise my eyebrows. 'Oh, when was this decided?'

'Yesterday,' answers grandma. 'We've got a cheap deal to Greece. We're going for three weeks.'

I shrug. 'Oh well. Good luck. Have a safe holiday. Just get back for my wedding.'

'Wedding? I won't be coming. You are a silly girl. I don't know what you are thinking about but I would have thought you would have learned by now! It's not so long since the last one finished!'

'That's not fair grandma!' I speak back with the same angry tone. 'I know what I am doing!'

'Huh!' says grandma. 'Do you? You are very easily led and immature young lady.'

'Immature? How dare you grandma! At least he isn't seeing someone else!'

'Now just a minute...' Grandma starts to get a little more animated.

'Anyway,' I say as I get my coat on and head for the door. 'Have a nice holiday!'

Edgar comes back into the room. 'Why are you upsetting your grandma? That's not nice!'

I scowl at him and then head out of the door.

Grandma shouts after me. 'Don't you come back if you go out of that door like that young lady! I'm warning you!'

I slam the door behind me and go home.

Despite my best efforts my grandma ignores my phone calls so I go round but she isn't in. I go round to Edgar's but there is nobody there either so I think they must be away in Greece. When I told Daniel about what she had said he wasn't pleased as he could see I was upset. But, he said that we should just get on with it and if she wanted to be like that then let her. We are happy, though, planning our wedding and I know that his mum and dad and sister will be there so that's okay. But, I return home one day from work, having been tormented a little by the nasty ward sister who must be having a bad day, to find Daniel very upset and his eyes are red.

'What's the matter darling?' I ask putting my arm around him.

'Daniel sobs a little. Mum went in for her operation today.'

I nod. 'Yes, I know. Is she all right?'

Daniel shakes his head. 'Not really. There are complications. I've been waiting for you so we can go and see her.'

I shrug. 'Come on then. Why didn't you call me and I would have stayed at work and gone to her?'

'Sorry,' answers Daniel in between small sobs. 'I never thought.'

We head out of the door and soon we are back at the hospital. His dad, sister and her husband are there already and they are all upset as his mum isn't well at all. After a while, though, it is no use keep sitting there and we all go home. I assure then that the staff know what they're doing and Daniel and I settle a little and eat our take-away curry.

'She's in good hands, you know,' I say to Daniel.

He nods but doesn't say anything. He also doesn't eat much of his tea and although I know why I am a bit concerned.

However, a few hours later we get a phone call and when Daniel puts the phone down he goes and grabs his coat quick and his eyes fill up with water.

Daniel looks at me . 'Come on. We need to go to the hospital. Mum is really poorly and they are worried for her life.'

Then the phone rings again and when he puts it down this time he puts his head in his hands and cries. 'Mum's died.'

I put my arm around him and after a while we carry on out of the door and go to the hospital.

Life after the passing away of his mum, and the subsequent funeral, is hard on Daniel as it is for the rest of his family. But we get on with life and carry on preparing for our wedding. It is now a few months on and Daniel's dad has met a very nice woman who he seems to be quite settled with. I still haven't spoken to my grandma. I have even sent her some flowers but I really don't know what she did with them, whether she got them or not. We have had a couple of drinks out with Daniel's dad and his new partner and she seems very nice and Daniel is glad that his dad's happy.

In fact, Daniel's dad is a lot quicker than us as he actually gets married before we do! Also, him and his new wife decide that they are going to buy a guest house in Blackpool so Daniel laughs that we can always have free holidays! On that subject, we decide to put our hard-earned cash to good use and go on holiday to Italy, flying into Lido di Jesolo for a week and loving Venice! When we get back home Daniel's dad has all but secured the guest house so we go and see him and have a look around the place – very nice!

A few months after we have almost made the final preparations for our wedding and the guest list is looking okay. Grandma and Edgar aren't on it though because I haven't invited them, not because I am angry or anything like that but I am very upset that my grandma doesn't want anything to do with me – it is a good seven months since we spoke. No matter, I suppose it can' t be helped and we have to get on with our wedding so I am glad that Daniel's family are coming.

I am sat one day at home – it is only two weeks to go to the wedding – and wondering why it is I am so bothered about what grandma thinks. It seems like I am scared of what she'll say, which is a terrible thing! That's what she makes me feel like though. The mere fact that I have tried to contact her and to speak to her says to me that I can hold my head up high but it isn't really any comfort. I am fully immersed in work but I am not really having a good time there either. The nasty ward sister is really not very nice with me and keeps giving me the horrible, long sittings with the very difficult people, especially on lates when she was in and I am never able to sit down properly. I am tired, stressed and very upset with the sister but I never let that show with the patients. I stick to my job in the same diligent way as I love my job but sometimes I sit in the chair and wonder what I've done wrong to this sister. I go into the kitchen to start the tea and when Daniel comes home I am crying a bit.

'What's wrong love?' he asks.

I wipe my eyes and then wish I hadn't as I am cutting up onions! 'It's that ward sister! Why is she so horrible to me? She's terrible to me Daniel but I love my job and I am not going to let the patients down.'

'Daniel puts his arm on my shoulder. 'Why don't you report her?'

I sigh. 'I could do, but then she might be twice as bad and I don't want it to affect the patients.'

'I can understand that,' offers Daniel nodding. 'Anyway, not long now until you are my Mrs!'

That makes me smile. 'I know! I can't wait!'

After tea we are going to see his grandma as he hasn't seen her for a couple of weeks. His grandma – this is the one on his mum's side – is a lovely lady and always gives us tea and cakes. She always has a smile on and we have a lovely chat every time we go. We have a lovely evening and as we are going I cannot help wondering why my grandma can't be like her.

Another week of work and then it is the Friday before our wedding. Daniel has gone out with his brother-in-law and his dad for a couple of drinks, a kind of stag do without the handcuffs! I am staying over at Raquel's, my friend from work and we are getting the chance for a girly chat. We also have a grumble about *the* ward sister so I am feeling a little bit better!

The next morning I am in great spirits as I am getting married! Raquel has been up about an hour and, true to friendship, she makes sure I'm up on time as well! She also makes sure I am ready and looking a million pounds!

'Come on then,' says Raquel, time to go and get hitched!'

Daniel's dad arrives to take us to the registry office so off we go. The wedding is wonderful and afterwards we are off to the restaurant, where we have cordoned off a number of tables for the reception. The reception is great as well and goes smoothly with no real secrets in the speeches! When everyone has sloped off at the end of the evening Daniel and I are left having a drink and his dad and wife and his sister and husband are at the bar but leaving us in peace!

I sigh. 'Well, that's it then. Back to work in a couple of days.' I grin at Daniel's surprised face.

'Well, that's a nice thought!' says Daniel. 'From married to work, soon come down to Earth haven't we?

'Still,' continues Daniel, 'at least we can buy the things we want.'

I frown a little. 'Why, what do we want?'

'Well,' says Daniel, 'we could have a holiday, or, we could buy a caravan.'

'A caravan?' I smile a bit. 'Now, that's not a bad idea. Lots of holidays!'

'Yep,' says Daniel. 'Between the guest house and a caravan we'll do pretty well!'

We chink glasses and give each other a kiss as a seal of future holidays and then the evening drifts to an end.

***

Daniel's idea of a holiday and a caravan materialise not long after we are married, well, not long in the time of life! We buy a lovely caravan and, at Daniel's insistence, a new car to pull it! Not what I would have planned and I am not quite sure if we can afford it – it will take all of our savings. But Daniel says we can always get the car on finance as we are both working so, reluctantly, I agree. Besides, it frees up some money for us to go on holiday so we book a nice week to Italy! When we get home we have a few days left so we hook the caravan up and park it for a few days near Blackpool. Daniel's dad and step mum spend their time getting their guest house in top condition and we help out a little bit during the day. Then its back to work for both of us and I decide it is time to try and do something about the nasty ward sister. I have a talk to a superior and then have a meeting to try to sort out her not bullying me any more. I am actually given a few options and start to be a little happier at work knowing I might be away from the sister. She is making me really unhappy and I feel used and bullied and it is starting to get me down at home. Daniel has noticed it and has fully agreed that I need to get away and get another position because he knows I like working at the hospital. It is a shame that she seems to have taken a dislike to me as I really like working with the patients I do. But, I can't go on being bullied so I have to accept that I need to move departments.

I am started to get worried about life a home as well as Daniel seems to be spending a lot of money that we haven't got on silly things. I keep thinking that I save our money and then *he* keeps spending it and it's not fair but what can I do? Whenever I try to talk to him about it he just says that we are both working so what am I moaning about? But, when we go with the caravan to places I really enjoy it so I keep quiet for much of the time. I try to contact my grandma as well and send her flowers but to no avail as I hear nothing back, which is no surprise really!

A few days later, however, I am walking near to Marks & Spencer when I hear a voice shouting 'Caroline?' and I look round to see my grandma.

'Grandma?' I go over to her. 'How are you?'

'I'm okay really,' answers grandma. 'Are you okay?'

'I'm not bad grandma.' I frown a little as I know I am going to have to tell her that Daniel and I are married, but I know she'll love it when I say it is not going very well! 'Daniel and I are married now.'

Grandma scowls. 'Married? Married? Are you stupid? What have you got married for, you silly girl!have you not learned by now?'

I shake my head. 'I knew you'd be pleased! It's the first time I've seen you in ages and you are having a go!'

Grandma throws her hand up in a dismissive gesture. 'Well! You know how I feel and I think you are a very silly girl!'

I look around. 'Shh! Not so loud please grandma!' I sigh. 'The truth is, grandma, it isn't going to well. So, I bet your happy about that then!'

'Don't you talk to me like that!' says grandma. She calms a little. 'Anyway, why is it not going well?'

'He spends money I've saved for us!' I answer sadly. 'I save a lot and put it away and then he goes and buys new clothes, or changes something on the car or even gets a new car!'

Grandma throws her head up and tuts. 'Well, you'll never get *me* harping on about money or spending it willy nilly! There are more important things than money young lady!'

I shrug my shoulders and point towards a coffee shop. 'Do you fancy a drink grandma?'

'Oh, go on then,' says grandma. 'Why not.'

We get a couple of coffees and a piece of cake and grandma can see that I am still not really very happy.

'You need to get rid of him then.' says grandma in between sips. 'If he is making you unhappy then he's no good!'

'I'm not really unhappy, just sick of him spending.' I sip my coffee. 'I am sick grandma of saving for nothing.'

Grandma shakes her head. 'You are unhappy if you are sick of him! I can help you if you don't want to be with him.'

I raise my eyebrows. 'Why would you want to help me grandma? You haven't seen me for ages!'

Grandma sighs and finishes her drink. 'That's why I suppose, Caroline, I think I owe it to you. If you want to go and see a solicitor I will go with you.'

I shake my head. 'A solicitor? Who said anything about a solicitor?'

'Well, you know where I am if you want me,' says grandma. 'She gets up and then gives me a little hug, complete with the pat on the shoulder. 'Give me a ring.'

As grandma goes out of the door of the cafe I finish my drink and then wonder what this particular relationship with grandma holds in store!

A couple of days later nothing has changed much and no matter how much I have tried to talk to Daniel about everything I don't seem to get any sense. So, much as I don't want to because of the inevitable, I am back staying with my grandma talking about my problems. I look around her lounge and think how much it seems to have changed, even though nothing has actually changed at all. It just shows how long we have not seen each other!

'So, what are you going to do about it Caroline?' asks grandma. 'You can't go letting him spend all your money.'

I shrug my shoulders. 'I don't know grandma. You taught me how to save very well and it just seems that he wants to spend it.'

Grandma nods slightly. 'Well, I think you should get rid! Divorce him. Another marriage gone wrong, I know, but it has to be.' Grandma actually smiles. 'If you want me to help you then I will.'

I don't know why but I go over to grandma and give her a little hug. 'Thanks.'

Grandma pats me on the shoulder. 'We'll go to the solicitors tomorrow. Get the ball rolling.'

I nod and then go into the kitchen to make a drink.

The next day grandma and I go to the solicitors in the morning, as I am working in the afternoon, and explain that I want a divorce under irreconcilable differences. There is a charge to pay of about one hundred pounds but the solicitor says I can take that back with some paperwork. There will be some more small costs so when we have finished grandma goes to the bank and gets me some money.

'See, don't worry about it Caroline,' says grandma handing me an envelope. 'There's some money for the costs.'

I take the envelope and then smile. 'Thanks grandma.'

The next week I have the paperwork filled in and have gone to work in the morning as, when I have finished work, I am going to the solicitors. I am walking down the main corridor when I hear my name called. I look round to see Daniel's sister coming towards me. She works in the hospital in the pathology department.

'How are you Caroline?'

I look at her with no real expression. 'I'm okay. Not that your brother has anything to do with that!'

Daniel's sister shakes her head slightly and tries to smile. 'I know he can be a bit of a pain but he does miss you.'

'Huh, I bet he doesn't miss all the money he spent that I'd saved.' I suddenly go wide-eyed as I know I just sounded like my grandma!

'I know, I know,' continues Daniel's sister, 'and there is no excuse for doing what he's done. But, I think he realises that he's been an idiot!'

I nod and then look at my watch. 'I really have to go. I'm in the middle of something actually.'

Daniel's sister nods and smiles. 'Okay, I understand. Well, nice to see you again.'

'Bye,' I say as I start to walk down the corridor again. I turn and call after her. 'You can tell Daniel he can ring me if he wants.'

She nods and then is lost in the crowd.

As the day goes on I decide that I won't go to the solicitors with the paperwork just yet, but I will wait to see if Daniel rings me. When I get home grandma is making a cup of tea.

'Have you been to the solicitors then?' asks grandma, handing me my brew.

I take a sip and then shake my head. 'No, I haven't actually grandma. We have had quite a serious incident at work and I am so tired after the shift that I came straight home.'

Grandma scowls. 'Well, the sooner you go the quicker the divorce gets done!'

I look at grandma and then shake my head again. 'Honestly grandma! I am on an early again so I'll go tomorrow.'

Grandma nods. 'Well, make sure you do!'

I frown at being told like a naughty schoolgirl but I say nothing, just finish my cup of tea and then start to go upstairs. 'I'm just going to get changed before tea grandma.'

I have had a wash and have just got my clothes on when grandma shouts upstairs that I'm needed on the phone. When I get downstairs grandma is looking a bit annoyed and holding the phone out to me.

'Who is it grandma?'

'It's Daniel! What on Earth does *he* want?'

I shrug my shoulders as I take the phone off grandma but I am smiling underneath. 'Hello?'

'Hello Caroline,' answers Daniel on the other end of the phone. 'How are you?'

'I'm okay,' I answer curtly, as I have to because grandma is listening.

'Listen,' continues Daniel, 'I know your grandma is listening so I wondered if we could talk sometime? I can meet you after work if you like?'

I purse my lips. 'Well, okay then. I finish at three tomorrow afternoon so if you come to the hospital you can give me the things then. Is that okay?'

'Fine,' says Daniel. 'See you tomorrow then. Bye.'

'Bye,' I say in return. I come off the phone and see grandma with a frosty look on her face. 'He has some things of mine that I have left at the house, some CDs and a few bits of clothing. He doesn't want them so he is meeting me after work to give them to me.'

Grandma tuts and goes into the kitchen. 'Make sure you get everything!' she shouts back.

The next day I finish work at four o'clock in the afternoon and then I go outside the main entrance of the hospital. Daniel is parked up and I smile as I get into the car.

Daniel smiles back. 'Hello you! Good day at work?'

I shrug. 'Same old same old! Not that busy actually. You?'

Daniel laughs. 'Same old for me too! Should we go and get a coffee?'

I look at him. 'What do you want?'

'I want to try again Caroline. I think we deserve another chance.' He sighs. 'I don't want us to end by me being an idiot and, yes, I do know that my sister has spoke to you!'

I keep on looking at him and shake my head a bit. 'I suppose we did have some good times Daniel! Do you really think we can work?'

Daniel nods. 'Yes, I really do. Look, I know I have been a complete idiot but please give me a chance.' He lowers his head and makes his lips into a mock sulk. 'Go on, you know we have some good times!'

I smile and shake my head. 'Okay then! I must be mad but I suppose we owe it to ourselves to give it a go!' I frown then laugh. 'Grandma will be pleased!'

Daniel raises his eyebrows. 'Oh, Pearl! What did you say to her when she knew you were meeting me?'

I smile. 'I told her that you was bringing some stuff to me that I'd left!'

Daniel nods. 'I like it! Nice one!'

Daniel drives off and we head for McDonalds for a coffee and a burger.

'So, do you really think we should give it another try, I mean, do you really think we can work?'

Daniel nods as we go into McDonalds. 'Yes, I do.'

I shrug. 'Okay then, let's do it! Should I move back in? Or, should we think about a fresh start?'

Daniel frowns and takes a bite of his burger. 'A fresh start?'

'Yes.' I hold his hand and smile. 'Why don't we move away from here and make a fresh start?'

Daniel shrugs. ‘Okay, where to?’

‘You said that you had friends in Accrington and that looks nice. Why not try there?’

‘Okay,’ says Daniel. ‘Let’s moved to there.’

Grandma is stood with her hands on her hips, *the* scowl on her face. ‘You are giving it another try? Are you mad young lady?’

‘Mad?’ I mirror the scowl. ‘I thought you would think it would be nice that we are trying to make a go of it instead of running away from it!’

‘Huh!’ says grandma. ‘Going to Accrington is running away! And what about my money? I suppose you are taking that away too! Fancy! Running away with my money!’

‘You what?’ I am now mirroring my grandma more by standing with my hands on my hips. ‘I can’t believe you think I am pinching your money!’

I carry on getting my things together as I am moving back with Daniel. I have got together the main things and am waiting for a taxi, as Daniel does not want to come near grandma’s, which is understandable.

‘Well, you are not using it for the solicitor so you must still have it!’ retorts grandma.

‘Oh, I will give you your precious money next week, when I get paid.’ I pick my coat up and start to put it on.

‘Oh, that’s it!’ says grandma with a loud voice. ‘Walk away like usual! *With my money!*’

I pick up my bag and go to the door. ‘I can’t believe you think I am running away with your money! That’s a dreadful thing to suggest grandma! Daniel and I are going to make a go of it, in Accrington, and I will give you your money back grandma!’

'Grandma? Don't you call me grandma! You are no granddaughter of mine running away with my money. If you go, *don't* think about coming back!'

'Fine!' I answer. 'Bye grandma.'

I get my stuff into the taxi and then we are off back to Daniel.

Daniel and I rent a house in Accrington and put our names down on the council list. As Daniel has worked for the council in Bolton and we were good tenants it isn't long before we get a nice flat offered to us. In the meantime, we have had a lovely holiday in Turkey with his dad and wife, his sister and her husband and little girl, a true family holiday! We have a great time and Daniel's niece is a real bundle of fun and I love playing on the beach with her! When we come back we set about making our flat to our taste and then settle into a nice life. I got a job in a care home in Accrington and Daniel commuted to Bolton still. We regularly went to see his grandma and auntie and uncle, with whom we used to go for rides. His other auntie and uncle had cats and dogs and we used to go and take them for walks. We also got another caravan and took it to quite a few places before we settled it at Southport for a while. We loved the caravan and used to go there in between work all the time. In fact, sometimes I stayed there and helped out in the kitchens, especially when there were parties or functions. Daniel used to come after work and it was a real home from home!

But, we started, or rather I started, to feel a bit out on a limb at Accrington and could not settle there at all. Daniel and I talked about this and decided that it had been a year away from Bolton and really it would be better if we moved back there. Daniel wouldn't have to travel so far to work as well, which was actually starting to tell on him, the hours journey every morning and night. So, Daniel makes some enquiries and we get a house in a nice area of Bolton. Ho hum, here we move again! The house is okay though and we set to decorating it nicely and the space – it is a semi-detached – is a lot better for us anyway. I manage to get a job at the hospital on the nursing bank and life settles down once again. We move our caravan as well, up to Yorkshire in Bronte country. The site is very nice and is right next to a railway line where steam trains go by every half-hour or so! We love the caravanning and make many friends, going up to it as often as we can.

There is a little problem, though. Daniel is starting to show signs of his money spending again as he suggests we get *another* car!

'What do we want another car for?' I ask him one day as we are sitting outside the caravan sipping a drink.

'Well,' answers Daniel, 'we have had this one a while now and I thought it would be better for pulling the caravan to change for another one, maybe a brand new one?'

I raise my eyes. 'A brand new one? We're not made of money.'

'We're both working,' answers Daniel, 'so why not? We don't want a car that long that it conks out when we are pulling the caravan!'

'But we are not pulling the caravan!' I answer with a slight shake of the head. 'We have sighted it here!'

'Ah,' says Daniel, 'but we are still travelling here a lot and that puts miles on it.'

I sigh. 'But the one we've got isn't that old Daniel! There aren't that many miles on it anyway.'

'All the same,' says Daniel matter-of-factly as he takes a sip of his drink, 'we could still do with keeping ahead of the mileage. Think about it.'

Nothing else is said and I go to sleep wondering what Daniel is on about – really!

We stay in Bronte country for another day and then head back home as I have to go to work. I am now on the nursing bank and some days it is very hectic, especially if I am assigned to the operating theatres! Some days I get tired a little and it is on these days that I just feel like Daniel is taking advantage of me a little, hitting me with the spending ideas when I'm down.

I get home from work that day – after quite a busy time on the wards where I have actually saved someone's life by being quick with the crash trolley – to find Daniel sifting through car books.

I frown. 'What are you doing?'

Daniel smiles and points to a page in the brochure, a Vauxhall brochure... 'This is a nice one! A nice big engine and a weighty car that will pull the caravan brilliantly!'

'A brand new car?' I throw my bag down and go into the kitchen to make a drink. 'We can't afford a brand new car! We're not on that much you know!'

Daniel holds his hand up and grins. 'Ah, well! I've solved that one. I have borrowed some money off my mate, which will help with some things, so we can afford monthly payments.' He grins. 'Anyway, I've put a deposit down and we pick it up next Tuesday! It needs the tow bar putting on.'

I raise my eyebrows. 'You've done what? Without asking me?' I shake my head. 'See, this is the kind of thing that causes problems! I save money and then *you* go and borrow money and then fritter it on monthly payments for... for a car we don't need!'

Daniel throws his hand out in a dismissive gesture. 'Pah! Anyway, it's done now and I'm sure you'll love riding around in it! Now, what's for tea?'

We pick the car up on the Tuesday, as intended, and I have to admit that it is a very nice car. But, as the weeks go on Daniel starts more and more to fritter money, only a bit here and there, but enough to start to affect our life. I have tried to talk to him but he isn't for listening.

I am also sending letters to my grandma again and even have sent a bunch of flowers to her but I have heard nothing back at all. At least I think it is high time we stop ignoring each other and I have tried to sort things out!

The next day, however, I am walking down the main corridor in the hospital when I bump into Daniel's sister Sally.

I smile at her. 'Hello. Are you okay?'

Daniel's sister nods. 'I'm not bad. How are you going on Caroline?'

I sigh, 'Daniel is at it again! Spending money when I'm trying to save it. He's even got a brand new car on finance when we don't need one!'

Sally shakes her head. 'I don't believe it! What a silly man.'

'Also,' I continue, 'he's only gone and borrowed some money off his mate, which I suppose *I'll* have to pay back eventually!'

Daniel's sister does not look happy. 'I'll kill him! You make an effort to sort things out and he does his old tricks!'

I put my hand on hers. 'I know he's an idiot but we'll sort it out.'

Daniel's sister smiles. 'Guess who I bumped into yesterday near Pathology? Your grandma!'

I draw in breath a little. 'Grandma? What was she doing here?'

'She was seeing a doctor about some problem or other. Anyway, I told her that you was upset at not seeing her and that you had been trying to get in touch with her.'

I sigh. 'Thank you. What did she say?'

'Well,' continues Daniel's sister, 'she wasn't very happy when I said that she should see you again.'

I laugh. 'No, I bet she *didn't* like that at all!'

Anyway,' continues Sally, 'I must have caught her on a good day as she said that you can ring her if you like, go down.'

I blow my cheeks out. 'Well, I can't believe that! It's been almost three years and now she says it is okay to phone her! Wonders never cease!'

Sally laughs. 'Good luck then!' She nods. 'I have to get these samples over to the ward so I'll see you later.' She starts off down the corridor. 'Let me know how you get on!'

I nod. 'I will. Bye and, thanks.'

I have the next two days off so the next morning I give my grandma a ring. Surprisingly, she is okay and says that it is all right for me to go down to see her, but not to expect too much. I can live with that so about mid morning I am knocking on grandma's door. As I go in I see that her fella Edgar is in the kitchen making a drink and I wish I could do magic and make him disappear!

I go into the living room and take my coat off. 'Hi grandma. Are you okay?'

Grandma nods. 'I'm not so bad.' She sighs. 'It's been a long time Caroline.'

'Yes, and your grandma has been really upset about it all as well!' cuts in Edgar.

I frown. 'What has it got to do with you?'

'Don't you talk to him like that!' says grandma. 'He's very good to me!'

'Look grandma,' I continue. 'Does he know that I have sent you loads of letters? Does he know about the flowers I sent you?'

'Yes, of course he does!' says grandma.

'Then he knows that it is *me* who has been trying to put things right. *You* are the one who has been ignoring *me*!'

'Huh!' says grandma. 'You should have listened to me in the first place! Running away with my money!'

'Er, I did not run away with your money!' I answer. 'I can always go and get it now if it's *that* important to you!'

Grandma shakes her head. 'It's okay. How is your marriage? That's more important.'

I sigh. 'He is up to his old tricks again. Spending money when I am saving it. He's even borrowing money from friends now!'

'Well, that's not good for you!' says grandma. 'You don't need to put up with that!'

Edgar nods, sipping his tea. 'No. it isn't nice at all.'

'Anyway,' I continue, 'we have a nice site for the caravan in Bronte country and it is just nice to sit and watch the trains go by.'

'Very nice,' says grandma, 'but you need to be happy. I can tell you're not happy Caroline.'

'You're right,' I say finishing my drink. 'I'm not really, but what can I do?'

'Do what you should have done anyway, get rid of him!' says grandma with some sort of satisfaction in her voice.

I get up and put my coat on. 'Nope. We have sorted it out once and we can sort it out again!'

Grandma gives me a hug and pats me on the shoulder as usual. 'Good luck then! You won't manage it though.'

I shake my head as I go out of the door. 'Bye grandma. See you soon. By Edgar.'

When I get home Daniel is in the middle of making a brew. 'Hi love,' he says smiling.

'Hi.' I get my coat off and look in the fridge. 'Have you had a good day?'

Daniel smiles. 'There's your brew. Not a bad day.'

I shut the fridge and shake my head. 'Why do you spend money that I've saved for us?'

'Oh, I see!' says Daniel. 'You've been to see your grandma, haven't you?'

'Yes,' I answer. 'This has got nothing to do with her though. It's me that is asking you. I am just getting a little bit tired of it love.'

Daniel frowns. 'Do you know, we are both working full time so I don't see the problem in spending our hard-earned money.'

'But what about the future?' I ask mirroring his frown. 'We have given ourselves another chance so I think we should save for the future as well.'

Daniel goes and gets his coat. 'I am going out for a bit, take the car to the car wash and then I might have a drink on the way home. Oh, and I think that the future will take care of itself, as long as we are both in sound jobs, which we are.' He goes out of the door. 'See you later.'

I sigh and then get a bit upset as we usually go out together. I get up to make another drink and think that, for once, grandma may be right.

The next day I am back at work and under a lot of stress it seems. I can't decide though whether I feel stressed because of work or because of Daniel's attitude. But, I can't let my problems at home affect me at work so I get on with it. One or two of the girls are asking if I am okay but I just smile and say that everything is fine. However, when I have periods on my own, such as lunch, I go a little watery eyed and a little bit upset as I know deep down inside that my grandma might just be right. Why is it that I try so hard to make people happy and try to get things right but it never works? Later on that day I bump into Daniel's sister again and she can see I am upset. I explain that her brother is playing his silly tricks again but it seems like she isn't really bothered this time and she makes her excuse to get on with what she was doing. We say goodbye on good terms though, as we always do.

A few more weeks of this situation and I really have had enough! The problem is that if I were to call it a day with Daniel I wouldn't have anywhere to live as he got the house through work so technically he would stay there. I am talking about this to my grandma and she nods a little.

'Go and make a cup of tea Edgar,' says grandma.

Mumbling, he goes into the kitchen and grandma turns to me and smiles. 'Now, Caroline. I don't mind if you move in here for a while but it can only be for a while though.'

I smile back and hug grandma a little. 'Thanks grandma. I will sort my things out and I should be in here in a couple of days. Is that okay?'

Edgar comes in with the tea and shakes his head a bit. 'Why are you having her living with you? You don't get on at all, always arguing and having a difference of opinion. Glutton for punishment suddenly, are we?'

Grandma stares at him and shakes her head. 'What can I do Edgar? I can't see my granddaughter on the street. It's only for a short time anyway. I'm sure we can get on for a short time.'

Edgar shrugs as he gives me my cup of tea and I frown. 'Well, I'm not playing referee. I wouldn't get paid and I don't know the offside rule!'

I drink me tea in silence but stare at Edgar, which makes him a bit uncomfortable. Then I smile at him, which makes him feel even more uncomfortable!

Grandma looks at her watch and drinks up. 'Come on Edgar. We need a bit of shopping so we could do with going now. Are you staying here Caroline or going back there?'

I get up and get my coat. 'I have to go and get my things together grandma and tell Daniel that we are done. I will get my things over bit by bit and then I should be in a couple of days from now.'

'Fine,' says grandma. 'Come on Edgar.'

The next couple of days are taken up with me moving my things between the house and grandma's. Daniel wasn't happy at all when I told him – in fact, he seemed quite sad really. But I told him he had had his chance and that I was sick of his stupidity with money. He did plead a little and I think he was genuinely very sorry. I know he wanted to really try but I just wanted to start again and I told him that it was over. When I am finally in grandma's I sigh in relief a little but it hits me that my marriage is over. Another two days and I go with my grandma to see a solicitor to start divorce proceedings.

It is tea time and grandma and I are sitting in the living room. 'I know that he wasn't a bad man really grandma. I don't really know why my marriage has gone.'

'Hmm!' says grandma. 'If he is messing with money then he has to be a bad 'un! I told you ages ago that you should have got divorced but you went and tried again. Now look at you! It's a lot worse you giving up on it now.'

I stare at grandma. 'But I had to try again. Isn't that what people should do first? Try to sort it out?'

Grandma scowls. 'You should have got rid of him before when you had the chance! You would have been far better off by now.'

'That's the easy way out grandma. At least I tried to make a go of it.'

'Yes, and look what he did as a result! No, you mark my words. Men like him are no good and you would do well to stick with what I say!'

I get up and go towards the stairs. 'I am going to my room grandma. Thank you for letting me stay here.'

I go upstairs and when I lie on my bed I can't help but get upset. I really do not know what the future holds for me now.

A Place Of My Own

Over the next few weeks I try and settle in and I get into a routine of going to work from a different home. It seems to be going very well but, after a few weeks, the 'I told you so' scenario is starting to creep into my thoughts. My grandma keeps having little digs about living on top of each other and just once or twice she has mumbled something about her and Edgar not having time to be together. But she was just being awkward as he only comes at night so I am a little upset at her attitude. Nevertheless, I have no choice but to put up with it at the moment and, actually, it isn't the most ideal situation for me anyway. With this in mind I have put my name down on the council list for a place of my own so we will just have to wait and see.

At work I still bump into Daniel's sister from time to time, if she was on duty, and whilst she was civil and nice to me we never spoke about Daniel or our breakup at all. I am enjoying my work and so I suppose things aren't all that bad really. I can put up with my grandma's moaning! In fact, I suppose she does have something to moan about as Edgar just goes in the morning and dumps her for the day. Mind you, grandma never goes out so she only has herself to blame!

I have been on an early shift this particular day and have arrived home to my grandma having a scowl on her face.

'What's the matter grandma?' I ask, throwing my coat on the chair for now.

'You know Caroline,' she answers as she goes into the kitchen, 'you really need to push the Council for a place of your own. You can't stay here forever!'

I stare at her. 'I'm trying my best grandma! They can't just give me anywhere overnight.'

Edgar shakes his head and buts in. 'You and your grandma are on top of each other all the time. It's not good for either of you, or me!'

'What is it to you anyway?' I ask him with a slight anger in my voice.

'Oh, ssh!' he retorts. 'I spend time here so it is a lot to me!'

'Don't shush me!' I say back.

'Don't you speak to Edgar like that either!' says grandma. 'Have a bit of respect.'

I raise my eyebrows. 'Like you treat grandma with respect, dumping her like that every day and pushing your way in at night!'

'How dare you!' says Edgar. He starts to come towards me a little so I get my coat and go to the stairs to go to my room.

Halfway up the stairs I turn my head back. 'You tell him to keep away from me grandma! I don't want him near me at all.' I go up a couple more steps and stop again. 'Oh, and just to let you know I have a day off tomorrow so I will go and see the council again tomorrow.'

'Good!' says grandma.

I sit on my bed and get a little bit upset as I can see my grandma starting to develop her old ways again. Why can't she be like my grandma, or even my mother, and look out for my interests? I sigh. I know the answer to that already – she is Pearl after all!

The next day I go into the council housing department and tell them that the situation is getting quite desperate!

The lady smiles and tells me that they have a couple of ideas in mind and it shouldn't be too long now before I have a place of my own. I go away smiling and afford myself a nice cup of coffee! I don't really want to go home yet anyway as I will probably only get moaned at again. The reason – it is one of those rare days where Edgar gets to grandma's in the middle of the afternoon, for whatever reason. When I get home grandma is in quite a pleasant mood for a change so I get myself a cup of tea and then tell her what the lady at the housing office has said.

'Good,' says grandma, 'that sounds a lot more positive!'

I smile. 'Yes, not too long now before I am out of your hair!'

The mood at the tea table is actually quite pleasant and I suppose it is because my grandma and Edgar know the time for me to be out is probably getting nearer – miserable beggars!

The next couple of days are ticking along nicely, mainly because I am on later shifts so I don't see Edgar or my grandma much. The day after the last late shift I have a morning in bed and when I get up grandma has a cup of tea waiting for me.

She points to the table. 'There's a letter for you there.'

I pick it up and start to smile as it is in a brown envelope. I open it and my smile goes even wider. 'It's from the housing department grandma. They are offering me a flat just out of town, near to the college. A ground floor one as well!'

'That's good,' says grandma. 'When can you move in?'

'Hm! Can't wait to get rid of me grandma?'

'Well, we aren't getting on that well being on top of each other are we Caroline.'

'Anyway,' I continue, 'you'll be pleased to know I can move in a week on Tuesday. Actually, I'll have to tell them the Wednesday as it is the first of two days off so I can get settled in. I'm sure you and Edgar can put up with me until then!'

Grandma shrugs. 'I suppose we will have to then!'

'Thanks a lot grandma!'

I put the letter in my bag as I will need to confirm tomorrow that I want the flat. As I go upstairs to get changed I shake my head and wonder what it is that I have done to grandma that is so wrong.

A week on Wednesday cannot come soon enough and I am nearly in by the end of the day. I look around and think how lucky I am to get this flat! It is in a nice area, a convenient area and it is lovely and quiet. Maybe my luck is actually starting to change at last! At the end of Thursday I have moved my things into the flat and am making myself a well-earned cup of tea. I am really pleased with my new home and I wonder when my grandma will come and see it. There are still a few bits of things to do but all-in-all it has all gone smoothly so far. Oh, and *no* Edgar any more! I haven't seen much of the neighbours, save for an elderly guy from upstairs at the corner saying hello and generally being nosey. Still, he seems okay though.

The next few days I am at work and it is wonderful to be coming home to my lovely new home. Good things are happening at work as well as I have made friends with a patient that I have been looking after, a lovely lady called Karen and we have said that we will go out and have something to eat. We are a little restricted as she is in a wheelchair and on oxygen so we can't exactly go dancing!

It is about a week now since I moved in and my grandma is actually here looking at my new home.

'So, what do you think grandma?'

Grandma looks around a bit more and then nods a little. 'Very nice. A little on the small side for me but I suppose it will do for you.'

'Actually, it is just the right size for me grandma,' I retort with a little sarcasm in my voice. 'Anyway, I am thinking of getting a little dog to keep me company. I have checked with the housing association and they say that it is okay.'

Grandma frowns. 'A dog? A dog? What do you want one of those for? You'll be tied to home all the time and what about when you are at work? You don't want a dog!'

'And why not?' I ask a little exasperated now. 'I'll keep me company but it will be nice and won't answer back!'

'Well,' continues grandma, 'don;t expect me to look after it! I am getting older you know!'

'Don't worry grandma. I won't be expecting you to look after it! Anyway, I will get out. I have met a new friend at the hospital and her and her husband are taking me for my dog next week.'

Grandma nods. 'Very good. Is she nice?

I nod. 'She's lovely. She is in a wheelchair so I will probably have to push her but that's okay...'

'A wheelchair!' interrupts grandma. 'Are you daft? You can't push someone in a wheelchair with your back. You can't be friends with her!'

'How can you be so nasty and cruel?' I ask grandma annoyed.

'How dare you speak to me like that young lady! After all the looking after you I do. That's gratitude!'

I go towards the door. 'I think you had better go now grandma! Thank you for coming and I will see you next week. I will probably come round to see you on Tuesday.'

Grandma nods. 'Okay, but you think on what I've said!'

I almost push grandma out of the door. 'I will. Bye.'

As she goes and I close the door I smile. Being able to tell grandma to go was great!

My friend Karen and her husband offer to take me to get a dog so a couple of days later we are looking around the pedigree puppy kennels. Choosing is difficult as they all look so cute and it is a little upsetting that I can't take them all home! I am getting to the despondent stage when a little white dog catches my eye, scampering up to the glass and wagging it's little tail. I ask the lady to get the little dog out for me and then I hold onto it and cuddle it. It is a little girl dog, a West Highland Terrier, and she licks me all over and sticks her nose in my face.

I smile a big smile and nod my head. 'I'll take her! She's gorgeous!'

Once the formalities are over we are on the way home in the car.

'What are you going to call her?' asks my friend Karen.

'I am going to call her Tammey!' I answer. 'She's wonderful and she looks like a Tammey!'

Karen nods. 'She suits Tammey!'

When we get home and my friend has left Tammey and I cuddle up again. I have a lovely little friend again. My mind goes a little bit back to Tootsie when I was young but I look at Tammey and she sticks her nose in my face again and licks my cheek!

'I think I had better feed you little darling!' I say as she starts to nibble my ear!'

My first day at work with Tammey at home is a little nervy as you hear the stories of little puppies chewing things so I really don't know what to expect when I get home. But, I open the door when I get home and little Tammey comes scampering to me and yelps her little bark! She is a little ball of white fluff and I scoop her up in my arms and give her a cuddle! I look around the flat and see that she has been a good girl and nothing is chewed or broken.

'Good girl!' I say. 'You're lovely aren't you?' I go to the fridge and take her puppy food out. She runs around my feet as I serve it out and then she is eating it as fast as her little jaws can eat! I get a cup of tea on the go and then start to get my meal cooking but it isn't easy when you have a little white ball of fluff hanging round your feet! Later on I am sat down reading the paper when it crinkles and a little white face peers over the top! I laugh and shake my head and then give her another cuddle. She's my little love and my little friend and I know we will be fine!

I take Tammey out but I have to carry her for a few days as she needs her injections but she is so cuddly I don't want to put her down anyway! When she goes to the vets she is a very good girl so I get her a few puppy treats! When I go to bed she cuddles up to me or lies on the pillow or at my feet so I know she is never far away! I wish the same could be said of my grandma! The thing is, Edgar has decided to move to another small village a few miles away from the town to be near his family. I get the feeling that my grandma doesn't want him to go but also she doesn't want to move away from me.

'But grandma, listen.' I hand her a cup of tea and a biscuit. 'I will be fine so why don't you move up there with him?'

Grandma shakes her head. 'You have got a few problems with your health Caroline so I want to be here for you. I don't really want to go up there.'

I sigh. 'I will be fine grandma. You know there is a bungalow next door but one to him so why don't you buy that? You can be next to him then and you can look out for each other. I can still come and see you with Tammey.' I wave my hand around. 'Besides, you don't really like it here any more.'

Grandma thinks for a moment and then nods. 'I suppose I will be better up there but I still don't like the idea of leaving you.'

I sigh an even bigger sigh. 'I will be fine grandma! It is a lot nicer up there and Edgar will be near you day-to-day so I know you will be looked after. You'll be a lot better off!'

Grandma does a smaller sigh then me. 'Okay. You're right Caroline. I'll start things off and see if I can sell this.'

As it turned out, grandma sold her house in three days so she moves next door but one to Edgar, a lovely little bungalow in a quiet cul-de-sac with lovely gardens around! I help her to settle in between work and she actually seems happy enough so I needn't worry.

Over the course of the next few months life ticks along quite nicely but at work I am starting to find my job getting a little harder, particularly making my back sore. Actually, I am getting quite a bit of pain in my back and neck but I just put it down to all the stress and carry on as best I can. However, I think I need to go to my doctor as I am also starting to get a muzzy head and I feel very tired a lot of the time. My face is going a bit numb as well and when I have a drink it is just like I've been to the dentists and the anaesthetic hasn't worn off! So, I go to see the doctor and after he gives me a thorough testing he arranges for me to go and see a neurologist. I still carry on working but it is starting to affect my back quite so I make a point of going seeing the occupational health doctor.

It proves to be a good move because I am diagnosed with spondulitis, a very painful condition and pretty much arthritis in a fancier word, in my neck and back. I sigh! I suppose it is through the lifting and twisting with patients all these years but I suppose I can't be sure. But, the occupational health doctor is straight on the case and insists that my job role is changed. After many conversations between the doctor and my ward matron I am given a new role in the discharge ward as a ward clerk. I also get a special chair and arrangement of workstation so I suppose they are looking after me. Also, I am given a very quick appointment at a specialist hospital near Manchester where I have a lot of tests, a scan and a lumber puncture, which were not very nice at all!

Funnily enough, the spondulitis is the only real thing they find so I can't understand why I feel like I do. It doesn't make any difference at work though as I have my special chair and workstation so I am fine.

Some time later Tammey is getting bigger and more cheeky, I am settled into my new job at the hospital and I am loving my flat. Some of the neighbours have proved quite friendly although I don't bother with them that much really. It isn't much of a problem going seeing my grandma either as my shifts mean I have quite a bit of time to go up and spend time with her. Grandma has also come across an old friend of my mother's, Doris, as she bumped into her in town. It might be nice to talk to Doris – she might be able to tell me some more about my mum. One day, when I had gone to my grandma's, she had a visitor, her niece Griselda and husband Lionel who we used to see at grandma's sister's all those years ago. I have no idea why they have been back in touch but as long as they don't bother me I am okay! Grandma and I seem to be getting along okay at the moment but the atmosphere drops to a bit of a miserable level when Edgar is around. I wonder why that is? I mean, it isn't like he is doing anything really wrong but it just seems like there is a sadness about when he is about. Some of the comments he makes are quite funny but it is so hard to tell whether he is joking or whether he means what he says. I shrug and think that it is grandma's choice so we have to live with it.

But, a couple of weeks later I finish work and go up to grandma's to see her for an hour. When I get there grandma is quite distressed.

'What's the matter grandma?'

She points towards Edgar's house. 'It's him! We have had a fall out and he has chucked me out of his house. I don't know what he's playing at. He's being a silly, silly man!'

I get hold of grandma's hand. 'Look, I'm sure it's just because you two have argued a bit.'

I go and make a drink and leave grandma sitting in her chair but all the time I'm in the kitchen grandma is silent.

I hand grandma her cup of tea and she nods a bit, takes a drink but says nothing and looks miserable.

'I'm sure he'll be back grandma,' I say sitting in the chair by the window. 'Anyway, what were you arguing about?'

Grandma takes a few sips of her brew and then coughs a bit. 'I had a go at him for keep leaving me when he goes to see his family. We have supposed to have been together for years but he never takes me!'

'Well hasn't he always been like that?' I answer shrugging my shoulders. 'I'm not surprised you have said something. It's about time!'

'Well,' says grandma, 'a lot of good it did me! He literally threw me out and I thought he would have killed me!'

I frown. 'He's very nasty grandma for throwing you out but I don't think he would have killed you.' I lean forward a bit. 'Has he been drinking?'

Grandma nods. 'He's had a lot of whisky.'

'Well then,' I answer smiling a little. 'When he sobers up he'll realise what he's done and come crawling back. You'll see grandma.'

Grandma shrugs. 'Huh!'

As it happens, over the course of the next few months grandma is actually proved right and she hears nothing from Edgar. Even though she really isn't showing it much I know she is upset about it so I try, in between work and Tammey, to go and see her as much as possible. The problem is I can actually see that it is affecting grandma quite a lot so, in spite of how she has been in the past, I feel I need to be there for her – but that's me all over! It is nearly Christmas time and I have decided to ask my grandma if she wants to stay with me for a little while. She agrees and so I know that at least she wont be on her own feeling miserable. Christmas is lovely as I have a fluffy little girl to buy presents for, and a grandma with me of course! The thing is, I start noticing that grandma is becoming a little strange in some of the things she is saying and doing.

One day I go into the kitchen to make a drink and when I go back into the living room grandma is twiddling her thumbs, mumbling and staring at the telephone and the television.

I stand holding the cups of tea and frown. 'What's the matter grandma?'

She starts rocking backwards and forwards. 'Why didn't you tell me you were on a mission? They're sending for you. Can't you see the lights blinking?'

I shake my head and my mouth is open a little. 'What are you talking about grandma?'

Grandma frowns and her tone gets a little frustrated. 'Those lights, over there, green lights blinking away!' Grandma points to the telephone.

I look and then shake my head. 'There are no blinking lights grandma! And why do you think I am on a mission?' I put the brews down and look at grandma. 'I'm not some sort of secret agent you know!'

Grandma stands up and puts her hands on her hips. 'How do I know that? You could be under cover and trying to fool me!'

Now I am worried! I wave my hand in a dismissive gesture. 'Grandma, of course I am not fooling you. Why would I want to do that? Now stop being silly.'

Grandma points towards me. 'Now listen here young lady! Just because you are highly trained doesn't mean you can talk to me like that! Anyway, I am going to the toilet.'

Grandma goes to the toilet and when she finally comes out I hear her laughing in the hall. I get up and go into the hall and then I frown as I see her looking at the wall near the front door.

'I didn't know you could ride a horse Caroline! See, there you go, riding fast to get away from that little dog!'

'Where grandma? Where are you looking?

Grandma points to the door and laughs. 'Over there! Blimey, you *can* ride fast! That little dog has no chance of catching you!'

I take hold of grandma's arm and lead her back into the living room. 'Grandma, you're starting to worry me. What are you going on about?' I go for the phone. 'I'm going to ring for a doctor. You're not well.'

Grandma pulls back on my arm. 'Doctor? The doctor? I am perfectly well thank you!'

'Then why are you seeing me riding a horse grandma?' I ask with an exasperated look on my face.

Grandma stares at the wall and then at me. She smiles a little. 'Can we have a cup of tea Caroline? I'll put the kettle on.' Grandma goes into the kitchen and starts to make a cup of tea. Suddenly, she looks very normal and I put the phone back, preferring to give her the benefit of the doubt for, now.

Grandma stays with me for another couple of weeks but half way through the week I am awoken In the night by grandma shouting for me. I rush into her and find her cowering on the chair.

'What's the matter grandma?'

She points to the floor near the television. 'Those worms. Where have all those worms come from?'

I look and of course there are no worms on the floor. I put my arms around grandma's shoulders but she shrugs them off with force and then paces around the lounge.

'Grandma? Grandma!' I get hold of her arm again but she pulls it away and then starts to shout.

'Caroline! Get that horse again and ride away. Take those worms with you!' She shouts louder. 'Get rid of the worms!'

I pick up the phone as grandma is now pacing quickly and staring sternly at me. As I dial for an ambulance she comes right up to me wagging her finger.

'Listen here young lady! Don't you touch me! I am your grandma and don't you forget it!'

I come off the phone and the ambulance is on its way.

'Grandma. I can't see any worms. Are you sure it isn't Tammey's toys?' I know it can't be but I am trying to take her mind off things.

Grandma shouts again. 'They *are* worms! They'll ruin your telly!'

Grandma continues to rant and rave but soon there is a knock on the door and the ambulance is here. I show the paramedics into the living room where grandma is still shaking a little.

'She's been acting really weird and shouting,' I tell the ambulance people.

'Shouting about what?' one of them answers.

I sigh. 'About seeing me ride a horse in the hall and then worms under the television!'

The ambulance man laughs. 'You would have a hard job getting a horse in the hall, never mind ride one! Er, what's your grandma's name?'

'Pearl.'

The ambulance man nods and then turns to grandma. 'Pearl, What's the matter then love? I believe you are having trouble with some worms?'

Grandma frowns at him. 'Worms? Why would I be having a problem with worms? I'm not in the garden you know!'

'Pearl, your granddaughter says that you've seen her riding a horse and that there are worms under the telly. She also says that you think that she is in some sort of secret service, that she is undercover!'

Grandma laughs. 'Undercover? The only undercover for Caroline is when she makes the bed! I don't know what she has been saying but there are no worms love! Anyway, when can I go home?'

The ambulance man indicates for me to follow him into the kitchen. 'Right love. Your grandma seems okay to me. I say get her a taxi and send her home.'

I scowl at him. 'But she has been screaming and shouting and seeing mad things! You can't send her home!

The ambulance man shrugs his shoulders. 'Look love, we can't find anything wrong with her.'

I shake my head. 'I'm not putting it on you know! She has been shouting and seeing things!'

'I'm sure you're not putting it on love,' answers the ambulance man, 'but there is nothing wrong with your grandma. You should get her home.'

The ambulance people get their stuff together and go, leaving me with a weirdly acting grandma.

'Are you going to get me a taxi home Caroline?' asks grandma.

Reluctantly, I nod my head and phone for a taxi. Then it arrives and grandma is going.

'Now think on Caroline. Stop the blinking lights and get some sleep.'

I shrug but what's the point in arguing. 'Ring me when you get home grandma. Let me know you're okay.'

Grandma nods and then she is on her way home. When she has rung and I know she's okay I get sorted for bed as I have to work tomorrow. I have to smile to myself! Secret agent, horse riding, worms! What the heck is going on?

The next day at work I am thinking about grandma and her silliness all day and I keep having to be given a little nudge to get on with things! When I get home there is a message on my answer phone. The message is from my grandma, asking me to ring her and she sounds a bit weird again.

I ring her back and when she answers I frown as she doesn't sound right.

'Grandma? What's the matter?' I am really puzzled actually.

'They're watching me Caroline!' Grandma sounds really flustered and upset.

'Who, grandma? Who's watching you?' I go for my coat again as I feel that I might need to go up to see her.

'The people outside!' answers grandma seeming to get more upset. 'The clowns don't help either! They keep laughing in my face and blowing frogs around the room!'

I am more than a little worried by now. 'Grandma, what are you talking about? Listen, I am getting on the bus and coming up to see you.'

I hear grandma getting more worried. 'No Caroline, no! They'll get you as well! I'm okay, really. The teddies on the bed will get rid of the clowns!'

By this time I have cut the call and am out of the door. By the time I get up to grandma's I gasp and my eyes go wide as she is wandering the car park in her nightie.

'Grandma!' I shout. 'Get back inside!'

Grandma sees me and stops still, only moving again when I link her arm and turning her round. When we get inside grandma rushes to her chair and then sits down in a cowering position. I pick the phone up and dial for the emergency doctor.

Grandma looks around and then blows out slightly. 'Thank goodness they've gone. I can get some peace now.'

I come off the phone and stare at her. 'Who has gone?'

'The Turkish dancers of course!' answers grandma. 'The music was far too loud and all those coloured skirts in my face!'

I shake my head and go into the kitchen. 'I'll make a cup of tea grandma.'

When I go into the kitchen I find it in a right old mess so I shake my head a little and start to clear up as the kettle starts to boil. I make a cup of tea for us both but we haven't been drinking it long when there's a knock at the door and the duty doctor is here. I show him in and then he sits down and looks at grandma.

'Can I get you a cup of tea?' I ask the doctor.

He shakes his head. 'No. thank you. I'm fine. Now then Pearl. What's been happening?'

Grandma points to the wall. 'It's them next door. Er, she used to be the Mayor but now she's taping me! They're watching me and taping everything I say.' She sighs. 'They must be working under cover!'

The doctor raises his eyebrows and then looks at me. I just shake my head.

'And what makes you think they have reason to tape you Pearl?' asks the doctor.

'Well,' answers grandma, 'first they send the clowns to watch me and then they put microphones in the teddies on my bed!' She leans into the doctor and wags her finger. 'I think they are trying to drive me mad so they can get their hands on my money!'

'I see,' says the doctor looking at me again. 'And why were you in the street in your nightie Pearl?'

'I was in disguise!' answers grandma matter-of-factly. 'And the Turkish dancing girls were too loud so I had to get away!'

The doctor gets up and indicates for me to follow him. 'Can you help me get some things from my car?'

I go with the doctor nodding.

When we get outside the doctor looks at me again. 'I am going to phone for the social worker and get your grandma into the hospital for some tests. She's obviously pretty sick. I'll make some notes whilst we wait for the ambulance. Can you get some things together for her?'

'Okay,' I say. I shake my head and start to cry a little. The doctor looks at me and smiles a bit.

'Don't worry,' says the doctor. 'She'll be fine. A little bit of care and some tests will get to the bottom of it. I think we will take her to the J wards and see if they can help.'

I frown and get a little more upset. 'Doctor, I work at the hospital and J wards are the psychiatric wards. She hasn't gone completely mad, is she?'

The doctor shakes his head. 'No. That's not why I am sending her there. It is because they will do the tests quicker which will be better for your grandma.'

I nod. 'Okay then. I understand. I'll get her things.'

So, that was that then! My grandma is off to the nutty ward to get assessed for seeing things! That man Edgar shoving grandma out of his life has really affected her. I am upset and feel sorry for grandma in a way but that's me. It doesn't matter that she has been rotten with me and ignored me for years at a time – she is my grandma and she shouldn't be like this.

She doesn't really want to go when the social worker turns up and kicks up a right fuss! But, the doctor convinces her it is for the best and that it is for some tests so she gets into the car mumbling and I get in with her, a bag of clothes and things in my hand. I glance across at Edgar's house and there isn't a sign of him. Not a surprise really.

Over the next couple of days grandma is settling into the ward and because I work at the hospital I can look in on her quite a lot. She seems to be doing okay but I know the nurses have put her on some medication so it has calmed her down. When I finish an early shift I go straight to see grandma as it is visiting time anyway. There are a mix of people in the ward at various different stages and grandma seems to be getting quite friendly with a nice man called Geoff.

When I see my grandma she is usually sitting at a table in a part like a hall near the door. She seems to like it there so if it makes her feel happy and comfortable then I don't see a problem. This particular day the bell rings as someone wants to come into the ward and then a man comes in and smiles at grandma when he sees her.

'Hi Pearl,' says the man. 'Are you okay today?'

Grandma nods. 'Not bad thank you.' She nods her head towards me. 'This is my granddaughter Caroline.'

The man smiles at me. 'Hello. How are you?'

'Not bad,' I answer smiling. He seems really nice and not bad either! 'Who are you here to see?'

'Oh, my dad Geoff.'

'Oh, Geoff! Grandma seems to like your dad. They're always talking.'

The man nods. 'That's my dad! Anyway. I must go and find him. My name's Phil. See you later. See you later Pearl.'

'Nice meeting you Phil,' I say as he goes off.

I look at grandma and she is smiling. 'What?' I ask.

'He's a nice young man Caroline. He's very good and loving with his dad.'

I shake my head at grandma. 'I don't know what you mean! Don't get any ideas!'

The next couple of days I get to see grandma as much as I can due to my shifts but I don't see Geoff's son Phil. I talk to Geoff though and he is a lovely man. He tells me he plays the organ and he likes a drop of Guinness! The next day though and Phil comes to see his dad, telling me that he has been working the last two nights so that's why he hasn't been.

'What do you do?' I ask him.

'I work in a CCTV control room as a security officer. I do two days, two nights and then four days off so I will be coming to see dad for the next few days.'

'I bet you don't get time to go out a lot,' says grandma to him.

'I go out when I can but it is about making sure dad is okay at the moment.' He turns to look at me. 'What about you Caroline? Do you get time to go out?'

Grandma smiles. 'Caroline works at the hospital here. She doesn't get out much either, do you Caroline!'

'Grandma!' I say, giving her a little nudge under the table with my foot.

Phil smiles. 'I'll see you later. I need to go and find dad. See you in a bit Pearl.'

'Bye,' shouts grandma, looking at me and smiling.

'What?' I say. 'Oh, grandma!'

At the end of visiting I am walking out of the ward when I hear Phil saying goodbye to my grandma. I look around and he has caught up with me. We walk out a little next to each other, down the stairs and as we are going up the corridor I see Phil looking a little sad.

Then he smiles a bit. 'It's not easy, is it? Having someone come here isn't easy at all.'

I shake my head a little. 'No, not really.'

'It's the second time in three years I've had to visit someone in here.' Phil looks a little sad again. 'My mum died of Alzheimers three years ago and she was in here as well.'

'Oh. I'm sorry to hear that,' I answer, continuing to walk.

Then there is a t-junction in the corridor and I start to walk one way as Phil goes the other out to the car park.

'You know, if you want to talk about it I have been here before,' calls Phil after me.

I look back at him and raise my eyebrows a bit. 'I'll think about it. See you. Bye.'

'Bye,' says Phil back.

As I walk down the corridor to get to the bus stop I get the feeling that he is looking at me!

The next day is pretty much the same at visiting time and Phil is there again, talking to grandma a bit as well as spending time with his dad. Geoff is actually a lovely man and, actually, so is Phil really. Grandma and I are sitting in the usual place and having a nice talk.

'That man Phil, Geoff's son was asking me if I wanted to talk. Don't know what for really but I feel a bit sad for him. His mum was in here three years ago with Alzheimers.'

'Oh, that's awful,' says grandma. 'To see his mum and his dad poorly like that can't be nice. Anyway Caroline, he's a nice lad so why don't you go out and have a chat with him?'

I raise my eyes and shake my head a bit. 'Grandma!'

'Well!' continues grandma. 'Why not! You've had some rotten men so a nice man would be a change!'

'Grandma, I'm not interested in a man, however nice he is!'

As it comes to the end of visiting I am walking out with Phil again and we have a nice general talk. When we get to the t-junction in the corridor again I turn the same way but Phil stops.

'Can I give you a lift?' asks Phil.

I am a bit stunned but I keep my cool. 'I'm okay thanks. I work here and I have to pick up some things before I go home. Thank you for the offer though. Bye.'

'Bye,' says Phil back as he heads off towards the car park. I still get the feeling he is watching me!

The next day I see grandma again but when Phil comes in I decide that I don't want to see him really. Grandma is in a different room so I spend the whole hour hiding from Phil!

I have no idea how I manage it in a smallish ward but I do! I am actually working the day after so I tell grandma that I will see her when I can and go home feeling a little bit proud of myself for avoiding Phil! I don't want to be bothered with a man, nice though he is!

Over the next couple of days Phil must be working and so I don't see him much. However, the next time I am in when he is I am with a friend, a lady that was my mum's friend called Doris. Doris is very nice but quite loud and a little overbearing to some people. She has very long hair in a ponytail and I really can't see, from what I have heard of my mum, how Doris and her could be friends. But they were and a few weeks ago grandma bumped into her in town so she asked me if she could come and visit grandma with me. Of course, I said yes so we are sat with grandma having a nice natter. Geoff has come and talked to us as well and then Phil comes in and says hello to grandma. He has a young lad with him, quite a big lad.

'Are you okay Phil?' asks grandma. 'Your dad's over in that room at the side. He's just been talking to us.'

'He hasn't been telling you his tram stories again has he?' asks Phil of grandma. 'Anyway Pearl, this is my son Richard.'

The lad nods and Phil continues. 'This is Pearl, Richard, this is Pearl's granddaughter Caroline and this is...?'

'This is Doris, an old friend of my daughter's,' says grandma.

'Hello love,' says Doris. 'Are you all right?'

'Not so bad,' says Phil. 'So, Pearl's daughter would have been your mum then,' Phil says to me.

I nod. 'Yes, that's right.'

Phil turns to his son. 'Come on matey. Let's go and find your grandpa. See you all later.'

As they walk away to find Geoff, Doris turns to me. 'He is a nice man, isn't he?'

I shake my head. 'Not you as well! Grandma keeps saying that he is and that I should go out with him! I'm not interested in a man.'

'Pearl's right,' says Doris. 'I can tell he's a good 'un so I think you should at least go out and see what he's like!'

I shake my head. ‘Blimey, I’m sick of you two going on! He might be nice but I am not interested.’

After a while Phil and his son come back and sit near us, with Geoff who laughs and starts to talk to us a little.

‘So, does your son live with you then?’ asks Doris.

Phil shakes his head. ‘No, he and my daughter live with their mother. We’re getting divorced.’

I see Doris look at me and smile and I give her a crafty nudge and shake my head a bit.

Phil’s son leans into Geoff. ‘If you look out of the window grandpa you’ll see dad’s new car.’ He points and Geoff looks. ‘That blue Renault there.’

I must admit I have a crafty look as well and it looks quite nice!

Then it’s time to go and we all say our goodbyes. Doris and I go one way, to the bus, and Phil and his son go to the car park.

‘You’re daft if you don’t go out with that one!’ says Doris. ‘He’s very nice you know!’

‘Doris!’ I am a little aggravated. ‘I said I am not interested in a man!’

‘I know,’ says Doris, but if you don’t go out with him you’ll have me to deal with! He’s a good ‘un!’

I carry on shaking my head as we head off down the corridor.

The next day at visiting Doris comes with me again and when she sees Phil come in and go to Geoff she is off again, telling me to go out with him. Oh, what the heck! For a quiet life I finally agree to let him have my phone number! Doris goes and gives it to him and then a short while later comes back with his!

‘See, I told you!’ says Doris. ‘He was really pleased that I gave him your number!’

When visiting is over Doris and I are going out of the door when we are joined by Phil.

'Can I give you ladies a lift?' asks Phil.

Doris nods. 'Go on then, as long as it isn't a two door car as I can't get in the back of one of them!

'No, it's got four doors!' says Phil smiling.

Doris grabs me. 'Come on then!'

Doris sits in the back and I get in the front. We drop Doris off at home and then we head off to take me home.

'Do you fancy going for a drink?' asks Phil.

I look at him and reluctantly nod. 'Okay then. Go on. Just one.'

We stop at a pub on the way home and go in for a drink.

There is a bit of music on and a quiz but we sit in a corner with a drink and start to get to know each other a bit. The thing is, we seem to be getting on okay and grandma and Doris are right – he is a nice man! He tells me that he has been separated for about six months and that he is renting a house off a friend, someone who lives across the road from where his dad lived. He has a daughter as well as his son and he is a security person.

'So, what do you do at the hospital Caroline?' asks Phil.

I take a drink and then smile. 'I was a carer but I have a back problem now so I work as a clerk in the discharge ward.' I take another drink. 'How long have you done security?'

'Not long really,' answers Phil. 'I was selling security systems but I got sick of selling so I had a word with one of my customers and got a job there, which is where I am now.'

'And where is that?' I ask, finding myself moving a bit nearer.

'In Cheshire.'

'A bit of a journey every day, isn't it?' I ask, raising my eyebrows.

Phil laughs a bit. 'I'm used to travelling to get to work and it's not that bad really. Anyway, it's not too far and there's not much traffic when I go to work!'

We talk about more general things and he is asking me about grandma and what has happened to her. I tell him a little bit about her and he smiles at some parts and we get on really well!

Phil takes me home and when we pull up in the car park of the close where I live.

'I enjoyed that,' says Phil. 'We should do it again. What do you think?'

I smile. 'Okay, I enjoyed it as well. You've got my number. Text me and let me know.'

'Okay, says Phil. Probably on Saturday? I have a rare weekend off so it would be nice to go out Saturday.'

I nod. 'Okay text me. Good night.'

'Good night,' says Phil.

It doesn't take long for Phil to text me! The next morning in fact! I am actually quite excited about him contacting me as, actually, grandma and Doris are right – he *is* very nice! A couple of texts later and it seems that he is asking me if I want to go out in a few days time, on Friday in fact. I say that is okay and then I am looking at my sent texts and smiling at the fact that I put I am missing him! Oh, what am I doing! Two days later I am at the hospital again and Phil is there with his son Richard. Grandma is actually sat with Geoff so we all have a really good natter! At the end of visiting we all go our separate ways but as I am waiting at the bus stop I see a black car stop and then Phil gets out.

'Hi, want a lift home?' shouts Phil.

I am a little bit hesitant but I come to the decision that it would be better than waiting for the bus! So, I get into the car. It is obvious that it is Phil's son's car and then they are taking me home. His son doesn't look all that happy but I suppose it has been dropped on him, judging by his reaction to his dad, but once home Phil says that he will ring me. I am quite happy actually and even more happy when he rings later in the evening! We have a lovely chat and then we agree that we should meet at a famous pub in town. But the next day Phil rings back and says that, if I want, he will pick me up and that we should go for a meal. I agree it's a good idea and then the rest of the week seems to go really slow.

And then Friday comes around and after work I hurry home and start to get ready, never easy with Tammey clinging like a dog with glue on! I have told Phil to text or ring when he is in the car park.

Then the phone goes and I read the text that Phil is outside waiting for me so I look in the mirror one more time before I go out, say goodbye to Tammey and then I go out to meet Phil. I am wearing a lovely flowery top and black pants.

I get into the car. So, where are we going?'

'Well,' answers Phil smiling, 'I hope that you like Italian food because I have booked a table in a lovely Italian.'

'I smile and shrug. 'Well, I like spaghetti bolognaise so that's okay!'

We set off and after a while I realise that we are heading towards the North end of town.

'I went earlier today and booked us in for about eight o'clock,' says Phil as we turn left at some traffic lights. 'It's a lovely little restaurant with a great atmosphere!'

'So long as the food is good that's what matters!' I say with a grin.

'I've never eaten there so I hope it's good as well!' says Phil.

We park the car and then it is a short walk to the restaurant. Phil is right, it is a lovely restaurant and, as it happens, the spaghetti bolognaise I order is very tasty. We talk about our lives, about how his mother was very ill before she died and I tell him that my mother died when I was ten, about our jobs and Phil tells me that he is renting a house from a friend of his but that it could be sold at any time! The talk and the food is very nice and I smile as I am having a lovely evening! When we have finished we head off to the pub we originally were to go but it isn't very nice so Phil takes me to a pub that he says he used to go to with his friends a few years ago.

We get a drink and I look around to see it is quite a nice old fashioned pub. We carry on talking about our lives a little more and he tells me that he used to have a business and has driven some famous people around, not in a show-off way though. I am really getting to like this man! At the end of a very lovely evening we pull into the car park as Phil gets me home.

'So, when are we doing this again?' asks Phil. 'I have had a lovely evening Caroline!'

I smile and look him in the eyes. 'I've had a lovely evening as well! You'll have to ring me and we'll arrange it when we aren't working.'

Phil nods. 'I'll ring you tomorrow evening as I'm on days.'

'Okay.' I lean over and give him a peck on the cheek. 'Night! Don't forget to ring me tomorrow!'

'I won't! Answers Phil. 'Night.'

I go into my little Tammey and then I am getting ready for bed. Then I decide that I will text Phil and I put that I am missing him! Well, I am! He lets me know that he is at home and then I am waiting for him to ring me tomorrow.

Difficulties And Distress

The next day at work the nurses and my work colleagues are asking me why I seem to be in a bit of a daze and then I tell them about my lovely evening.

'Ah!' says one of the nurses. 'We might have guessed there was a man involved!'

I shake my head. 'He's actually very nice!'

'Single?' asks another one cheekily.

'Well, separated and going through a divorce,' I answer.

'Any kids?' asks the first one as I am making my way out of the ward to get some patient files.

'Two,' I shout back, 'but one of them, his son, is twenty so he's not a kid.'

I am glad of the time away from the ward for a bit as I can have a rest from all the questions!

The rest of the day is pretty much the same so when I finish I am glad to get the bus and get away from the questioning, although I know that they are just being nice really! When I get home I am greeted, as always, by my little white ball of fluff and then I am getting my tea and waiting for Phil to ring. It gets to about half past seven and he still hasn't rung but about ten to eight my mobile rings and it is him!

'Hi,' I say. 'I thought you'd forgotten me!'

'No, of course not,' says Phil. 'I don't finish until seven and the traffic was murder tonight! Have you had a good day?'

I smile. 'Not bad! A lot of questions and ribbing from the girls at work!'

'Oh?' asks Phil. 'And why was that?'

I sigh. 'They say I have been walking around in a bit of a daze and that they guessed a man was involved!'

'So I made a good impression then!' says Phil.

'Not a bad one!' I answer.

'Okay,' says Phil, 'so when are we going out again? The next day I have off is in a couple of days so I am usually in bed until early afternoon so I could pick you up later?'

I am nodding to myself. 'That would be nice! Where are we going?'

'Do you like shopping?' asks Phil. 'Or, is that a daft question to ask a girl?'

'Hey, don't be so cheeky!' I say with a slight tone. 'I don't mind shopping really. Where were you thinking of?'

'The Trafford Centre!' answers Phil. 'There are some nice places to eat there as well!'

'Okay,' I say with a big smile. Are you picking me up then?'

'Yep! I'll pick you up at around five o'clock?' says Phil.

'That's okay,' I answer. 'You can knock on the door if you want!'

'I'll see you on Wednesday then!' says Phil.

The phone call finishes and I am smiling a big smile! 'Come on Tammey,' I say to my lovely little faithful friend. 'Let's go for a walk and then get some tea!'

Wednesday afternoon cannot come soon enough and I spend a good while getting ready. Then, at about ten minutes to five the knock comes on the door and Tammey starts to bark. I open the door and she runs out to Phil, wagging her tail.

'Hello Tammey!' says Phil. He looks at me and smiles. 'Hiya! Aw, she's gorgeous!'

'Well I think so!' I say looking at Tammey. 'Come on Tammey, in the house now. Come in Phil.'

We go into the lounge and I get my coat on. Phil seems to have his hands full with Tammey which makes me smile! But, he seems to genuinely love her so that's okay.

'Have you had a dog before?' I ask.

Phil shakes his head. 'No. Actually, I have always had cats but I love dogs just as much.'

I make a yukky expression. 'I don;t really like cats. I wouldn't harm them but I don't like them.'

'Cats look after themselves really,' continues Phil. 'They also bury what they do as well! Oh, except when in the tray in the kitchen!'

I shake my head. 'Too much information Phil!'

Phil strokes Tammey. 'I'll see you again little girl!' He looks up at me. Are you right?'

I nod my head. 'Yep. Come on then. Bye Tammey.'

Shopping is very nice and it is really unusual to go out with a man that doesn't mind shopping! We buy each other little presents and then we are sitting in an Italian waiting for our meals. Phil tells me a little more about his life and one fascinating thing is that he has written a book, a science fantasy novel and he wants to get it published! I have only met his son up to now but I might meet his daughter soon. She is only thirteen though so I don't know. I have told Phil that I haven't got any children so he doesn't know about my girls. We have a lovely meal and then Phil takes me home. We agree that we should carry on seeing each other and arrange to go out on Saturday, as Phil actually has the weekend off. He suggests that we go to the pub across from where his dad's house is as it's a country style pub and a great atmosphere apparently.

Saturday comes and I have bought a new dress. Tammey knows I am going out again and I feel a little sad for her but I want to see this lovely man so she'll have to put up with it for a bit! She's always okay though. Then the taxi comes and I am on my way. Phil says that he will meet me there as he can walk to the pub in about twenty minutes from where he lives. The taxi pulls up at the pub and as I am getting out I see Phil walking up the car park! That's timing for you, or definitely fate! We go in the pub and Phil is right – it is a lovely pub, very lively with a great local atmosphere. As we talk we get closer together in spirit and then, when Phil says that he is falling for me I respond with the same and that is that! We are a proper relationship! After the pub we go back to Phil's house he is living in and I must say it is very nice actually, a large semi with a very big kitchen! We have a brew and then we have a lovely evening together. I finally get my taxi home at four in the morning and as I am going Phil makes me promise to ring him when I get home which I do. As I cuddle up with Tammey I smile and think how right my grandma and Doris were. Phil *is* a lovely man and I am so lucky to have met him!

We start to see each other as much as we can, sometimes at my house where Phil is really making good friends with Tammey or at his, where he does some cooking and makes me dinners! Sometimes, he sees his son or daughter but that's okay because I might be working anyway. We are in Phil's house one day and he is cooking dinner, chatting away and we are having a great time. I am helping him to prepare some of the dinner as well and doing a bit of washing up.

'Do you know what?' asks Phil.

'What?' I answer.

'I would like this to be us in thirty years time!'

I look at him and then I have a big smile on my face. I am so happy he said that!

Also, when Phil is at work on nights he always gets a break later in the evening so he has a particular walk near work and he always phones me! He comes to see me on his way to work to do nights and sometimes we just sit, Phil, Tammey and me and cuddle up until Phil has to set off for work. Life is starting to seem a little bit better and I am smiling more!

The next time Phil has his four days off we are going out for the evening but he rings me as he is held up by having a long phone argument with someone. I am very disappointed but Phil rings me as says that he won't be long and to stay ready! I am so pleased as I have got my glad rags on and was really looking forward to our night out. When he gets to my house Phil has his glad rags on as well and we are off out at last!

We go for a drink first and then we go to a nice Italian restaurant and we can talk a little.

Phil smiles. 'You know what? I think I might be nearer to getting my book published. I might have the money to help it along a bit.'

I finish my mouthful of spaghetti as I raise my eyebrows. 'That's great! When did you write it?'

Phil smiles and nods.'I've had it written for a few years and it is a dream of mine to see it on the bookshelves, or in a book shop window.'

'What's it about?'

'Science fiction and fantasy,' answers Phil. 'I've had the idea since I was a teenager and finished writing it a couple of years ago.'

I smile. 'That's pretty clever! I am going out with an author! Any more surprises?'

Phil shakes his head. 'No. I don't think so. The rest is me. Honest!'

I smile and nod.

We finish our meals and then go to another bar for a drink. It doesn't get too late and when we get home Phil comes in for a drink. He stays a while and we chat.

'I am going to my aunty Griselda's tomorrow so you can pick me up there if you want,' I say cuddling up to him.'

Phil nods. 'Where does she live?'

'In Accrington,' I say, 'actually, Clayton-le-Moors. 'Do you know it?'

Phil nods. 'Yep! I used to work round there.'

I roll my eyes s little. 'Thought you might have. You seem to have been everywhere!'

'Not quite!' answers Phil.

After a little while more Phil has to go home. I don't want him to but he can't stay here so I kiss him goodnight and then make him promise to ring me when he's home safe.'

The meeting between Griselda and Phil seems to go well and the fact that they both have a love of Disney seems to help! On the way home Phil tells me that it might be an idea to move into his dad's house that he has started doing up. I am quite excited about this but, as it happens, he doesn't really think in the end it is a good idea, mainly because of the fact that he doesn't think he can ever get it very liveable and his mother became very poorly there so a lot of bad memories. Also, it is on a very busy road surrounded by four pubs! We carry on and out relationship seems to be growing and we seem to be getting closer and closer and more in love! There are a few hiccups though. For instance, we arrange to go out and I get very much dressed up but Phil rings and says his son has been hit on the head by his car boot and he has to take him to hospital! Phil does turn up eventually, not too late, and I can tell he is stunned by me! In fact, we go to Manchester and when we are in the restaurant he tells me that he is out with the most beautiful girl of all of them! There are some very nice moments too, like when I am at home with my friend and the door goes. I open it to a very large bouquet of flowers sent by Phil! No man has done that for me before.

Sometimes, though, things are put into your head by people not being nice, people who you thought were okay, and Auntie Griselda says that flowers from men are only because they want something or they are guilty of something. I take no notice but, as will become apparent, the thought really never goes away. But, we carry on getting closer and closer and then there is a bombshell dropped! Phil says that night that the friend he is renting the house from has sold the house and he has to look for somewhere else to live! He asks me to help him look and we do this for a couple of days. However, he comes down one day to pick me up to go out and I am smiling broadly.

'What are you so happy about?' asks Phil.

'I know you are not having much luck finding somewhere to live,' I answer, 'so, why don't you move in here with me until you find somewhere?'

Phil looks quite amazed.

'What?' I ask. 'Is it not a good idea?'

'Well, yes. I think it is a lovely idea,' says Phil. 'But, are you sure? I mean, you have lived here a while.'

'I give Phil a kiss. 'I don't mind at all! I would love you to move in here! I love you and it would be great for us!'

Phil hugs me and then smiles. 'Okay! I will start to move my things in tomorrow.' He frowns. 'I have got quite a bit of stuff you know!'

I nod my head and smile. 'I know, I have seen it, remember! Don't worry. We'll work it out!'

The day comes soon and Phil moves in and although it seems a struggle we manage to fit everything in. But, remember me saying that there are very often some hiccups. Well, there is a major one in that Phil is being threatened by his ex for moving in but he says stuff her and he will sort it! So, everything is looking fantastic for us and we begin to build a life together!

A few days later and grandma is coming home from hospital, going home to her lovely bungalow with a care package being put in place. I am giving my grandma as much help as possible and when Phil comes with me to help he says that it is great to go to a grandma's house again, with all the little quirky things that grandmas seem to have! My grandma and Phil get on really well and they seem to be like kindred spirits. We are still going to the hospital to the same ward as Phil's dad is still in there. Phil is quite upset at how his dad is and I am also as his dad is a lovely man and I get on really well with him. It is, however, only three years since Phil's mum died, after being in the same ward, so I know how difficult it is for him.

After grandma is well settled in we are out for a night at our favourite pub – it is on the way home from grandma's – so we have been to see her and are having a nice drink.

Phil looks at my hands. 'You have a lot of rings!' he says.

I look down and smile. 'Yep, I suppose I have.'

Phil has a drink and then grins.

'What's the matter with you?' I say smiling.

Phil holds my left hand and sighs. 'I suppose we will have to get a ring for this finger as well!' he says holding my third finger.

I stare at him. 'What?'

'Well,' says Phil smiling, 'This finger doesn't have a ring on it so we need to get one for it!'

'But, that finger is the wedding finger,' I say still staring.

Phil nods. 'I know. Will you then?'

I still continue to stare and then smile.

'Will you marry me?' asks Phil.

I sit, eyes glazed for a while and then nod. 'Yes, of course I will!'

We kiss and then sit together, happy and in love!

The next time Phil is off we decide to have a day in Liverpool. We go to the dock area to look at the quirky shops and then we head off to the proper shops. The only thing on my mind, however, is looking for an engagement ring and we are constantly going into all the jewellers! We draw a blank but a couple of days later we end up in the large shopping centre in Manchester and finally we find a ring that I love! We go home and Phil tells his son and daughter and I ring up my auntie, Griselda, who just said a very unenthusiastic congratulations and that was that. But, as with every part of my life, there was always a problem and I get a call the next morning from the care company that my grandma had fallen at home. In fact, she had fallen last night and had been on the floor all night! The ambulance had taken her to hospital and we rushed over there to be with her. But, grandma was really awful with me and kept saying that if I took her things away from her, especially her purse, she would be finished with me! I have heard this before of course and even though I explained that the hospital would not let her keep her purse there, for safety, she was still insistent that I was taking it from her! I take no notice and try to do the best I can for her. We go to see her as much as we can, in spite of her off-handedness towards us and in between we are working our shifts. One day, however, it is quite sunny and Phil is on a day off. We are sitting outside at home when he gets a call from his son to say he is popping round to drop something off. When he gets to our house Phil goes to the car to meet him but then they both appear around the corner and I smile.

'This is Richard,' says Phil introducing his son properly, although I have met him briefly before.

'Hi Caroline,' says Richard.

'Hello again,' I answer. 'Nice to see you again.'

Richard nods.

Phil goes and gets Richard a drink and a seat and then we are all outside again.

'I'm sorry that I haven't been before now,' says Richard. 'It's not that I haven't wanted to it's just that it is awkward with my mum and family.'

Although I am a bit disappointed I nod. 'It's okay Richard.'

He takes a drink and then smiles. 'Let's have a look at this ring then!'

I show Richard the engagement ring and he nods approvingly. We get on really well and chat away quite happily.

'Are you up for going away for a week?' Phil asks Richard.

Both Richard and me look a bit questioningly but I realise finally what Phil means.

'I am going to Majorca with my auntie Griselda and her husband in October.'

'Yes, so I thought we could go away as well!' Phil says to his son.

Richard nods. 'Yeah, whatever. That would be good dad. Where are we going?'

'Should we go to Scotland? We could get a bed and breakfast in a pub in a little village!'

Richard laughs and I just shake my head. Typical!

A few days later and my grandma is coming out of hospital again! I tell her that Edgar has been ringing and asking how she is, so, when we get her home he comes round to see if she is all right. After a while I leave them together as I think that Edgar will look after her okay. Phil and I leave and Phil says that he thinks Edgar seems okay. On the way home the phone rings in the car and it is Phil's daughter, Kate, asking if he would go and see her as she has been very upset. I nod and they make a time for a couple of days.

'She seems a nice girl,' I say when she has gone.

Phil sighs. 'I don't know what's gone on there but she has ignored me for a few weeks now.' He shakes his head. 'I will find out though.'

A couple of days later Phil has been to see his daughter and he says that she has been upset at a few things but they have sorted them out a little so everything seems okay. When we get home, though, things start to go through my mind and for reasons that I don't know I start having a go at Phil, saying that he went running to his daughter after she had ignored him and left me in the process! Phil says not to be so silly and when I carry on he says that I don't understand because I have not had any kids. This makes things worse as I start to hurt a little, knowing what happened to my two girls but I decide to say nothing. The argument blows over and we start to talk about our upcoming little holiday that we planned for all that time ago, when Phil was living in his friend's house. We have booked five nights in a bed and breakfast right next to the sea in a little village on the coast near the border with Scotland. Suddenly, I can't wait!

The next day Phil is at work on day shift and when he comes home he is on the phone – again! I guess from the conversation that it is his daughter again and when he comes off he looks at my stern face and frowns.

'What?' asks Phil.

'Well,' I say, 'I'm looking forward to you coming home and there you are on the phone to her!'

Phil scowls. 'What do you mean 'her'? That's my daughter you are talking about!'

I bang about a little. 'Like I said, she ignores you and then you are always talking to her!'

'And like I said,' says Phil in an angry voice, 'you've never had kids so you don't understand!'

I start to go watery eyed. 'Actually, I *do* have kids. Two girls!'

Phil looks stunned. 'What?' he says after a few moments.

I sit down and start to cry a bit. 'I have two daughters but I can't see them any more! They don't want to see me either!'

Phil looks at me for a while and then sits next to me, putting his arms around me. 'Go on Caroline. Tell me all about it.'

I tell Phil the story of my girls, of the supposed abuse by their father and how they were taken away so cruelly. I tell him of how I tracked them down and met them again but how they felt that they had lived new lives with new families and that is how they wanted to stay. I look at Phil and he looks really sad and upset for me.

'So, they don't want anything to do with you?' asks Phil. 'I think that's a bit harsh, seeing as how much work you went through to track them down. And, they know it wasn't your fault that things went like they did!'

I sob and nod. 'I know, but they have new established lives now, so, that is that.'

'Have you any photos?' asks Phil.

I nod and go to the bedroom. I return with the pictures of my daughters. 'They will be twenty-eight and twenty-seven now.' I sigh. 'They are okay though.'

Phil looks at the photos for a long time and then gets up to make a drink.

A couple of days later Phil is phoned by his daughter asking him to go and help her with maths homework. He agrees, as apparently he is good at maths, and he goes up to her house. When he comes back about an hour later he says that they sat in the car to do the homework.

'That isn't very good,' I say. 'You should find somewhere indoors that's better for you both. Why can she not come here?

Phil shakes his head. 'She isn't ready for me being with someone else,' he says. 'She's only young so we need to give her time.'

I frown and get quite annoyed. 'Well, Richard comes so what's her problem?'

Phil mirrors my frown. 'I have just told you why! Richard is an adult and he has had relationships of his own. He understands better!'

I start to feel quite annoyed and really start to have a go at Phil. He scowls and then walks off, muttering about wondering why I am having a go when he is being nice! We end up having a bit of an argument and I throw something, although I quickly forget what, and then the air is really bad.

Today is going to be nice as grandma is coming to spend the afternoon with us and have her tea. We are talking nice together and watching television when the news comes on. We all stop talking as there is an item of news that makes us all prick up our ears. There are bombs going off in Majorca where me and Aunty Griselda are supposed to be going and I look at grandma and Phil and I can see that they don't look too happy about it!

'What should I do?' I ask.

'Well,' says Phil, 'I would be worried to death that something would have happened to you or that you would have been stuck in Majorca!'

Grandma nods. 'I think so too. I wouldn't be happy if you were in danger there!'

'I think I am going to ring Auntie Griselda,' I say. 'I am going to tell her that I am not going.'

I ring my auntie but I'm not prepared for the way she reacts. She is extremely upset and says that I am being soft and daft and stupid! Phil and grandma talking to her doesn't make any difference and Griselda is tutting and saying again that I am stupid and it will be okay. But, I have decided that I am not going and that is that!

I come off the phone and look a bit dismayed. 'What about that then? Do you think that I have made the right decision?'

'Yes, I do!' says grandma. 'You can't go where there are bombs!'

'I'm glad you decided not to go,' says Phil. 'I would be worried as well.'

I sigh. 'But I've paid for it now. What do I do about that?'

'Don't worry love,' says grandma. 'I will give you the money back if it means you are safe!'

We are quiet for a while and then grandma says that she would like to go home. We take grandma home and decide to call for a drink on the way home.

'Don't worry about not going,' says Phil. 'You are better safe than sorry.'

I nod. 'I know.'

Over the next few weeks life trundles on and we get on with working shifts and settling into our life together. As the day comes for Griselda to go to Majorca the bombings have stopped and I begin to think that I probably should have gone! But Phil says that it is still holiday season though so they could start again at any time. So I smile and think now that I have made the right decision.

It is a Sunday in the middle of October and unfortunately I am working. But I am finishing in the early afternoon so we have decided to go to a wedding fair at a nice hotel on the other side of town. Phil picks me up and we are on the way when some traffic lights change when we are approaching them. Phil stops sharply but not suddenly and we have just stopped when there is a big crash and someone hits the back of our car. They hit us very hard and after Phil has had a right go at the other driver, a young lad, and then exchanged details he gets back in the car and I start to feel my neck is hurting.

'What an idiot!' says Phil. 'He thought we were going to jump the red light and accelerated to go through after us.' Phil looks at my face and is quite concerned. 'Are you okay darling?'

I shake my head and then wince a little as it hurts!

'Do you want to go to the hospital?' asks Phil.

'No, it's okay,' I answer. 'Let's carry on to the wedding show. I'll be all right.'

But I am not! After about half an hour at the show I am in quite a bit of pain and Phil can see this.

'Let's go to the hospital and get checked out,' says Phil.

I nod. 'Okay. Let's go then.'

At the hospital we are told that we have really bad whiplash and that also my back has been banged quite badly. This is bad as I already have a very bad back problem, so bad that I am registered as disabled at work even though I can get around okay. Phil is also badly affected and goes off work on the sick. He has, however, been for an interview for another job which he should get so he probably won't go back to work at his current job, so he says. It is a bad time for Phil to have a bump anyway as he is going into hospital in about a month for an operation!

There are some issues starting to creep in, though and I really don't know why. There are more times that we shout at each other and there seems to be a lot of frustration about. I am even saying to Phil that he is no good, only with me because he has nowhere to go and all sorts of things like that! Afterwards, when I think about what I have said I can see that it is nonsense and that it upsets Phil. He really doesn't do anything at all so what is going on? The weeks go around and Phil comes off work and goes in for his operation. It is only for a day though and when he comes home I have to feel sorry for him as he does not look too well! He will need dressings changing so I use my experience as an auxiliary nurse. But, Phil shows a soft side and whines like a baby when I go to change it! Softy!

It takes Phil a couple of weeks to recover and then when he is right it is the first of December of that year and he starts his new job. But, the job is mainly at nights with some days and while I don't really like the idea I remember me working nights so I really can't complain. It *is* more money as well! Grandma seems to be going a little bit strange though as she keeps having a go at me when I go to her house. I take Tammey with me a lot of the time but grandma still seems to be acting funny. Edgar seems to be coming back into grandma's life more and more and while I think nothing of it at the time him and grandma's odd behaviour seem to be linked. Even stranger, though, I seem to be starting with little panic attacks and this is very odd as this hasn't happened to me for quite a while. Phil is always there for me though so they really do not last that long. Christmas is coming up quick as well and we are both looking forward to spending our first Christmas together!

As it happens, Christmas brings about *another* bout of disappointment and hence more arguments. Phil thinks he has bought nice, thoughtful presents for me but they are not! In fact, I feel that he hasn't put any thought to them at all! I mean, I have bought him lovely presents, things that he has mentioned along the way but the ones I get I've either already got or they are a disappointment. I can see Phil is quite upset and he keeps apologising, which winds me up even more! But Phil actually has to go to work the next day so we sort of forget about it, have our tea and then go to bed as Phil is up early for work in the morning. A couple of days later we are doing a dinner for my grandma and Edgar and the conversation at dinner goes through many things, from how my grandma is to presents and cards and also about Phil's book. They seem very interested in his book but we get the feeling that they don't really think it will amount to much. Is it jealousy? I don't really know but I suppose we will find out in time.

Phil is off at the New Year and we have booked to go to a New Year's Eve dinner and dance. We get dressed up and get a taxi to the place, a lovely old manor hall but we are in the annexe function room at the side. The night goes really well and we seem very much in love! As it gets past midnight and into 2010 we seem to have a whole life of happiness and love in front of us, something that I have not had for a little while! The night takes on one of our little disasters though as the taxi we have booked to take us home hasn't turned up! We are on the phone time after time but after two hours in the cold, with snow on the ground, there is still no taxi! We get to desperate measures and try to book another one but, after one says he will come back for us for a dearer price we finally get a taxi from the company we booked with originally! The whole journey is taken up with us complaining to the driver and he apologises but takes no real notice. When we get home I am freezing and I immediately get pyjamas on and get a hot drink! A couple of days later and Phil is back at work for a few nights. I don't like him being away at nights really but I know it can't be helped. I don't know either whether this night working is causing it but over the coming months we have a number of quite heated arguments – and one or two bad ones! Phil storms out of the house a few times and rings members of my family and Doris because, he says, he cannot understand why I am being terrible to him when he has done nothing wrong and just loved me. I suppose he has a point but unfortunately I don't really see it that way. I just shrug it off and tell him not to be so soft! But things get worse before they get better as, during a very heated argument and us having a go at each other, somehow Phil's finger gets broken! So badly, in fact, that the end of it is completely bent over! Phil, however, snaps it straight back on, which makes me cringe! We rush off to the hospital straight away and when it is x-rayed the doctor says that the end has broken straight off and that Phil did a good job in putting it back! We go back home and then wonder why this has happened. There seems to be no reason for it and I know that it is not really me acting like this. I just hope Phil knows.

Phil is also upset at his dad getting worse with the dementia and we go to see him at the home as much as we can. Phil's dad is great though and we always have a laugh with him when we go! The other bright thing happening is that we have booked a holiday to Tenerife, and we will be away on my Birthday! We do the best we can for spending money as Phil's dad's house is going through the motions of being sold so we are really waiting for some money coming from that. We have a fantastic time in Tenerife but, true to form, we end up having an argument over my present, which is very silly really! Also, Phil's son Richard rings up very upset as his other granddad has died. Phil tries to comfort him but there isn't much we can do when we are on holiday. When we get back the house sale still hasn't completed so we have to dip seriously into our savings to get Phil's son Richard a car, us having his. Phil says that he will give it straight back when the house is sold – the money was promised to his son by his dad – but because I have been listening to other negative people I do not believe him and accuse him of using my savings power! This starts another argument and Phil storms out again. What is going on? The arguments go on right throughout the summer, which is strange because we are planning our wedding for the next year and when we act good together it is the best relationship ever! In the summer we find a little bit more money so we book *another* holiday, this time to Tunisia! We also come up with some ideas about selling Phil's dad's house, even though one of the people who lives local to it has said he will buy it. But, weknow that nothing is assured so I have an idea that we should put a notice in the window, 'house for sale!'.

Tunisia comes and we are off to the sun! It starts off badly as I have a nasty infection in my mouth and Phil says I look like one of the Munsters! But, it is a superb holiday and we have a great time. Tammey also seems happier as we have found a nicer kennels for her! When we pick her up she is lovely and clean, with a new haircut, smelling sweet and with a bow! I make comments about her being my baby – Phil thinks I'm daft! We also have started saving for our honeymoon and we have decided we are going to go to Hollywood! Phil has also self-published his book and it looks fantastic! He has found an excellent illustrator to do the cover through an old college friend and when it is printed and published we get some copies to give to friends and family. I get the first signed copy, of course, and then Phil gives the next ones to Richard and Kate. We also book Phil's first signing session at a local book store and there is another author that Phil has his photograph taken with for the local paper! We also show my grandma and Edgar, who seem interested but still a little unbelieving. But we also give a copy to Aunty Griselda who says she is looking forward to reading it. However, a few days later we get a phone call, which Phil answers. It is Aunty Griselda and she starts to rip Phil's book to pieces, telling him that it is terrible and there are so many mistakes that she is going to ring the publishers to complain! Phil comes off the phone and I can see that he is very annoyed! He rings her back and really tells her what he thinks! I think it is terrible and also she doesn't even ask to speak to me!

A couple of days later we are telling grandma about it.

'Well!' says grandma. 'I think that's terrible! And, she didn't even want to speak to you? Give me the phone!'

Grandma rings Griselda and really gives her a piece of her mind! When she comes off she is really annoyed and I go and make a cup of tea.

'She told me not to fall out with her!' says grandma. 'Well, *I* don't want to know her now! She has been really horrible and she's not speaking to you like that!'

She didn't speak to me anyway so it didn't really matter but I know what grandma means!

Christmas is different this year as Phil is working but we have been out and bought each other presents, as well as presents for grandma and Phil's kids. Phil has bought really good presents for me this year! He is working New

Year as well so we don't get much time together at all over the festive period. I do a dinner though for us and invite grandma and Edgar and there are some very good photos taken! Into 2011 and I start to feel that some things are not right with the way Phil and me are acting together, particularly me and I don't know why. We are having quite a few more rows over silly little things really but things start to come to a head. We have an argument one particular day and I throw a cup of tea and my phone, then shout and tell Phil that he is no good and that he is only there for convenience! However, he is going out to work for the night shift so he storms out of the house and I am left to wonder what is going on. We try to phone one another but we never really connect and then I hear nothing else until he comes home in the morning. A few nights later and the police are at the door – I really don't know why though – but they tell Phil that he will have to go and sleep somewhere else that night! When he has gone I am starting to get scared as I don't want to be on my own. I ring him and he says that he is going to go to a guest house, but, I find out the next day that he slept in the car all night! What a proper mess!

A few weeks later Phil comes home from work in the morning and, for some unknown reason, I start on him again and keep stopping him from going to bed, as he is on the night shift again! I don't really know how but the police knock on the door and question us, which is shameful really! Again, they tell Phil to go and find somewhere else to go and not to come back until the day after! What have I done to him? Phil goes and stays in a guest house and I ring him to ask when he is coming home for tea but he says that he has been told to stay away! When he is at work at night I ring him.

Phil sighs on the phone. 'I have had to sleep in a guest house, Caroline. It's not fair you know what you do to me and I can't take it any longer!'

I start to get upset. 'What are you saying Phil? Does this mean it's the end of us?'

'I think so,' says Phil. 'I am not putting up with it any longer!'

There is a silence and then I speak first. 'I don't really want us to end Phil. Is that what you want?'

'No, not really,' answers Phil, 'but we can't go on like this.' He thinks for a moment. 'Caroline, it could work but you need to get some help! We have to find someone who can find out what is happening to you and why you are doing these things.'

I nod to myself. 'So, you're saying that if I get help you'll stay with me?'

'Yes,' answers Phil. 'I love you and I can't understand why you are doing it.'

I sigh. 'Okay, I will go and see someone. Do we see one of those counsellors?'

'That's the best idea,' says Phil. 'Let me get this run of shifts over with and we will go and see someone.'

'Do you want me to try and find someone?' I ask.

'You can if you like,' says Phil.

The next day Phil is at home and he gets up just after lunchtime, as he always does first day off after nights. I show him that I have written a letter to Griselda, telling her what I think and what I now know she's been doing all these years!

'You know she won't listen to you, don't you?' says Phil.

I nod. 'I don't care! She needs to know and I am going to send it!' I smile. 'Anyway, I have found a counsellor in Newly House, called Gail. She can see us at ten o'clock tomorrow. Is that okay?'

'That's fine,' answers Phil. We can go straight on to Morrisons shopping afterwards.'

So, that's it then! We are off to see a counsellor, something I *never* thought that I would be doing! But, if it helps our relationship then I really don't mind.

The next day comes and we are sitting in the waiting room of Gail the counsellor's office when she comes out of a room and I see Phil raise his eyes.

'What's the matter Phil?' I ask.

'I know that woman, the counsellor!' answers Phil.

'Where from?' I ask.

'She used to be the partner of an old school friend,' answers Phil.

I frown a little. 'Do you not want to see her then?'

Phil nods. 'Yes, it's okay. I don't mind. We're here now and I'm sure she won't mind.'

After a short while Gail calls us in. Once we are in Phil tells Gail that he knows her and she remembers him and they bring each other up-to-date. We explain the situation to her and all the story of what's gone on and Phil tells her that he has had enough of how I treat him. But, I also say that I don't know why I am like this! I show her the letter I have written to Griselda.

'I wouldn't send it,' says Gail. 'Have the satisfaction that you've written it and then burn it!'

'Why?' I ask.

'Well,' says Gail, 'it will only cause trouble and they are looking for a fight. I would just leave it alone.'

We spend the rest of the time in trying to sort ourselves out and at the end of the meeting Gail says we have made some progress as we are sitting closer together and holding hands, whereas at the beginning of the meeting our chairs were quite a way apart!

We arrange another meeting with Gail for a month's time and then we are off to do some shopping.

There is another problem, though. Edgar is starting to be a real nasty man, telling me to shut up when I go to see my grandma. He is always laughing when he says it so I just keep thinking it is some sort of joke. Phil, however, sees things differently when he is with me and Edgar is around!

'That man is very rude!' says Phil. 'He is not treating you and your grandma right at all!'

'What makes you say that?' I ask.

Phil frowns. 'He is always telling you to shut up and shouting. Not very nice at all!'

'Oh, he's only joking,' I say.

Phil shakes his head. 'No, he isn't. He is a bit of a bully and he isn't joking at all! You need to watch him. You'll see I'm right!'

Actually, there are many instances over the next few months that make me think that Phil *is* right about Edgar! We always go and see Phil's dad in the home, which is round the corner from my grandma's, and we come away from seeing his dad quite happy. But, when we get into grandma's and Edgar comes in there is always *something* that makes the mood worse and it usually is to do with something that Edgar says or does! This usually makes me upset but, the strange thing is, my grandma doesn't seem to care and sides with Edgar. Phil keeps saying that he told me so and I am beginning to believe him!

But, it still keeps affecting me as well and the month comes around and we are seeing Gail again. I also have to tell her that Griselda has written a nasty letter back. Gail says that she told me it would be wrong for me to send the letter and that they were looking for a fight! She was right and I wonder why I didn't listen to her! Why do I not listen to people? We leave Gail after making some more progress, though, and carry on with preparing for our wedding. In fact, we go onto the travel agent after we have seen Gail and pay some more off our honeymoon to Hollywood!

Over the course of the next few weeks Phil has some signing sessions of his book at some stores of a well-known bookshop! It is quite fun promoting the book and in one place it becomes the best seller for the week! But, it is tiring for me to sit around in the store for a few hours but I do it to support him. However, I am wondering if it is a bit of a dream too far and am remembering what people have said about him being too much of a dreamer! But, we will see and Phil has never said that he is relying on the book for a job. Instead, Phil is working hard at his security job but it is still mostly nights, which I don't like very much at all but it is a job and it is paying all our bills and we are able to save a bit. But, I seem to be worsening with panic attacks and I don't really know why. They are really hard to deal with as they usually come in the middle of the night when Phil is at work. I am really scared when they happen and am on the phone to Phil, crying and not being able to breathe, scared and wishing he was at home with me! We are also going to see Phil's dad at the home but he seems to be getting a little worse now. He is still joking though and he still knows who we are. However, one night at work Phil gets a phone call from the home to say that his dad has been rushed into hospital;. He gets cover at work and sets off home, ringing me on the way to tell me to get dressed as we need to go to the hospital straight away. Phil picks me up and soon we are at the Accident and Emergency department. Phil's dad is in X-ray but soon he is back and joking. But he is hooked up with lots of tubes and oxygen and he does not look in a good state at all. Phil has rung his son Richard but has said he will ring back if anything changes. The doctor takes us into a side room and, to put it bluntly, tells Phil to ring any family he needs to as his dad may not last the night! Phil rings Richard, who is there in a very short time and rings his dad's sister. His aunty and uncle are soon there as well and we all go to a separate room with dad and then we are just sat. Then, by early morning dad has passed away and we are all so very upset. Phil held dad's hand when he went and I can see Phil is distraught.

The funeral is a couple of weeks after, as there needs to be a post-mortem, and when dad's ashes are given to us Phil, Richard and I scatter them in the place where his mum's ashes were scattered five years before. I have the great idea though of burying the bag that the ashes were in under the tree outside our front door at home and we create a little garden for him! There are some solar lights as well and one in particular shines whatever the weather! We know dad is with us and, as will become apparent, we will need him! The thing is, you see, my grandma is starting to get very funny with me and I am sure that it is that man Edgar that is putting the ideas in her head! He has made her get rid of her home helpers and I am sure if he could get rid of her home-delivered meals as well he would! My grandma also has an elderly lady called Alice from a befriending service who comes and talks to her once a week. Alice is a really lovely lady in her nineties and she is wonderful, as she still drives her car and does all sorts of activities with her church! But, as usual, Edgar keeps coming in and I hear when I go up that he keeps telling my grandma that she doesn't really want to be talking to Alice, telling her all of her business! He seems to be trying to get rid of her as well, but Alice and me and Phil are becoming really good friends! We actually start to call her 'Gran Alice'! There is also the episode with Edgar when my grandma's friend of many years, Mary, dies and we are all invited to the funeral. Edgar convinces grandma that the people are all drinkers, which is very unfair, and that she doesn't really want to go to the party after. He makes the excuse that he doesn't know where the venue is and they end up going home. When I ring my grandma he gets on the phone and he is *still* telling me to shut up! Phil tells him off and then he has gone off the phone and we stay for a while and then go home.

Things come to a head, however, one evening when Phil is at work. He has dropped me off at grandma's on his way to work and everything is okay, grandma Edgar and me going into Edgar's garden as it is a nice evening. However, the conversation goes into how my grandma is treating me and finally I tell her that Edgar does not love her and he is only looking after her out of guilt. He calls me a nasty name and slaps me across the face! Then he goes to hit me with a watering can but I shy away and then I hear my grandma gasp! I tell my grandma that she is a nasty witch and ring Phil. Edgar tries to talk to Phil but Phil tells him in no uncertain terms to put me back on the phone. Phil says that he is coming over from work and to ring the police, which I do when he has gone off the phone. Phil gets there at the same time roughly as the police lady and she takes a statement and then goes in to see Edgar and my grandma, who has stayed in his house with him. The police lady comes back and says that they look like two frightened old people and I know that he has pulled the wool over her eyes. The police lady says that she has cautioned Edgar but nothing further will be done. I am so very upset and then Phil takes me home and then goes back to work. I can tell Phil is *not* very happy at all!

Actually, as the weeks go on the situation gets worse as my grandma takes more and more notice of Edgar. Phil and I go to see his son's wife to tell her what has gone on and, although she seems to agree it is not very good of Edgar, her sympathy isn't real! After a few weeks we go and see grandma and she is shaking her head.

I shrug and look at her. 'What's the matter grandma?'

'I have something to tell you,' says grandma. 'Edgar and me are going to get married! We are going to go away together and get married where you don't know!'

I look at Phil and we both raise our eyes.

'Oh, that's lovely, grandma,' I say.

Grandma frowns. 'I know you don't approve Caroline but we are going next week to somewhere and when you see me again I will be married to Edgar!'

We humour her and when we have gone I shake my head, but Phil can see I am getting upset.

'I don't think they will allow them to get married,' says Phil. 'They are two old people and there is something with your grandma – social services said that – so they won't allow it.'

'Do you think that?' I ask.

Phil nods his head. 'I am sure of it.'

The next day, however, I get a call from social services to say that they think I should stay away from my grandma. I am really upset and when Phil comes home I am crying! He helps me to get in touch with the social services department and we arrange a meeting with the manager there. A couple of days later and we are in the room with them and as much as we try to convince them that Edgar is the one that is causing the trouble, and Griselda, they will not change their minds and tell me to still stay away from my grandma! I am distraught and start to cry, panicking and getting really upset. The manager tells me I should go and see my doctor as I think I am saying that I don't want to live anymore! When we get home we get a phone call and it is our doctor ringing us, saying that she has been told I am saying I want to be dead and getting in a right state! Why are they telling me to stay away? I think of Christmas that is coming up, spending it without my grandma, and that I might never see her again before she dies. What am I going to do?' Phil is trying to be kind and helpful but I am so upset he can't get through to me! The situation gets worse as my panic attacks are getting worse and worse going into the New Year and I am starting to have a go at Phil more and more. He and Richard are trying to be there for me but it seems like I am inconsolable! Phil is still missing his dad and he has a car accident coming out of work so it is a right mess all round! We decide, however, to book a holiday and we decide that we will go to Cornwall in the July, about four months away. We are still seeing Gail the counsellor and sometimes we actually need her! I have got out of the car a couple of times and run off and also keep throwing things, sometimes at the wall and sometimes at Phil! We try to get along and we go and see friends and, on the whole, we get along fine.

Cornwall comes along and we are very excited! We have booked to go on a holiday park in a chalet and when we there it is nice and secluded at the top of the park. We settle in and then for the rest of the week we go to all the nice fishing villages and we are having a really good time! But, near the end of the holiday we have a really big argument and then Phil notices that his laptop has gone out of its bag. He asks me where it is and when I don't tell him he accuses me of pinching it! I am very angry and tell him I have put it under the bed for safety. Phil gets onto his knees to get it and then I kick him very hard in his shoulder! It is the shoulder that is hurting him after the car accident and he is in great pain, almost crying because it is hurting him! I pull on his clothes and then my hands are round his neck, squeezing and hurting. I top it all by getting the dog lead and then Phil rings the police. When they come they arrest me and take me away! I end up in a cell at the police station and I am really scared. What have I done? Of course, I don't know that Phil gets his things together to go home and when I get out I see him taking the keys to the chalet to the reception.

'Where are you going?' I ask.

'I need to get home! You have to stay away from me!' says Phil. 'The police have told me to go home on my own so you can't come with me!'

'I start to panic. 'But how am I going to get home? What am I going to do?'

Phil shrugs his shoulders. 'I don't know! You are going to have to find your own way home. Anyway, I won't be there when you do get home. This is the last straw!'

Phil goes away and I can see that the security man is making sure that he is okay. I walk off to drown myself but I am stopped and then realise that it is silly! Phil drives off and I am left to wonder what has gone so horribly wrong!

I wander around the next day and the day after that and finally I get a train home from Cornwall. When I get home Phil has gone and so has most of his things. I am at home when he comes back with Richard and the police to get the rest of his things. He has taken the television off the wall in the bedroom, as he bought it, and then he is off and I realise that I will never see him again. He is taking a soft teddy with him that has been his for a long time but the teddy was my comfort, especially in the police cell, so I really have had everything taken away! Phil is staying in a bed and breakfast at the other side of town and I keep trying to text and ring him but he is telling me to go away. However, a couple of days later and I am in a right mess! I get a letter through the post from my grandma's solicitor telling me that they want me to account for every single penny that I spent when I was looking after her money. I don't know when to start and I am so upset and frightened. I ring Phil but he tells me that it is none of his business anymore and not to keep ringing him. But who else do I ask? I ring him back again, this time really crying and getting distressed but he says again that he doesn't want anything to do with me. Then, a few days later I have been out to see someone about it and when I am walking down my road Phil and Richard are driving away in the car. They stop and, because it is a nice day and it is a convertible we bought, we end up talking.

'How is Tammey?' Phil asks.

'She isn't eating,' I answer sadly. 'She's really missing you!'

Richard shakes his head. 'Come on, get in! We can go to the supermarket and have a coffee and talk about this.'

We sit down with a drink and Richard says that Phil is really upset and has been crying because he is missing me! I smile as I realise that there might be some hope that I have not lost Phil forever!

'I have a plan to keep you together!' says Richard. 'My dad can get his own place and then you can keep the flat and you can start to see each other again!'

I think about it and smile. 'That sounds like a good idea. Are we going to look for somewhere then?'

Phil nods. 'You can move there with me and if you feel you need to go back to the flat you can!'

We finish our drinks and then Phil takes me home and then goes back to his digs with Richard.

Phil has also been doing a legal certificate this past year and I don't know where he is up to with it but he has sent in all he needs to so he is hoping he will pass.

New Beginnings

There is a new problem starting as Phil is starting to run out of money as he is out of work at the moment! I think that he is silly for living hand-to-mouth and I am wondering what he is going to do. He and Richard come round to talk and we decide that it would be better if Phil moves back into the flat, as it is half in his name after all! But, we know that things have to be different now and there has to be no more fighting and bad arguments. We also decide that, seeing as how Phil has got most of the money back from the honeymoon and the wedding we should go on holiday! We book to go to Turkey for a week and then we are really excited about going away again! We also decide to change the car as I think it is a good idea for us to buy a touring caravan! Over the next few days we have a look at cars and caravans and I wonder if Richard is sick of looking around! But, he loves his cars so he isn't really bothered! We find a nice car and have a tow-bar fitted and then we find a lovely caravan and so we are set!

Turkey is a fantastic holiday but the weather is scorching! I have been before but Phil hasn't and he loves the place and the people, who are very nice people! When we come back Phil is still out of work but we are getting by and going for weekends away in our caravan. We find a lovely place in the Derbyshire Peaks, right next to a village with a great pub! We go there a few times, as well as to Southport to get some sea air, and things are really good at the moment. I am still not seeing my grandma, though, which is still upsetting me but there is nothing I can do about it. I am still feeling upset with panic attacks so my doctor refers me to a specialist to see what is going on. When I see her she is a nice lady and she tells me that it is my grandma that has made me feel like this. The funny thing is, though, that after I have seen her I stop having the panic attacks! Maybe she has hypnotised me! I have also started developing a few odd symptoms, feeling very tired a lot of the time and getting tongue-twisted in what I am saying. As the symptoms get a little worse we are looking on the internet for answers. Suddenly, Phil mentions that it sounds like I have got a condition called M.E., or Myalgic Encephalomyelitis, also known as Chronic Fatigue. We read about it and it explains that it is a nasty illness, caused by a problem with the brain and central nervous system in the body. It also affects the immune system and causes weakness of the muscles and, from what I am experiencing, it seems like I *do* have the symptoms of the condition! We continue to go away in our caravan a couple of times but the weather is getting a little bit cooler and more rain is coming down so we decide that it is probably best if we leave it until the spring. But, then we come up with the idea of going away in the caravan for the New Year, so, we look around and find a site in Garstang where there is a do on in the club house on New year's Eve! We book it and then we are excited that we are going away again! We are also excited as Phil has passed his legal course and he can put the letters after his name!

I continue to feel tired a lot more and I decide after a few weeks of this that I need to go back to my doctor. It doesn't help that I still have had no contact with my grandma and I am still heartbroken at the fact that I might never see her again before she dies. The doctor agrees that I cannot go on with these symptoms happening so he refers me to have a brain scan in the New Year. I am *really* not looking forward to that as I hate those scanners, but, we need to get to the bottom of why I am feeling like I do so I suppose I will have to grin and bear it! We muddle on and we are occupied as well in finding a job for Phil. But, the time comes for us to go away and when we get to the caravan park it is lovely. But, it is raining and they put us on a grass pitch at the bottom of the park! To top it all, the electric hook up is across grass and the power keeps going off so Phil has to trudge in the mud and switch it back on again! We decide that we have too much on so we leave something off when we have the microwave on! That should sort it out! In fact, Phil makes the point that we haven't really gone away in the caravan when it isn't raining and I suppose this sort of proves his point! There is worse to come, though. We get ready and we are looking forward to the New Year party, but, when we get into the club house it is crowded and they are playing bingo of all things! The worse thing is I had gone into Garstang in the afternoon and paid a lot of money to have my hair done! We are not happy but we decide that we should go into Garstang and get something to eat o take back to the caravan. We get pizza and garlic bread and take it back to the caravan to have with our wine and beer! It proves to be just as enjoyable and after we settle down in bed and watch telly. But, I drift off to sleep and then Phil is waking me up to wish me 'Happy New Year', which is nice but I am not happy as I have been woken up! Phil is quite upset and I can't think why I went to sleep so quickly and for so long. I did drink a lot of sherry so I just put it down to that. In fact, we guess the day after that it could be something to do with me having this M.E. and seeing the doctor. So, when we get home we check on the internet and we see that people who suffer with M.E *really* do have a problem with drinking alcohol! So, it seems like I might have the condition after all and no wonder I fell into such a deep sleep! But, we will only know when I have had the scan and seen the doctor.

A few weeks later I get my appointment for my scan and I am now waiting another few weeks until I go. There are no more panic attacks but I am still feeling tired a lot and very often want to go to sleep in the afternoon. The good news is Phil gets an interview for a job with a large company so we are looking forward to that and Phil prepares for it. He gets the job with the big company but it is going to be in a couple of months when he starts so we will have to struggle with finances a little longer! But, the time seems to come around quite quickly and Phil seems to enjoy getting into his new job, in spite of the fact that he says the training is really hard and comes home shattered most nights! We are also trying to put the final stages to our wedding preparations and have decided to send out the invitations in a month or so. But, Phil ends up being off work for a day during his training course as he is quite sick! Richard has been at our house for tea when Phil suddenly collapses and ends up in the A & E department with a suspected heart attack! He is kept in overnight and Richard and I go to his workplace to explain. It isn't a heart attack though, which is a big relief, but we are wondering just what has happened. I have also got my appointment to see the neurologist for the August so everything seems to be moving along there okay.

Phil gets more into his job and starts to learn properly now he is out of training. But, things take a really dramatic turn as I get a phone call one morning from the police to say that they have been contacted by a company in the town where my grandma lives and they have got her in their office! The police say she has been wandering around all night and could I go to get her. Phil and I get into the car and are soon at the company, where we find my grandma very confused and rambling on about buses and wandering! We get her in the car and take her home and then I ring the social worker, who advises we take her to the hospital to get checked out. The hospital say that she is okay though so I decide that we will take her to the social services office in her home town. We meet with the social workers there and my grandma tells everyone she wanted to get away from Edgar! Oh, it is starting again I think to myself! The social workers make arrangements for my grandma to go into a home and they put her immediately into a temporary place, to both get her from roaming the streets and to observe her to see what is going on. She is not happy but we can't do anything about it and we go and see her every day. The problem is, however, that they are allowing Doris and Edgar to go and we know that this will cause problems but what can we do. The problem is proved when, on one occasion, Edgar *and* Doris have been and my grandma is very rude and nasty towards me. But, not just me, she is being nasty to Phil and his son Richard. In fact, Richard is so annoyed that he storms out and sits in the car! I am really upset and Phil and I storm out. I am not going seeing her again!

I tell the social worker but she doesn't seem to be that bothered, instead just keeping saying that if it is my grandma's wishes then they have to be allowed to go! I am not happy! However, a couple of days later I am going to see my grandma and Doris asks if she can come as well. So, we pick Doris up and take her to the home to see my grandma. In fact, Phil isn't staying as he is taking Tammey for a walk with his daughter. So, Doris and I go in and see my grandma and Phil goes off with Tammey. But, not long after I am ringing Phil as, horror of horrors, I see Edgar coming down the path! I can't stay when he is coming but Doris is telling me to stay. I am really scared and can feel myself getting worked up! So, I tell the nurse and I am ready to go out of the door when he is in the entrance the same time as me! I freak out a little and looks around as if he doesn't know what is going on! But, he is a kidder as we know and a really nasty man so I just want to get out. Also, Phil has rung Richard who, apparently, is ready to jump in the car and rescue me! Why is this all happening again? Why won't they believe me? Anyway, in the end he is told he has to go so I go back in to see grandma. Doris is still there but I really don't want to talk to her! Phil eventually picks us up and he says that his daughter told him to go to me but Richard was coming instead. However, Edgar has gone so everything turned out okay – for now! In fact, a couple of days later the social worker says she has found my grandma a place in a nursing home near to where her house is. When she gets in the place is really nice, a converted old country manor house type building with all the original features! Grandma complains an bit but she is soon settled in and the staff are really nice. She makes a friend called Betty who is really nice and, in fact, Betty's daughter works at the hospital and I know her from working there! Although grandma is settling I seem to be getting a little worse all the time and also I now have my appointment with the neurologist for a month's time. To make matters worse I have found a letter in my grandma's handbag, written in Griselda's handwriting, saying that her and the warden at my grandma's bungalow were plotting to take my grandma to a sheltered home in Leigh and I would not know where she is and *never* see her again! What a dreadful thing to do! How dare they even think about doing that! I am *so* upset and when I tell Phil he is furious! But, like he says, we have the letter and we have rumbled their plot so nothing can happen there. Also, my grandma's interests are now protected so we really have nothing to worry about. Phil's job is going okay and he is getting into it well now. He also has a second job in security and he goes all over the North to different events. The time comes for me to see the specialist and he is actually a very nice man! He examines me and tells me that my scans have come back normal, with no brain damage he comes to the conclusion that I most likely *do* have M.E! He also asks about our wedding and are we having a party? I explain that we are having a small party at home so he wishes us good luck! He also explains that he is referring me to a colleague of his, another specialist who has had more experience of working with M.E. so I am happy that I am finally getting somewhere with it. I am also going to a luncheon club with some very nice ladies once a month and I am making some nice new friends there. However, things take another bad turn as, one day, Phil comes home from work and he says since he left the building at work he has been shivering but feeling very hot to touch. I just say that he must have a bad cold and to take a tablet but he insists that he wants to go to see the emergency doctor. So, we go and when the doctor has examined Phil I have to feel a little ashamed as she is referring him to hospital straight away! He has a very high temperature and an infection in his gall bladder and liver! In fact, Phil is in hospital for *six* days and at the end he is told by the surgeon that he needs to have his gall bladder removed! Phil has another three days off work and when he goes back his manager is not very happy. He has to have a meeting the next day and when it is over the company have sacked him! It is dreadful behaviour by them and Phil is so upset! But, we have to carry on and, as it happens, he gets another job within three days! But, our wedding is coming up soon and so is Phil's operation so he doesn't have to start the new job until we come back from our honeymoon – a week in Cornwall in the caravan! I am also trying to cope with my condition as well but it is difficult when I get so tired and fatigued.

But, our wedding day comes around and the night before I stay at home whilst Phil and Richard have hired a room at a nearby hotel and go to the pictures. Well, the groom cannot see the bride the night before the wedding! Richard is also the designated driver of the official wedding car, which is actually Richard's car! In the morning I get ready and the hairdresser comes to the house. Phil and Richard are getting ready and then Richard drops Phil off at the registry office and comes for me and Gran Alice, who is accompanying me in the car, which I am really glad about! The wedding goes really well and everyone says I look beautiful in my dress. Richard signs for Phil and Phil's best friend's wife signs for me and when we have had some photos done at the registry office we go back to our home and everyone comes back for a buffet and drinks. The ladies from my lunch club are there, as are some of Phil's family and friends. A couple of the nice neighbours are there as well and the do is a really lovely day! When everyone has gone we take Gran Alice home and then Phil, Richard and I go for a nice meal, just the three of us! We get back to be fairly reasonable as we are setting off in the morning for Cornwall. Tammey has gone to the kennels the day before so everything is set and arranged! We have a special teddy, George, that Phil has had for a long time and he is coming as well as he goes everywhere with us!

So, the next day we pick up Tammey, hitch up our caravan and we are off to Cornwall! The journey is a long one though because we have to keep stopping to give Tammey a walk and something to eat we don't mind! It takes us ages and when we reach the caravan park it is dark! The place is down a few country roads as well so doubly tricky! The man at the site helps us to get the caravan in place and then we just do a brew and then we go to bed as we are shattered! The next morning we see that we are not really next to the sea at all, which we thought we would be! But, the day is fine but cloudy so when we've had breakfast Phil puts up our new porch awning – or tries to! He has to ask the man near us to help but soon it is up and then we are off to look around. But, in the afternoon the weather takes a turn for the worst and we find out that we are in the tail end of a hurricane that was in France! Looks like Phil is right about it being bad weather when we are in the caravan!

But, we have a great week and get to visit the villages that we didn't visit the year before! We have a much better time as well and take quite a few photos. By the end of the week we are tired and then we have an horrendous journey home that takes us nearly eleven hours! We decide that it is the last time we go to Cornwall for a while!

When we get home some of the wedding things are still up in the house so we decide to leave them up, just for a couple of days! Phil starts his new job and I go and see grandma but she is quite nasty with me! The staff tell me that Edgar has been to see her and I shake my head as I now know why she is being funny. I also find out that Griselda has phoned, asking questions and *demanding* answers. Is it any wonder that grandma is so confused and I am feeling quite ill? A couple of weeks go by and Phil goes in to have his operation. He is only in for the day and at night Richard and I go to pick him up. We find him dozing but he wakes up and then we can take him home. He is in some discomfort and has got some stitches but he is okay! But, we get one person out of hospital and then another goes in! We get a call from the home to say that my grandma is having a go at the other residents and is being very aggressive towards other people! We don't know what is going on but, unfortunately, she has to go into hospital to get checked out and to be observed! This is dreadful as this is what happened to her the last time! We have our suspicions, though, that it is Edgar that is upsetting and confusing her so, again, it is him that has put her in hospital! She is actually going into a private separate building in the hospital grounds. But, Phil tells me that she is going into the place where his mum died, so we have mixed emotions.

Grandma is not happy at all when she gets into there and we have to laugh at some of the things she says, such as the staff drug them and take them upstairs and keep them tied in beds! There is no upstairs! It is a real shame for her and I feel quite sad but it is Edgar that has caused this! However, she won't be I that building for long as the patients are being moved into a ward in the main hospital building that has been renovated, which is good in one way but bad in another as parking is terrible at the hospital! But, the great thing is that I have been granted a disabled badge from the Council so we should be okay. Grandma will be in the new ward before Christmas as well so we are glad she will hopefully be quite settled by the New year.

Christmas gets nearer and we are preparing for that when things take another twist, probably for the good actually! Phil gets a call from a company that he applied to for a job ages ago asking him to go in for interview! Phil says he is quite excited as it is a patrol job, which he wanted anyway, *and* it is working on the ship canal so it is working with big ships as well! Phil gets the job and he finds out that he will also have a licence to work on the docks so we feel that things are really looking up! Phil starts his new job and things are looking really good there. But, I have now been to see the second neurologist and he confirms that I have got M.E.! I am also getting terrible pains in my right leg and have to have the occupational therapist in to assess me. She advises that I need a stool for the kitchen, for when I am preparing food, and that I would benefit from a wheelchair! I am totally devastated and when she has gone I start to cry. I *never* thought I would need a wheelchair and I don't know whether I can cope! I start to say to Phil that it is not fair on him but he says that he loves me and that he is not bothered about me needing a wheelchair for long distances. In fact, when I get it he is not bothered about pushing me at all! He is silly though, at first, as he is still recovering from his operation so he is well-and-truly told off! I tell my grandma about it all and she can't believe what has happened to me! It is starting to affect my life a lot and all the ladies at the lunch club, as well as Gran Alice, can't quite believe it either. In fact, I feel sometimes that Gran Alice doesn't believe that I have got anything wrong at all, which quite upsets me! But that isn't the only thing that upsets me! Edgar is being allowed to visit my grandma at the hospital and we have a meeting with the doctor to say that this is a bad idea! In fact, we can refer them to the home grandma was in as the staff there noticed that she changed when he had visited. But, the doctors are not listening to us and keep saying that it is my grandma's wishes as she keeps asking for him! We say that this is only because he has brainwashed her over twenty years bit they are not listening! The doctor also says that my grandma is quite poorly, as she has got evidence of Alzheimers and Dementia *and* anti-psychotic tendencies! I am very upset at this and all I can think about is my poor grandma and what has happened to me! I am beginning to get into a terrible mess!

Phil is working Christmas Day and Boxing Day so we have my grandma for Christmas dinner on Christmas Eve instead! I do a lovely roast dinner, even though it kills me and wears me out completely, and then we relax before we take my grandma back to the hospital. Grandma doesn't want to go back at all and I have to kid her a bit and say that we have to call at the hospital before we go home! Aren't I terrible! But, she has to stay there so she'll just have to complain a little. The New Year comes and I am actually awake this year to see the new one in! We go into the New Year full of hope that things are going to be better. But, my leg and my illness are getting worse so I join the local M.E. Society and find that there are other people who are like me, some are worse even, and I now have people who are like me I can talk to. We are also stopped from seeing my grandma for nearly two weeks as there is a nasty bug in the hospital ward! There are still some quite bad arguments between Phil and me, though, and after we calm down I can't understand why I am like this. I keep hurting him and he really is a nice husband to me so I suppose he has a right to be upset. Why do I keep telling him that I a going to run away one day? Maybe my illness is getting to me in ways I didn't know. The way we are also affects Richard, which is really not fair as he is a great lad and is always here for me, just like Phil! On a brighter note we are told that we can start to look for a new nursing home for my grandma so we visit a few and decide on one, a lovely place that has nice people and staff and is run by BUPA! We reserve a lovely room and we tell the hospital so they make arrangements for the home to assess her. In the meantime, Edgar has visited again and my grandma has started to get nasty again and quite ill after his visit! Unfortunately, this means that she has to stay in hospital and she loses the room in the home! We are happy at all and call an emergency meeting with the doctor, only to be told that they have had a meeting with the solicitor and social worker and have concluded that it would be good for my grandma to have him visit as well as us – and Griselda too! Why will they not listen to us? In any case, after another few weeks of my grandma complaining that she is perfectly healthy and should not be in there we can finally move her into the BUPA home! We have found another room for her and she will be moving in another couple of weeks. Phil is in quite a bit of a pickle though as his patrolling job is temporarily stopped so he has to scratch around for work on different sites within the company. He does okay for hours but some of the work is on the docks overnight and he says that it is freezing! He does learn different roles though so some of his hours are at more money, which is always good! Actually, we are in a very great mess with money as I have been told that I will not get any disability money so our bills and life have to be paid for just by Phil's wage. I feel angry and useless and although Phil says that he is okay with doing extra hours I am annoyed that I can't help! This causes more aggravation between us and I start again saying the usual rotten things to him. I still don't know why I keep hurting him! But, we will get through somehow. Phil has decided that he is going to send his book off to some publishers to try and get it republished, along with the second book in the trilogy, which he has now finished! He is also going back to the doctors as he is having trouble with co-ordination and some headaches. Given his family history we think it is a good idea he gets checked out. So, we are feeling a little bit mixed up at the moment.

The Future?

So, we are nearing the end of my story, but there are still a number of things happening which I need to tell.

Grandma has moved into her new home, which is not far from where we live and is next to where *she* used to live! I have got her 'back home' and, although she is complaining all the time I know she will be happy in it! We move her chair and unit in, along with her telly and pictures and it now feels homely, cosy and friendly! I am happy now that *she* will be happy, even though Edgar is still being allowed to visit but we can't do anything about that. Just as long as he doesn't upset her!

Phil's report from his doctor is not good though. His brain scan revealed vessel damage in his brain that is quite advanced so we don't know what the future holds there, but, we will have to get on with it. I need him to be right to look after me because I can't walk hardly now and I am in a really bad state. I have been given a mobility scooter for nothing, though and a new set of batteries now means I can have my freedom to get around! Phil and his son Richard say they are going to do it up as I drive it like a sports car anyway! Cheeky beggars!

And the future? It seems like my grandma will be happy and okay and at least I know that she is being looked after and she is safe. Phil is on medication for his condition and he is actually in line for a new job with the same company, that is more money and he will be happier with! He has also got a publisher interested in his book so we may be looking at a much brighter future anyway, with him being able to work from home and look after me!

And me? Well. My journey has come to a nice stage at this moment but I have been left very ill by my life and what has happened in it. But, I now have my grandma back, have a man that is wonderful to me and, although I am very ill and don't show any signs of getting better, I think I might have a brighter future now. In fact, it's looking like I have! Maybe, at last!

BUT YOU NEVER KNOW!